OXFORD
UNIVERSITY PRESS

Great Clarendon Street, Oxford OX2 6DP

Oxford University Press is a department of the University of Oxford.
It furthers the University's objective of excellence in research, scholarship,
and education by publishing worldwide in

Oxford New York
Auckland Bangkok Buenos Aires Cape Town Chennai Dar es Salaam
Delhi Hong Kong Istanbul Karachi Kolkata Kuala Lumpur Madrid
Melbourne Mexico City Mumbai Nairobi São Paulo Shanghai
Taipei Tokyo Toronto

Oxford is a registered trade mark of Oxford University Press
in the UK and in certain other countries

A CIP catalogue record for this book is available from the British Library

ISBN 0 19 831477 9

Cover illustrations by Darrell Warner show (left to right) Charles Dickens,
Geoffrey Chaucer, John Milton, Charlotte Brontë and William Shakespeare

Typeset by AFS Image Setters Ltd, Glasgow

Printed in Great Britain by Bell & Bain Ltd, Glasgow

Orders and enquiries to Customer Services:
Tel. 01536 741171   Fax 01536 454519

Contents

• •

Acknowledgements

• •

The author is grateful to O. P. W. Martin for contributing theological materials on the Tudor period, and for help with the metaphysical poets; and to Jan Nikolic for her supportive and careful editing. Special thanks are due to Dr Corinne Saunders, who wrote Unit 1: Medieval Contexts.

The author and publisher are grateful for permission to reprint the following copyright material:

A. C. Bradley: extracts from *Oxford Lectures on Poetry* (1909) and *Shakespearean Tragedy* (1904), reprinted by permission of Macmillan Publishers.

Emily Dickinson: 'Apparently with no surprise' and 'To make a prairie' from *The Poems of Emily Dickinson* edited by Thomas H. Johnson (The Belknap Press of Harvard University Press), copyright © 1998 by the President and Fellows of Harvard College, copyright © 1951, 1955, 1979 by the President and Fellows of Harvard College, reprinted by permission of the publishers and the Trustees of Amherst College.

H. D. (Hilda Doolittle): 'Oread' from *Collected Poems 1912–1944* edited by Louis L. Martz (Carcanet Press Ltd, 1984) reprinted by permission of the publishers.

E. M. Forster: extracts from *Aspects of the Novel* (Arnold, 1927), 'Notes on the English Character' in *Abinger Harvest* (Arnold, 1936) and *Room with a View* (Arnold, 1908), reprinted by permission of The Provost and Scholars of the King's College, Cambridge, and The Society of Authors as the literary representatives of the E. M. Forster Estate.

Nicholas Roe: extracts from *John Keats and the Culture of Dissent* (Clarendon Press, 1997), copyright © Nicholas Roe 1997, reprinted by permission of Oxford University Press.

William Soutar: 'Ballad' from *Poems of William Soutar: A New Selection* (Scottish Academic, 1986) edited by W. R. Aitken, reprinted by permission of the Trustees of the National Library of Scotland.

The publisher would like to thank the following for permission to reproduce photographs:

Corpus Christi College, Cambridge (page 7); The Bridgeman Art Library International Ltd (page 13); University of Bristol Theatre Collection (pages 43, 138 top, 141, 142); Ancient Art & Architecture Collection Ltd (page 48); English Faculty Library, University of Oxford (page 68); The Bridgeman Art Library (pages 83, 86, 102); Grant & Co, London (page 100); The Royal Collection (page 119, top); The Imperial War Museum, London (page 119, bottom); The Raymond Mander & Joe Mitchenson Theatre Collection (page 138, bottom); The Trustees of the V&A Museum (page 139); John Tramper and Shakespeare's Globe (page 149)

We have tried to trace and contact all copyright holders before publication. If notified the publishers will be pleased to rectify any errors or omissions at the earliest opportunity.

Section I
Literary Contexts
1 Medieval Contexts

●●●

The writing of Geoffrey Chaucer, more than that of most other writers, medieval or modern, creates a vibrant and memorable sense of the author's voice. Even now, when his language is not our own, his work has an extraordinary vividness and dramatic quality. Few readers are likely to forget the comedy of the *Miller's Tale*, or the high tragedy of his long poem *Troilus and Criseyde*. He is a writer with a remarkable ability to move from a high to a low style, from elevated, grandiose language or abstract philosophical discussion to immediate, earthy dialogue or colourful description. He is as much at home with elegant French and Latin phrasing as he is with robust Anglo-Saxon words; indeed it is to Chaucer that we owe many of the French words in our language. Similarly, he is as able to tell a tale of a sorrowing woman as he is of a cuckolded husband, to offer a serious sermon as well as a comic beast fable.

For us, Chaucer is the father of English literature. In his age, he would have been seen as the inheritor of a great tradition as well as the inventor of a new one. His models were the classical writers, especially Ovid and Virgil, and he refers to them and draws on them often. His great mission was to use English in order to follow in the footsteps of the ancient writers. Whereas before the fourteenth century serious literature had been written in Latin, and courtly literature in French, Chaucer and his contemporaries made English into a sophisticated literary language. It is partly because earlier writing in English did not tend to have a high status that Chaucer stands out as one of the few writers known by name. In this era before printing, literary works circulated in rare manuscripts, copied out by scribes who did not record and probably did not know their history or author. Chaucer's popularity, however, was notable: his poems were swiftly and widely circulated, and there remain some 50 manuscripts of his complete works, a very large number for this period.

Chaucer is also unusual in that throughout his work he shapes a literary identity for himself, creating the persona of a detached, self-deprecating, bookish and slightly naive observer: often the gap between this voice and the story it tells creates the celebrated quality of Chaucerian irony. In Chaucer's early dream-vision poems, the *Book of the Duchess* and the *Parliament of*

Fowls, he presents himself as a disappointed lover; in *Troilus and Criseyde*, his stance is that of the servant of lovers, not daring to be one himself; in the *House of Fame*, the plump and bookish 'Geoffroi' is caught up in the claws of a giant eagle, who offers to teach him the secrets of the universe, but he insists that he prefers to read about them instead. In the *Canterbury Tales*, Chaucer represents himself as one of the pilgrims – but as a rather over-trusting observer figure, whose contributions to the story-telling competition leave much to be desired. His first attempt, the tale of *Sir Thopas*, is so doggerel-like that he is is eventually cut off by the Host, *Namoore of this . . . thy drasty rymyng is nat worth a toord*, and his second attempt, the *Tale of Melabye*, is little better, an immensely long, prose moral treatise.

Chaucer's life

These vignettes of the failed story-teller must have amused those who knew the real Geoffrey Chaucer, a very different figure: he was a scholar and widely read, but as well led a highly sophisticated, public life as courtier and diplomat. Born in the early 1340s, Chaucer belonged to a new upper middle class: his father was a successful vintner in London, who had served as deputy chief butler to Edward III (keeping the king's wine cellar). The young Chaucer probably attended a grammar school in London. His writings reflect his knowledge not only of Latin literature, but also of history and philosophy (he translated the classical philosopher Boethius' *Consolation of Philosophy*, c.1381–86) and subjects like astrology, considered a serious science in the Middle Ages and the subject of a treatise by Chaucer.

His public career began in a noble household: a record of 1357 documents the purchase of an expensive suit of page's clothes for Chaucer by Elizabeth, Countess of Ulster: his travels in her employ included service in the military campaign in France of 1359–60, when he was captured and ransomed; he also carried letters from France to England, a diplomatic role that would continue.

Chaucer's links with the court were both public and personal: in 1366, he married a knight's daughter and lady-in-waiting, Philippa de Roet, whose sister was to become the third wife of John of Gaunt (the powerful Duke of Lancaster, uncle of Edward III); the next year, Chaucer became a member of the royal household of Edward III, one of perhaps 40 men in the king's service, whose duties would have ranged from household tasks to diplomatic missions; he made a large number of journeys to the Continent, including to France and Italy. French poets strongly influenced Chaucer's early works, in which he used the popular dream vision form: *The Book of the Duchess* (c.1368), *The House of Fame* (c.1378), *The Parliament of Fowls* (c.1380); he also translated part of the French dream-vision *The Romance of the Rose* (1360s), and a later work, *The Legend of Good Women*, uses the same form (c.1386–87). In Italy, he would have discovered the poetry of Dante, Petrarch and Boccaccio, which he frequently drew on – his epic romance, *Troilus and Criseyde* (c.1381–86), translates a work of Boccaccio.

In 1374 he was given the important public office of comptroller of the customhouse, and made responsible for the collection of an export tax and other taxes, although his diplomatic missions to the Continent continued. Eventually he left London for Kent, where he was made a justice of the peace and member of Parliament; he then became Clerk of the King's works, responsible for the construction and repair of all the royal residences and king's holdings; finally he became overseer of the royal forest in Somerset. It was during this later period that he undertook the *Canterbury Tales* (c.1387 onwards).

Chaucer's numerous appointments suggest his great success as diplomat and civil servant in a turbulent political world; his friend Thomas Usk, by contrast, was beheaded for treason. A contemporary record describes Chaucer as *our beloved esquire going about divers parts of England on the king's arduous and pressing business*.

Despite our considerable knowledge of Chaucer's life, there are many gaps: we don't know how to interpret, for example, the mysterious record of his release from *raptus*, a charge that can mean either rape or abduction, by one Cecily Chaumpaigne – the record is connected with other legal accusations brought against Chaucer by two London citizens, so the charge may well have been part of a financial dispute of some sort. Chaucer appears to have had two sons, 'little Lewis,' to whom his *Treatise of the Astrolabe*, an astrological instrument (c.1391), is dedicated, but about whom we know nothing, and Thomas, who like his father led a highly successful public life, and one of whose daughters married the powerful Duke of Suffolk.

For the Middle Ages, Chaucer's life was relatively long: his tomb records the date of his death as 25 October 1400, when he would have been about 61. In the last year of his life, Chaucer had leased a house in the parish of Westminster Abbey, and thus was buried there – the beginning of Poets' Corner.

Medieval England

The variety of Chaucer's life reflects the more general turbulence of the Middle Ages. The world of medieval England was one of extremes, of high sophistication and idealism but terrible cruelty and violence, of deeply ingrained social structures and conventions but extreme mobility and unrest. The population of England was small – only about two million people, and of these as many as 90 per cent were peasants, only one or two per cent nobility, and the rest townspeople. Primitive technology meant food was never produced in abundance, and bad weather, floods or natural disasters could have catastrophic effects. Famine was a very real threat, as was the rising cost of bread. Chaucer's contemporary William Langland, in his poem *Piers Plowman*, describes how hunger takes a man by *the mawe* [stomach] / *And wrong him so by the wombe that al watrede his eighen* [eyes] (174–75). The world beyond the court or city presented other dangers: towns outside London were small and separated by large tracts of forest and wilderness, dangerous places perhaps inhabited by outlaws or thieves. Illness was a constant threat in this age of primitive medicine, and life expectancy was not high. Many children died in infancy from commonplace ailments, and women were weakened by frequent childbirth. Chaucer's early poem *The Book of the Duchess* was a lament for Blanche, the wife of John of Gaunt, who died aged 28, having had five children. In Chaucer's lifetime, the greatest killer was the plague or Black Death, an epidemic carried by rats from Asia to England, where it recurred for over a hundred years: in 1348–49 it killed perhaps as much as a third of the population. The medieval historian Henry Knighton writes, *The grievous plague . . . struck as it were by sudden death; for there were few who kept their beds more than three days, or two days, or half a day; and after this the fell death broke forth on every side with the course of the sun.* Chaucer was fortunate to have survived.

English society had also to contend with political unrest both within and outside the country. Popular dissatisfaction over poverty, high taxation and corruption within the Court of King Richard II reached its peak in 1399. On his uncle John of Gaunt's death, the king seized his lands to fund a campaign in Ireland, and Gaunt's son Henry Bolingbroke returned from exile while the king was in Ireland to gather an army against him. Popular support for Bolingbroke was great, and many of the king's army deserted; finally, Richard was captured, imprisoned and deposed, and Bolingbroke was crowned King Henry IV.

Military campaigns

Internal strife, then, could not have been greater at the end of Chaucer's life; but there was no period during his lifetime when England was not at war. The Hundred Years War against France, begun in 1339 by Edward III against the provocative French King Philip in an attempt to regain the French throne, lasted (with occasional treaties) through the reigns of five kings, until 1453. Chaucer took part in the campaign of 1359–60, and in the *General Prologue*, the Knight's son has been on various campaigns against France, *in Flaundres, in Artoys, and Pycardie* (86). As well, there were military campaigns against Scotland and Ireland.

Military service could also be combined with the pursuit of spiritual ideals. Chaucer's Knight has fought most of his battles in the name of God, taking part in various Crusades to defeat Jews and Moslems (or 'Saracens') and win back the Holy Land from those considered to be 'pagans'. From the eleventh century, when the Greeks in the Holy Land called on the Pope for military assistance against the Turks, an extraordinary number of men had set out to fight for Christianity in the East, and themselves gain heavenly reward. The French chronicler Fulcher of Chartres records the Pope's summons in 1095: *Undertake this journey for the remission of your sins, assured of the imperishable glory of the kingdom of heaven.* Jerusalem was won in 1099 and a series of new Crusading states was set up in the East, but the empire was a vulnerable one, and Jerusalem fell once again to the Moslems in 1187.

The possibility of winning it back fuelled a further series of Crusades in the twelfth and thirteenth centuries, and as the Turks began to move into Europe other 'holy wars' were launched, which continued right up to the mid-fifteenth century.

The truth of military behaviour was sometimes far from Christian, as, for instance, the cruel sack of Alexandria (participated in by Chaucer's Knight) demonstrated, yet the ideals remained. It is in this context that we must see the Knight, who in the late fourteenth century has fought in as many Crusading campaigns as span Chaucer's life: against the Moslems in Spain, North Africa, the Near East, and the Baltic, where Henry IV himself fought (Chaucer's description mentions Lithuania and Russia) and against hostile pagans in Turkey. The Knight is thus of the highest order of warriors: he fights for Christ in a society that still believed absolutely in the establishment of God's kingdom on earth.

The military background of Chaucer's Knight and his tale, then, is a realistic one. War was a constant financial drain on the English economy, and expensive too in terms of lives; this in part caused the Peasants' Revolt in 1381. A popular lyric of the time complains of widespread corruption: *Truth is set under a lock and Falseness reigneth in every flock.* Discontent over taxation, low wages and high rents reached its height when a poll tax was levied to pay for the war. Rebellions began in Kent and Essex, led by Wat Tyler. Eventually the rebels descended on London itself, calmed only by the intervention of the king. Chaucer's writing, however, is remarkably apolitical and he refers only light-heartedly to the Peasants' Revolt in his *Nun's Priest's Tale*, where the people pursuing the cock stolen by the fox make more noise than one of its famous leaders, Jack Straw (3394).

The Church

The Peasants' Revolt was partly fuelled by tensions between Church and State. The Church was the other great force in medieval England; even the king, as God's representative, was subject to divine rule. Though ruled by Rome, the English Church was extremely powerful in its own right. Its structures and monastic houses had been established since the Anglo-Saxon period, and it was responsible for much administration, as well as funding schools and hospitals. Everyone was expected to attend church, and for many the sermon – the only part of the service not in Latin – would have been their only form of instruction and access to the written word. The Church had its own courts, regulating matters such as marriage, wills, tithes and immorality charges (Chaucer's Summoner would call people to the ecclesiastical courts).

Religious inspiration and devotion find concrete form in the powerful art of the Middle Ages: the great Gothic churches; the painting, tapestry and stained glass; the beautiful, ornate manuscripts; the gold and precious objects adorning churches; and much of the literature – the life of Saint Cecilia told by Chaucer's Second Nun is a good example. The promise of eternal life in an uncertain age was powerful, and many chose to lead holy lives, either in monasteries or convents, or independently, like the anchorites Dame Julian of Norwich and Richard Rolle.

Dissident religious groups, the Lollards and Wycliffites, emphasized the importance of the prayer of the common man, for whom the ploughman (a figure included by Chaucer in the *General Prologue*) became an emblem. Religious idealism was sometimes accompanied by criticism of the wealth and corruption of the Church, particularly once the 'Great Schism' of 1337 – when two popes vied with each other for power – had exposed the Church's politics.

Chaucer's religious figures span the two extremes of the ideal and the corrupt, with the ascetic Parson and Clerk balanced by the Monk, a highly worldly prelate, and the ambiguous figure of the Prioress, with her elegant dress, gold brooch, and lapdogs fed on white bread. The Pardoner, selling 'pardons' from sin for his own profit, exemplifies religious practices at their most corrupt. The Friar represents a member of one of the new 'mendicant' religious orders, whose members were not based in monasteries but made their livings by wandering and seeking alms – thus supposedly pursuing true poverty and promoting the charity of others. The Friar demonstrates just how unruly and corrupt such figures could become: his only interests are profit and pleasures of a very secular kind.

The 'three estates'

In the *General Prologue*, Chaucer draws on a traditional theory of society as made up of 'three estates,' the nobility, the Church, and the peasants – those who fight, those who pray and those who work. The Knight, the Parson, and the Plowman are idealized representatives of this interdependent hierarchy, and to these estates belong the more individualized figures of the Squire, the Knight's son; the Franklin, a member of the lesser, country aristocracy; the Clerk, an ascetic Oxford scholar; the Nun's Priest and undescribed Second Nun; and the Yeoman, the Squire's servant, who is a forester or game-keeper.

The 'estates satire' was a familiar medieval literary genre. Such satires listed examples of members of the three estates, with descriptions of their typical virtues and vices. Chaucer plays with this tradition in his use of both idealized portraits and descriptions of highly flawed members of the estates, most obviously the worldly Monk, Prioress and Friar, and the corrupt parasites of the Church, the red-faced Summoner and the sinister Pardoner.

But the *General Prologue* also moves beyond the notion of the three estates to depict the growing middle classes. The strong spirit of commercial enterprise in medieval England is evident in the figures of the Shipman – with his own ship the 'Maudeleyn' – the Reeve, the manager of a northern estate, and the Miller, affluent from his dishonest sale of corn. Although England still had a largely agrarian economy, a considerable movement to the cities had begun: the population of London was about 45,000, and it had large suburbs as well, like Stratford-atte-Bowe, the home of Chaucer's Prioress. There was a new sense of civic community and urban needs – government, planning, architecture, roads, cleaning and sanitation.

A new merchant or bourgeois class was emerging – most obviously represented in the *Canterbury Tales* by the Merchant, but also by the Wife of Bath, who has her own cloth-making business, and Harry Bailey himself, the keeper of the Tabard Inn at Southwark. Other, more elevated civic figures, members of the professional classes, are present too – the Physician, the Man of Law and the Manciple, a business agent of an Inn of Court. The pilgrimage includes as well a group of working-class city dwellers – a Haberdasher (hat-dealer), a Carpenter, a Webbe (weaver), a Tapycer (a weaver of tapestries), and the Cook.

The notion of the city and the spirit of bourgeoisie interweave with the traditional model of the three estates. The audience for Chaucer's poetry would have been similarly mixed, comprising both the court and the new middle classes, who were unlikely to read French or Latin but eager to own books and avid for literature written in English.

Activity

Consider the frontispiece of a manuscript of Chaucer's poem *Troilus and Criseyde*, reproduced below, which depicts the poet reading to his audience. What kind of audience is it? What is the setting? What would be the effect of the poet reading to his fellow courtiers? How would the situation differ from one where there was a bourgeois audience or reader?

*The frontispiece of
Corpus Christi's manuscript of*
Troilus and Criseyde

The Canterbury Tales

Chaucer's depiction of society finds its focus in the Canterbury pilgrimage, which has drawn followers from all walks of life, whose motives range from highly religious to completely secular. The ideal of the penitential journey to visit the *blisful martyr*'s tomb and find spiritual regeneration is balanced by the use of the pilgrimage as a money-making enterprise by the Pardoner and Friar, and the Wife of Bath's search for a sixth husband, while for the Monk and Prioress the pilgrimage seems more a pleasure-seeking expedition than a spiritual experience.

Like the Crusades, the idea of a pilgrimage, a journey to a holy place – most often a shrine sacred to the relics and memory of a saint – had enormous impact in the medieval period. Startlingly large numbers of people journeyed to shrines within England such as Walsingham or Canterbury, to Continental holy places like Rome, Lourdes and Santiago de Compostela, and even the Holy Land. The Wife of Bath's several pilgrimages were surpassed by those of the medieval mystic Margery Kempe, who among many journeys went as far as Jerusalem itself. Pilgrimage offered the chance to do penance by undertaking an arduous journey, and to reanimate spiritual life by worshipping in holy places; it offered too the possibility of adventure, experience and self-realization.

The search for the spiritual is a recurrent theme of the *Canterbury Tales* as a whole, recalled in the various religious tales and the highly moral sermon of the Parson at the end. The image of the pilgrims' goal, the great cathedral at Canterbury, hovers over the work, reminding us of the world of the sacred beyond, of Christian principles and belief, and of the struggle of good against evil. Thomas à Becket, the saint whose shrine the pilgrims seek, was murdered in his own cathedral in 1170 after many political conflicts with the king, when four of Henry II's knights acted on his question, *Who will rid me of that turbulent priest?* The tale of Thomas's martyrdom and the miracles associated with his shrine drew worshippers from all over Europe.

Activity

> Read the opening of the *General Prologue* (1–18). What imagery does Chaucer use? What asssociations does the spring have? Can they be spiritual as well as secular? Is sexuality an idea you associate with spring? Note the ambiguous term 'corage' (11), which can mean either spirit or heart, and can imply either spiritual or sexual desire. Can you assess the motives of the individual pilgrims for setting out to Canterbury?

Collections of stories

The story-telling competition that ensues, like the descriptions of the pilgrims and the springtime setting, is rooted in a literary convention. Chaucer would have been familiar with many kinds of story collections – legends, saints' lives, fables, classical myths, in particular Ovid's *Metamorphoses*, and the Bible itself. None of these, however, uses a frame narrative like the pilgrimage, nor does any use individualized narrators, or the range of genres of the *Canterbury Tales*. The most similar work is Boccaccio's *Decameron*, written in the 1340s and presented as a collection of stories told by a group of Italian nobles to while away their stay outside the plague-ridden city of Florence. This contains a number of tales analogous to the *Canterbury Tales*, though Boccaccio does not develop the relationships of the tellers or the possibilities of literary variation – and it is by no means certain that Chaucer knew his work.

The idea of the story-telling competition is original to Chaucer, and it allows for the natural inclusion of a large number of diverse tales, which captures the diversity of pilgrims, *Diverse folk diversely thy seyde*, but, at the same time, excuses Chaucer from responsibility in the 'immoral' tales. The reader can always *turne over the leef and chese another tale* (*Miller's Prologue*, 3177): *Blameth nat me if that ye chese amys*, says Chaucer (*Miller's Prologue*, 3181).

The teller and the tale

The interplay between pilgrim and tale, but also between pilgrims, is a crucial part of the *Canterbury Tales*; early critics tended to see the *Canterbury Tales* almost exclusively as a kind of 'roadside drama'. Recent criticism, however, has emphasized the limits of such a view – we do not know what form the final drama would have taken, since Chaucer (perhaps unsurprisingly) did not finish the projected design of two tales told by each pilgrim, one on the way, another on the way back. Twenty-four tales survive, not all completed, no two by the same pilgrim, and there is some evidence that the links between tales and narrators were not yet definite. Nor was manuscript culture like book culture: the 55 manuscripts of the *Canterbury Tales* are copied in different ways by scribes, with different spellings, often lacking parts, and in different orders. We know the order of only small groups of tales or 'fragments' that are found consistently together (for example, the Knight's, Miller's and Reeve's tales), and thus the notion of the interaction between pilgrims cannot be taken too far.

Despite this, camaraderie and rivalries, already hinted at in the prologue, are evident: the Miller and Reeve, like the Friar and Summoner, tell tales against each other; the Miller responds to the Knight, the Clerk addresses the Wife of Bath in his story of patient Griselda. The tales serve to illuminate their narrators, sometimes in surprising ways: we don't necessarily expect the Prioress to tell a highly anti-Semitic, graphic tale of the violent death of a little boy, or the Wife to tell an Arthurian romance. Just as we cannot see the work exclusively in terms of the drama of the pilgrims, however, it is reductive to see individual tales purely as a function of their narrators, about whom, in some cases, we have little or no knowledge – the Second Nun or the Nun's Priest, for instance. The tales are complex, sophisticated pieces of writing in their own right, which frequently move beyond characterization of their tellers. Thus for all its bawdy humour, the Miller's tale is an elaborately crafted, brilliant structural response to the Knight's tale, which plays on courtly conventions with a literary self-consciousness that we cannot reasonably attribute to the Miller.

The *Canterbury Tales* allowed Chaucer to experiment with all extant medieval genres: romance, *fabliau*, beast-fable, saint's life, miracle story, sermon, moral treatise. Frequently, tales are not quite what they seem: they subvert convention, or gain an ironic quality through their relations to their own narrators and to other tellers and tales. Criticism analysing and comparing tales in terms of genre has proved a useful way of approaching Chaucer's work.

The power dynamic of the narrators is especially obvious at the start, as the Miller constructs his tale to *quite* or outdo the Knight's tale which precedes it; the Reeve's tale continues the pattern of *quityng* as the Reeve, angered by the Miller's mockery of a carpenter (his own profession), narrates a tale whose villain is a miller. The Knight tells a tale eminently fitting to his rank, a long classical romance (a term meaning a courtly narrative, rather than exclusively a love story, in this period). The tale uses elevated language, full of rhetorical devices, to tell of the tragic love of two noble kinsmen, Palamon and Arcite, for the lady Emilye, and it is set against a backdrop of war, imprisonment, tournaments and chivalry, and the classical gods.

The Miller's Tale

Harry Bailey chooses a suitable respondent for the Knight, *telleth ye, sir Monk . . . / Somwhat to quite with the Knyghtes tale* (3119), but instead, the Miller intervenes drunkenly with *lewed dronken harlotrye* (3145). His story is a *fabliau*, a comic, bawdy story of low life, far from the saint's life that the Miller's phrase *a legende and a lif* (3141) promises.

Most of Chaucer's writing has some kind of literary source, and much Chaucer criticism addresses this question of sources: there are many Continental *fabliaux* analogous to the *Miller's Tale*, though none is a direct source and none is so brilliantly comic. The tale turns courtly values and genres upside down on every level: the classical world of the Knight's tale, with its noble inhabitants, is replaced by contemporary *Oxenford*, peopled by craftsmen and clerics. At the same time, the stories parallel or balance each other. The Miller employs the same triangular structure of two men and one woman as the Knight: the rivalry of the two male figures for Alisoun allows Chaucer to create a burlesque of the courtly romance form.

Whereas in the Knight's tale the two protagonists are imprisoned both literally and by love, in the Miller's narrative Alisoun is *caged*, married to a much older husband (3221–26).

Activity

Consider the description of Alisoun (3233–70). What kind of imagery does Chaucer use? Is Alisoun compared to noble, courtly objects? What effect does the description create? Is sexuality a theme? What do the words *likerous* (3244), *popelote* (3254), *wenche* (3254) imply?

The sexuality hinted at in the description of Alisoun fuels the plot of the *Miller's Tale*, from the moment when *hende Nicholas* takes hold of Alisoun, *prively he caughte hire by the queynte, / And seyde, 'Ywis, but if ich have my wille, / For deerne love of thee, lemman, I spille'* (3276–78). The scene becomes a burlesque of courtly romance, which repeatedly employs the notion of love as a wound or malady that causes the victim to swoon, sigh, weep, and even die: the true lover becomes the abject servant of the lady, and love a sublime, refined emotion with its own code of behaviour, best described in the terms of medieval romance as *fin'amors*, refined love. Tales such as the Knight's and Franklin's treat the notion of *fin'amors* seriously. Nicholas uses conventional images of suffering and service, but his actions are rather more direct than those of the courtly lover: he seizes Alisoun *harde by the haunchebones* (3279), and his plea, *Lemman, love me al atones, / Or I wol dyen* (3280–81), seems to express desire for sexual fulfilment rather than sublime love. Alisoun's denials are swiftly set aside, and the music that might accompany a lover's expression of his grief in a courtly romance becomes a sexual image as Nicholas plays his sawtrie *faste, and maketh melodie* (3306).

Activity

> The overt and natural sexuality of Nicholas and Alisoun finds a contrast in Chaucer's portrayal of Absolon. Compare the description of Absolon (3312–3338) with those of Alisoun (3233–70) and Nicholas (3199–220). How are Absolon's physical traits described? Is his behaviour courtly? Why does Chaucer include the lines *he was somdeel squaymous / Of fartyng, and of speche daungerous* (3337–38)? Does Absolon have any redeeming features?

The story also plays on the opposition of social classes. Nicholas, *a poure scoler* (3190), is set up against John, *a riche gnof* (3188), a rich churl: the cleric's learning is opposed to the craftsman's ignorance, *A clerk hadde litherly biset his whyle, / But if he koude a carpenter bigyle*, says Nicholas (3299–300). The deception depends on Nicholas's astrological predictions of a flood, his prophecy of the end of the world, and his use of biblical comparisons and examples. The barrels John builds for their escape from the Flood are a concrete emblem of John's carpentry as well as the means of his final cuckolding and public shame. He becomes the victim of his ignorance and his inability to comprehend human relations – most evident in his choice of Alisoun as wife. It is notable that only Alisoun goes scot-free in the tale, while the male figures all suffer wounds of different types. In this tale as in a number of others, referred to by the early critic G. L. Kittredge as 'the marriage group', the freedom of the woman within marriage is addressed. Recent criticism has placed particular emphasis on Chaucer's treatment of women, and there have been a number of feminist studies of Chaucer.

The Merchant's Tale

The Merchant's Tale also addresses the issue of marriage, and again parodies the conventions of *fin'amors* by interweaving romance and *fabliau*. Chaucer uses a similar narrative pattern of the marriage of the young and beautiful woman to the aged, undesirable man – the very names of his characters, January and May, make the theme explicit. January's folly is evident in his excessive praise of marriage as a worldly paradise and of young wives, whereas his friends rehearse the traditional anti-feminist position often emphasized in clerical writing. The tale engages with the possibility of arranged marriage, a very real one in the Middle Ages. The female body is bought as an investment by January for the union of *Oold fissh and yong flessh* (1418).

Activity

> Consider the description of the wedding night of January and May (1805–57). What is its effect? Is it comic or horrific? What imagery is used? What is May's response? How is she described?

The tale illuminates the disturbing possibility of reducing the woman to sexual object and commodity. As the story unfolds, however, May's role shifts from victim to adulteress, and we come to question her apparently virtuous passivity. Like May's suffering, her suitor Damian's love first appears courtly and idealized, and Chaucer uses traditional images of illness and wounding: he is struck with Venus's brand so that he comes close to madness *for the verray peyne* (1775); he swoons, weeps and laments, taking to his bed with the malady of love.

Activity

> Consider the wooing of May by Damian, and her response (1875–1954). Is their relationship courtly and refined? Where does she read Damian's letter, and what is the effect of this setting? How is her plotting to deceive January described (1977–2008)? What is Chaucer's reason for the details he uses, for instance regarding the key to the garden (2116–24)?

The garden itself is a recurrent image in medieval romance, the traditional setting for lovers' meetings (see for example the depiction of lovers in a courtly garden on page 13). January uses the elevated, religious language of the Old Testament *Song of Songs* or *Song of Solomon* (a collection of erotic love poems usually read allegorically as God's call to the Church or soul) to call May into the garden (2138–48). Such excess serves to remind us how far we are from a tale of idealized divine or secular love; this garden is neither the biblical paradise nor the courtly garden of romance, but a parody of Eden, where the blind January assists in his own cuckolding by helping May into the pear tree in which Damian waits. We can't help noticing the echoes of the familiar story of the snake waiting by the Tree of Knowledge to provoke the Fall of Adam and Eve, and hence the first sexual sin. Courtliness is overturned, and January's power usurped.

In a sense, the adultery seems to be justified by the inequality of the marriage, yet it is also disturbing: women are shown to be as treacherous as men, and gender relationships are built on deceit and betrayal. The story plays on the misogynist stereotypes of women hinted at by January's friends earlier on, both in the portrayal of May and in the sub-plot, a dialogue

Lovers in a garden from Book of Hours, *or the* Golf Book, *c. 1520 (from the workshop of Gerart Horenbout and Simon Bening)*

between the two figures from classical myth whom Chaucer inserts into the garden, Pluto and Proserpina. Classical writers like Ovid tell how Pluto abducted Proserpina to the underworld to become his queen, but here Pluto has become a henpecked husband and Proserpina a shrewish wife; we totally forget, as the critic Jill Mann has pointed out, that *this is a rapist talking*. Pluto, like January, becomes the victim. The tale leaves us uncertain about the place of women – are they innocent victims, or shrewish adulteresses?

The Wife of Bath's Prologue

In *The Wife of Bath's Prologue*, Chaucer addresses the question of women at some length, thus exposing a lively cultural debate. The Wife sets up her own *experience* against the *auctoritee* of clerical writers (1), whose perspective on women could be a very negative one. There were undoubtedly strong female role models in the period – including the female saints, the women of classical legend, and powerful historical figures like Eleanor of Aquitaine. But women were also seen as different by nature from men.

According to the Book of Genesis, whereas Adam was created when God breathed life into the dust of the ground, Eve was formed from Adam's rib and identified from the start as his possession. The woman was associated definitively with the body, and appropriately was the bearer of children, whereas the man was associated with the rational and the soul, and viewed as having the right to rule women. The woman's frailty was proven by her role in the Fall: singled out as the weaker vessel by Satan, *she took of the fruit therof, and did eat, and gave also unto her husband with her; and he did eat* (Genesis 3:6). Because the Fall resulted in the first act of lust, woman was connected with sexual temptation. Saint Paul's epistles repeatedly warn against women as frail, tempting and inferior, the *second sex*; later Saint Jerome notably condemns the natural provocativeness of women, writing of the woman's insatiable capacity for lust, and there is a plethora of other damning writings against women by medieval clerics. A twelfth-century life of a fictional Greek philosopher, for example, contained the following popular definition:

> *What is Woman? – Man's undoing; an insatiable animal; perpetual trouble and non-stop combat; man's daily ruin; a storm in the home; an impediment to peace of mind; the wreck of a weak-willed man; instrument of adultery; expensive war; the very worst creature and heaviest burden; fatal snake; human property.*

> (*Life of Secundus*, 36–37, trans. Blamires)

Fortunately women also had a positive role model in Mary, the Second Eve. Crucial to Mary's perfection was her virginity: she had conceived without participating in the sexual act, and was unpolluted. Those who chose to become nuns and lead lives of virginity followed Mary, and were empowered by sloughing off the taint of the lustful body. Although it was recognized that not all could pursue this life, there was no doubt that virgins were at the top of the hierarchy of chastity, with widows next, and chaste wives lowest. Women were polarized, with Eve at one end of the spectrum and Mary at the other. The virtuous, rewarded woman tended also to be the passive, suffering, virgin saint – often a martyr, since only the dead virgin was totally free from the threat of the body.

The Wife of Bath's Prologue engages directly with the problem of connecting virginity and virtue, *Virginitee is greet perfeccion* (105), she says, for those who please to be *clene, body and goost* (97); but this life is not for all, *Wher can ye seye, in any manere age, / That hye God defended* [forbade] *mariage . . . Or where comanded he virginitee?* (60–62). Her Prologue defends earthly marriage and sexuality: God bade us wax and multiply; He made no mention of numbers, indeed, biblical figures like Solomon, Abraham and Jacob had more than one wife; and if we were all virgins, how should the human race propagate; what are sexual organs made for?

The Wife enumerates recurrent and destructive stereotypes of married women common to clerical writing: they are spendthrift; gossipy; proud; assailed by all men if fair; desirous of all if not; chiding and shrewish; in *peril of . . . chastite* (339) if they dress nicely; possessive and destructive, their lust like *wilde fyr; / The moore it brenneth, the moore it hath desir / To consume every thyng that brent wole be* (373–75). The woman is compared to the worm that destroys the tree, a reference back to the serpent.

The Wife lists legendary examples of wicked women, whose stories are told by celebrated misogynist writers such as Valerius and Theofrastus, who attack marriage, and Jerome, who passionately defends virginity. Jankyn, the Wife's fifth husband, reads a typical anti-feminist work, which describes Eve's betrayal of mankind, and the betrayal by women of famous men like Socrates. The Wife's prologue equates to her act of tearing out the leaves of Jankyn's book of wicked wives; she turns the tools of misogynist clerics back on them, albeit in a way that might greatly have distressed thinkers like Jerome, using the Bible and other authorities subversively to defend sex and marriage through her own experience. Her use of a celebrated fable, of the question asked by a lion on looking at the painting of a man killing a lion, sums up her approach: *Who peyntede the leon, telle me who?* (692). If women had told the stories, they might be rather different.

Activity

> The Wife's persona has received a varied and conflicting critical response. Do you see her as a positive or negative figure? Does Chaucer's portrayal of her confirm or condemn patriarchal stereotypes of women as lustful and shrewish? How do we assess the Wife's open sexuality and readiness to welcome her sixth husband? Is the *Prologue* an anti-feminist or feminist work, or neither?

The Pardoner's Tale

The Miller, the Merchant and the Wife all engage in different ways with the secular, with the topics of desire, love and marriage, and with the nature and predicament of women. With the Pardoner and his tale, we enter a very different world, that of the Church and corruption within it.

The tale chillingly recognizes the possibility of hypocrisy and the seductiveness of evil. The granting of pardons or indulgences, as they were often called, was particularly open to abuse: pardons could be given by the Church in return for penance or good deeds, which often took the form of monetary donations, and the money gained through this practice was considerable. Professional pardoners like Chaucer's sold pardons irrespective of merit and for their own profit. Various medieval writings condemn the practices of pardoners. William Langland, for example, describes a pardoner who *preched . . . as he a preest were*, using false letters of indulgence to gain rings and brooches and then sharing the proceeds with the parish priest rather than the poor (*Piers Plowman*, 68–82). Chaucer follows in this tradition in a uniquely dramatic way, by allowing the Pardoner himself to narrate the story of his corruption. His prologue tells his own tale: his sale of false relics, his false prayers and use of Latin and Church documents to drive home his bargain, and his ability to play on human sins.

The Pardoner makes clear that he is highly skilled in the art of story-telling – an art that was indeed essential for preachers in the Middle Ages. It was common to use *ensamples* (435) or moral stories that illuminated the theological points made in a sermon. The tale takes as its model the medieval sermon: it centres on a biblical text, *radix malorum est Cupiditas* (334; 'greed is the root of all evils'), and develops this topic of greed, one of the seven deadly sins. The subject of the seven deadly sins (categories under which all sins could be classified) was a familiar one in sermons and other religious writings, and the Pardoner opens with a vivid description of tavern sins – gluttony, gambling and false-swearing – sins especially relevant to the pilgrims. His rhetoric is recognizably that of the preacher, as he catalogues human sin, recalls the Fall, and points a finger at different individuals, such as the man in Cheapside. He offers a series of biblical examples to support his condemnation of these sins. He then illustrates his main text through an extended moral *ensample*, the story of the three rioters who seek death. The tale is a well-known one with various Continental versions, but the Pardoner's telling is unique.

Activity

> What is the effect of the Pardoner's prologue on his tale? Note his comment, *For though myself be a ful vicious man / A moral tale yet I yow telle kan* (459–60). Is it possible that the tale can still be read positively, as teaching a moral lesson? Can you think of any modern parallels in either politics or religion?

The story is rhetorically highly effective, and tightly constructed in vivid dramatic terms, with the image of the *privee theef men clepeth Deeth* (675), the mysterious old man who seeks death and directs the riotours *up this croked way* (761) to find it; the glittering bushels of treasure; the careful plans of the three companions; the description of the poison; and the grimly neat ending. Its message is chilling and its mode effective: yet because the Pardoner has already told the tale of his corrupt practices, it is also deeply shocking. Because the Pardoner has revealed his own sinfulness, in a very odd way the tale works against him. His prologue has identified his besetting sin as greed: this is evident not only in his selling of false pardons, but also in his love of the tavern. Yet he tells a story of three young men overly fond of the tavern, who destroy each other through greed. Are we to see the Pardoner's existence as questioning the power of morality, or his story as damning him eternally? His highly self-conscious narration is disturbing: he repeatedly reminds us of the tale's literary status and his role as narrator, with phrases like *now wol I telle forth my tale* (660), boasting of his hypocrisy. We become aware of the destructive power of evil and the need for moral government.

Small wonder that the pilgrims respond negatively to his concluding offer to pardon them for avarice, if they will purchase his relics and pardons. Harry Bailly's response when the Pardoner suggests he come up to kiss the relics – that he would prefer to castrate the Pardoner – is perhaps understandably savage. The Pardoner personifies abuse of Christian practice and belief, and we are made keenly aware of the danger of separating the physical manifestations of Christianity from their spiritual significance. Desire for economic profit replaces spiritual desire here, and we are a long way from any sense of a meaningful pilgrimage to Canterbury.

Chaucer's achievement

Chaucer, then, in creating the *Canterbury Tales*, presents us with a vivid and memorable vision of medieval society in all its variety. The idealism of the Knight is balanced by the corruption of the Pardoner, the asceticism of the Parson by the worldliness of the Prioress, the authority of the Clerk by the experience of the Wife of Bath. The tales, like their narrators, span the different spheres of society, from secular to religious, from the lower-class world of the Miller's tale to the aristocratic one of the Knight's; they span too the sweep of history, from ancient Greece to the fourteenth century. Similarly, they range over and engage with the different genres of literature popular in the period – the romance, the *fabliau*, the sermon, the clerical treatise – often combining or subverting these genres. Chaucer plays at realizing his own society on the page, with an objectivity and realism that allow him to shape a most distinctive voice, sometimes ironic, often sympathetic, always believable. Like Shakespeare after him, he is a writer of dazzling diversity, who balances wit and learning with a startling immediacy and ability to range from robust comedy and light-heartedness to profound emotion and existential questions.

2 Renaissance Contexts

● ●

> *Kings and Princes, as well the evill as the good, doe raigne by Gods ordinance, and that subjects are bounden to obey them . . . Kings, Queenes, and other Princes . . . are ordeined of GOD, are to bee obeyed and honoured of their subjects: that such subjects, as are disobedient or rebellious against their Princes, disobey GOD, and procure their owne damnation . . . Is not rebellion the greatest of all mischiefes?*
>
> An Homilie against disobedience and wilfull rebellion, *1571*

The defeat and death of Richard III at the battle of Bosworth in 1485 brought thirty years of civil war to an end. His conqueror Henry VII was the first Tudor king, and in the succeeding years of Tudor rule memories of the Wars of the Roses were a potent warning about the instability of regimes. Tudor propaganda sought to secure and legitimize hereditary rule, under conditions that continually threatened rebellion.

The Tudors

The major destabilizing force in the sixteenth century was the religious upheaval known as the Reformation. Protestantism came to England as a result of Henry VIII's decision to divorce his Queen, Katherine of Aragon, who had failed to give him a son, and to marry his pregnant mistress Anne Boleyn. In defiance of the Pope, who would not grant him a divorce, Henry appointed himself Supreme Head of the Church in England. Until 1533 Henry had been a supporter of the Catholic Church, and early converts to Protestantism were tried and burned at the stake as heretics. After 1533 it was the turn of Catholics who would not take the oath of allegiance to Henry to be persecuted and executed. On his daughter Mary's ascension to the throne in 1553, she restored Roman Catholicism, married a Catholic king and persecuted Protestants. During her reign nearly 300 people were burned as heretics and many Protestants fled abroad. When Elizabeth I became Queen she re-introduced the moderate Protestantism of Henry VIII. In her cautious religious settlement of 1559, the Book of Common Prayer was reintroduced and services were conducted in English instead of Latin. Gradually, religious tensions eased, but even under Elizabeth there were rebellions.

There were often underlying economic reasons for rebellion: resistance to taxation under Henry VII and Henry VIII; resistance to enclosures under Henry VIII and Edward VI; distress caused by high prices, food shortages and leaping inflation in the time of Edward VI, Mary and Elizabeth. But in most cases, local groups were stirred to rebellion by the unease they felt as accustomed religious practices were overturned. Every Tudor monarch faced rebellion, although they tried to moderate and dispel grievances by propaganda encouraging obedience. The loyalty of subject to monarch was promulgated as a Christian virtue. Disobedience was a sin, even when a monarch's demands were unjust – it was for God to punish an unjust king. The Tudor message was preached from pulpits and spread by broadsheets and pamphlets. Homilies were read every Sunday in church, like the one quoted at the head of this chapter. The theory of obedience spread into all relationships: servant to lord, apprentice to master, child to parent, wife to husband. *The rule of obedience that is betwixt the magistrate and the subject holdeth betwixt the husband and the wife, the father and his child, the master and the servant*, wrote Elizabeth's Archbishop Whitgift.

Another powerful piece of Tudor propaganda was the image of the monarch as the loving head of a united family. Erasmus, in his *Institutio Principis Christiana*, 1516, wrote: *The good prince ought to have the same attitude toward his subjects as a good paterfamilias toward his household . . . for what else is a kingdom but a great family? What is a king if not the father to a great multitude?* Tudor monarchs repeated this idea constantly to encourage support from the people. The Lord Protector Somerset, replying on behalf of Edward VI to the demands of rebels in 1549, wrote: *We be content to use our princely authority like a father to his children.* Mary, appealing to the citizens of London for their support at the dangerous time of Wyatt's rebellion said: *Certainly, if a prince and governor may as naturally and earnestly love her subjects as the mother doth love the child, then assure yourselves that I, being your lady and mistress, do as earnestly and tenderly love and favour you.* Tudors also carefully cultivated the concept of the *body politic*, in which the King was portrayed as the head of a human body and the lords and gentry as its members or limbs. In speeches, print and pictures, the phrase *body politic* was used to reinforce the idea of an indissoluble unity of king and populace.

Printing presses spread rapidly in the sixteenth century and the control of print was a powerful political weapon. Plays too, even though they were unprinted manuscripts, were censored and any reference to *matters of religion* or *governance* was suspect. At the start of Elizabeth's reign in 1559 a proposal was drafted to regulate performances:

> *The Queen's Majesty doth strictly forbid all manner interludes to be played either openly or privately, except the same be notified beforehand, and licensed . . . her Majesty doth likewise charge . . . that they permit none to be played wherein either matters of religion or of the governance of the estate of the commonweal shall be handled or treated upon.*

From 1578 a fair copy of the manuscript of every play had to pass the censorship of the Master of the Revels before being licensed for performance. Since it was known that nothing blasphemous or seditious would pass, self-censorship operated powerfully on Elizabethan playwrights. No living monarch could be represented on the stage. Nothing threatening the stability of the throne was acceptable. It was blasphemy to swear using the name of God, a restriction the playwrights got around by invoking classical deities like Ceres, Juno and Jupiter, or using more neutral phrases such as *heavens*, or *gods*, or *fates*, or *providence*, like Hamlet's *There's a special providence in the fall of a sparrow* (V.2.158).

Drama, censored and licensed, voiced Tudor fears about rebellion and disobedience. Dramatic incidents in Shakespeare often start with a problem of loyalty – of subject to king, servant to master, wife to husband, child to parent. Rebellion within the family leads to discord; within the state it leads to death and disaster. The structure of the comedies naturally impels the plays towards harmonious endings. It is more revealing to consider the histories and tragedies, and note how their endings resolve and dissipate the dangers of discord and rebellion. Tragic heroes die, but the plays conclude in a state of peace, even if it is an exhausted or *glooming peace* as the Prince describes it at the end of *Romeo and Juliet.*

Activity

> Consider any Shakespeare play containing a household. Is it a place of harmony or discord? What are the rewards of living in a harmonious household, and what troubles arise in a discordant one?

In the late sixteenth century, the population was increasing rapidly and nowhere more so than in London, the fastest-growing city in Europe. From the countryside where the growth in population put pressure on land, people migrated to London in the hope of employment. London's population swelled from around 60,000 at the start of the sixteenth century, much what it had been for over a hundred years, to 200,000 or more by 1600. It was the political and the economic centre of the country. The Tudor Court settled in London, attracting nobles and gentry to the city. The export of woollen cloth, the basis of the country's economy, operated mainly through the ports of London. John Stow wrote in his *Survey of London* (1598):

> *As for the retailers, therefore, and handicraftsmen, it is no marvel if they abandon country towns, and resort to London, for not only the court, which is now-a-days much greater and more gallant than in former times, and which was wont to be contented to remain with a small company, sometimes at an abbey or priory, sometimes at a bishop's house, and sometimes at some mean manor of the king's own, is now for the most part either abiding at London, or else so near unto it, that the provision of things most fit for it may easily be fetched from thence; but also by occasion thereof, the gentlemen of all shires do fly and flock to this city.*

As Stow noticed, gentlemen flocked to London and hung around the Court, partly in hope of preferment and employment, partly to complete their education. Education expanded during the sixteenth century with the founding of many grammar schools and increasing numbers of students at the universities. Historians believe that at no time until the late twentieth century were so many students in tertiary education as under Elizabeth I. Falstaff, Justice Shallow and Silence in *Henry IV Part 2* were all students at the Inns of Court in London. Silence has a son at university. It was the standard upbringing for a young gentleman, and to have access at Court, to be able to speak to a great lord, was a privileged position. Falstaff, on hearing that Hal is King, believes he can command favours for himself and all his friends. *A friend i'the Court is better than a penny in purse*, says Shallow in *Henry IV Part 2* (V.1.26).

At the other end of the scale were the poor, who also flocked to London in the late sixteenth century. Tudor statutes against vagrancy reveal the authorities' concern about *masterless men*, the poor but able unemployed. They attempted to return such people to the parishes of their birth. The Act of 1531 states that:

> *if any man or woman being whole . . . in body and able to labour having no land, master, nor using any lawful merchandise, craft, or mystery, whereby he might get a living . . . be vagrant . . . then it shall be lawful . . . to arrest the said vagabonds and idle persons and to bring them to any of the Justices of Peace . . . (who) shall cause every such idle person . . . to be tied to the end of a cart naked and be beaten with whips . . . and after such punishment . . . to return forthwith without delay . . . to the place where he was born, or where he last dwelled.*

The 1590s, when Shakespeare's plays were first appearing on stage, were a time of hunger, plague, unemployment, inflation and high food prices. There had already been some poor harvests in the 1580s, and between 1594 and 1598 there were five continuous years of bad weather, heavy rains, and crop failures, leading to starvation and plague. Poverty is always treated sympathetically by Shakespeare, culminating in King Lear's anguished recognition in the storm scene that he has taken too little care of *poor naked wretches*. In any Shakespeare play, even in those where the poor and dispossessed do not appear on stage, there is a sense of the fragility of life that makes the security of a harmonious household precious. In *Twelfth Night*, Feste's refrain *the rain it raineth every day* hints at a bleak life outside Olivia's protection. Though he breaks bounds occasionally, Feste chooses to return to her household.

Another troubling group for the authorities were the aliens or *strangers*, amongst whom were Jews and 'blackamoors'. Historians now recognize that after the expulsion of the Jews in 1290 some remained or returned, and from the fourteenth to the seventeenth century there was a small Jewish population. The numbers were tiny and there is no obvious reason why they should have been so vilified, but hated they were and horrific stories against them were believed – that Jews ritually murdered Christians, killed children, poisoned wells and extorted interest on loans, which was forbidden by the Bible. There was an even smaller number of 'blackamoors', yet in 1601 Elizabeth ordered all *such slaves* to be transported out of England (there is no evidence that this happened). The reasons given in the Order may explain the authorities' anxiety: the fear was that strangers took work from unemployed Englishmen. These fears and myths feed into literature, where the figure of a Jew or 'blackamoor' signified a villain, like Barabas in Marlowe's *Jew of Malta* or Aaron the Moor in Shakespeare's *Titus Andronicus*. It is difficult for us today to recognize how mould-breaking the presentation of a heroic Moor was in Shakespeare's *Othello*.

Elizabethan drama

Playwrights and actors joined the stream of artisans who made their way to London in search of work. Actors gained their livelihoods on the margins of legitimate employment. Unless they had the protection of the monarch or a great lord, players were at risk of being classed as vagabonds, with all the penalties that lack of status attracted. The playing companies which thrived were all technically the household servants of a named aristocrat (see Unit 8, *Theatres and Playing Spaces*). They served a populace that had never before been so concentrated into one civic area, and in the last quarter of the century they were able to build themselves permanent playhouses.

Christopher Marlowe and William Shakespeare were the same age, both born in 1564. Ben Jonson was a little younger, born in 1572. Marlowe was the son of a Canterbury shoemaker, Shakespeare's father was a glover in Stratford upon Avon and Jonson was the stepson of a London bricklayer. All three had a good humanist, classical education at their local grammar schools and, in time, moved up the social scale from artisans to gentlemen. Marlowe went to university. He won a scholarship from the Archbishop of Canterbury to Corpus Christi College, Cambridge, which automatically conferred on him the status of a gentleman at graduation. Shakespeare and Jonson, lacking higher education, attained the status of gentleman late in their lives.

Christopher Marlowe

Marlowe's student years at Cambridge have mysterious episodes. It was standard practice for students who were secretly Catholics to stay on at university for an MA and then to disappear just before graduating to Rheims in France, where they were trained as Catholic priests and returned clandestinely to England. Marlowe disappeared just before taking his MA but reappeared later. The university authorities were reluctant to allow him to graduate until ordered to do so by the Privy Council. The directive stated that *it was not her Majesties pleasure that anie one emploied as he had been in matters touching the benefitt of his Countrie should be defamed by those that are ignorant in th' affaires he went about*. Lord Walsingham ran an efficient spy service for Elizabeth I and biographers suspect that Marlowe, who was a friend of Walsingham's nephew while at Cambridge, accompanied Catholic students to Rheims, pretending to be one of them while in fact spying for the Queen. He was murdered in a tavern at the age of 29 while he was on bail on a charge of treason, with evidence against him of atheism, and this has added to the mystery surrounding him.

Dr Faustus

The heroes of Marlowe's plays are Renaissance high-strivers, gifted men who make their way in the world from modest beginnings to the heights of their professions; brave men who push their remarkable talents to the limit and test, by their failures, the ultimate boundaries of personal ambition. Dr Faustus is already a learned scholar when the play opens. His studies have reached an impasse – he is dissatisfied with the conclusions of his scholarship and is driven to seek forbidden knowledge. Intellectual curiosity and a capacity for learning are his spectacular abilities, but they are also the qualities that destroy him.

Activity

> *Dr Faustus* is rooted in scholarship and an awareness of the potential power of knowledge, but the great learning that Faustus possesses leads him into a pact with Lucifer. The knowledge that costs him his soul is put to trivial use. How does *Dr Faustus* convey both interest in and concern about the advancement of learning during the Reformation? What do you feel is the attitude of the play towards scholarship?

The core of *Dr Faustus* is religious belief, and here too the messages of the play are complex and questionable. This has led to critical debate, further complicated by the mystery of Marlowe's life and the insecure nature of the two differing printed texts of the play, for which no original manuscript survives. The teasing question is: where do the sympathies of the play lie? The Catholic Church taught that sinful man could claim God's grace to achieve salvation. Christ died bearing the burden of human sin and would give his divine favour, his 'grace', to a repentant sinner who was a baptized member of the Church. People could forfeit their chances of grace by unbelief or by unrepented mortal sin.

After death, the blessed went to heaven and the sinners went to hell, often described as fiery torment, although Marlowe uses the academic, theological idea of hell as permanent separation from God. Unfortunately, humans are not so neatly divided into thoroughly good and bad, so, in the twelfth century, the doctrine of purgatory was devised. This was a sort of half-way house to heaven, where sinners could pay for any outstanding sin by undergoing suffering. By good works, prayer, fasting and almsgiving, people could earn remission of this time in purgatory. It is interesting that although so much of the play's attitude to the afterlife is traditionally Catholic, the idea of purgatory is ignored. As soon as Faustus calls up Mephistopheles and enters into the pact with Satan, he has committed a mortal sin for which there is no other destiny than an eternity in hell unless he repents.

The half-century before the writing of *Dr Faustus* saw constant argument about the destiny of the soul after death. This came to a climax in London in the late 1580s and 1590s, when the play was written. With the Reformation, out went the idea that you could earn your salvation by merit. Lutherans argued one could earn grace by faith alone. If your faith was whole and strong, you would be saved and you would show this in your good works. As soon as Faustus turns from God to follow Satan, therefore, under the Lutheran doctrine he is damned. His arrogance and actions demonstrate his lack of faith. Calvinists were more extreme – they argued that God knows everyone's destiny from the beginning. Those whom He knew to be 'predestined' to salvation were called the 'elect'. This could be an agonizing doctrine if you did not feel confident that you were among the elect. Faustus's final dilemma, when he faces up to his fate in hell, must have resonated for some people in the first audiences who felt that they might be similarly destined, with no hope of late repentance to avoid eternal punishment.

Marlowe made use of pre-Reformation elements in his story. The Good and Bad Angels are figures from older Morality plays. The traditional Catholic views of a human being's personal responsibility for his afterlife are vital to the dramatic power of the play. Faustus turns away from God to follow Satan. His arrogant belief in his intellectual powers and his decision to use them to achieve a purely self-centred happiness lead him on, but there is always a possibility that he will heed the warnings of the Good Angel and the Old Man. The plot would be much less dramatic if there were no possibility of help for him.

There is some sense, though, that Faustus is damned from the start. He might be seen as a man born with tremendous intellectual powers in which lie the seeds of an inevitable downfall. With the Reformation, the Bible became the fundamental basis of Protestant belief, and people were urged to read it for their salvation. When Mephistopheles claims to have engineered Faustus's downfall, he gloats: *'twas I, that when thou wert i' the way to heaven, / Damned up thy passage. When thou took'st the book / To view the Scriptures, then I turned the leaves / And led thine eye.* (V.2.103–6) Faustus was already at the Devil's mercy. It is as if Marlowe, like many men of this time, was not clear about how far man's salvation was predestined and how far it lay in his own hands.

An Elizabethan audience would have been in no doubt about Faustus's damnation. The practice of black magic by itself would not have condemned him, although it would have called up the fears and superstitions Elizabethans felt about witchcraft. It is the pact with Lucifer and intercourse with Helen of Troy, a spirit and therefore a manifestation of the Devil, which are damnable. The Good and Bad Angels spell out Faustus's spiritual choices in what appears to be a simple, straightforward manner, but the plot and poetry pull against each other. The best arguments and the best lines are given to Faustus, leading many critics to feel that the play, consciously or unconsciously, is on the side of the questioning mind.

Activity

> After studying the religious background to passages and speeches of your own choice, consider the dramatic effect of the language. Do you find anything to admire in Faustus's deeds and words, or is he a human soul descending further and further into deserved damnation? Is it possible to hold both views at the same time?

Shakespeare's history plays

Shakespeare came to London some time in the 1580s and probably joined a company headed by James Burbage (see Unit 8, *Theatres and Playing Spaces*). His earliest playwriting activities were contributions to plays written by other authors, like *The Play of Sir Thomas More*. This was a common enough practice at the time. By the 1590s he was writing his early comedies and the history cycles, starting with *Henry VI* about the Wars of the Roses, which haunted the Elizabethan imagination. He celebrated the Tudor dynasty in *Richard III* which ends with the victory of the future Henry VII, grandfather to Elizabeth I. Finally he wrote the Lancastrian history cycle, *Richard II* to *Henry V*.

The history plays deal with rebellion, with the rights and wrongs of overthrowing a king, with the troubles of civil disorder, and the ideals of peace, firm rule and effective law and order. *Richard II* was the most problematical of these plays for the authorities because it showed a hereditary king being deposed. While Elizabeth lived, printed texts of the play deleted the deposition scene, and some scholars also think it was cut on stage. Evidence of the perceived power of theatrical performance is shown by the fact that supporters of the Earl of Essex paid the Chamberlain's Men to stage *Richard II* on the eve of Essex's rebellion in 1601. The players escaped punishment, although one was called to testify at Essex's trial. The rebellion's leaders were executed.

Essex's supporters obviously thought *Richard II* a persuasive piece of theatre which helped to justify rebellion. The debate over whether a king can be justly deposed lies at the play's heart – necessarily so as Tudor theory had to accommodate the historical fact that kings had lost their thrones alongside their own propaganda encouraging the idea of hereditary monarchy. The Master of the Revels made cuts in the rebels' speeches in *Henry IV Part 2*, particularly those by the Archbishop of York. The Elizabethan Church was expected to denounce rebellion as unchristian, not support the rebel cause as the Archbishop does in I.3.85–108 and IV.1.53–87.

Activity

> What picture of the country is shown in the opening scenes? How is the atmosphere of disorder created, both in private and in public? What is threatened by disorder? Who is troubled by it and why?

Tudor concerns about Elizabeth's successor surface in a mood of anxiety throughout the play (see Unit 9, *Approaches to Drama: Shakespeare*). Most of the characters are anxious and many of them are elderly – Hal is one of the few young men on stage. His energy and exuberance contrast with the king's failing health, Falstaff's diseases and the backward-looking conversation of elderly friends in Shallow's orchard. The need for reinvigorated leadership is clear, and the age-versus-youth and disease-versus-health themes point up the problem for the country if wild, young Hal refuses to mend his irresponsible, rebellious ways.

Numerous references to Falstaff show that he was a most popular character in the seventeenth century. In the eighteenth century, the role was taken by leading actors and played for laughs until his final scene, which was performed to excite sympathy. Eighteenth-century criticism concentrated on Falstaff. Did his warmth and wit excuse his vices? For the stage reformer Jeremy Collier in 1698 (see Unit 8, *Theatres and Playing Spaces*) it was morally right that Falstaff be *thrown out of Favour*. Nicholas Rowe in the preface to his 1709 edition of Shakespeare felt that audiences were *sorry to see his Friend Hal use him so scurvily when he comes to the Crown*. Samuel Johnson, holding twin points of view, argued in 1765 that *no man is more dangerous than he that with a will to corrupt, hath the power to please*.

Nineteenth-century critics, still concentrating on character, questioned whether Hal and Hotspur were heroic or self-interested. Interest in the two young men merged with the nineteenth-century passion for things medieval. Whatever their perceived faults, both were glorified as *the essence of chivalry*, as William Hazlitt described them in 1812. Of Falstaff he wrote: *He is represented as a liar, a braggart, a coward, a glutton, etc., and yet we are not offended but delighted with him*. Changes in literary theory in the early twentieth century altered the nineteenth-century perception of literature as the portrayal of character to an understanding of literature as a collection of linguistic constructs, in other words a body of texts made from words organized into meaning. Changes in theory shifted critical attention from character to the structure and language of texts.

How does a study of its structure affect our understanding of *Henry IV Part 2*? First of all, the play is part of a larger history cycle in which the deposition of Richard II and the usurpation by Bolingbroke lead, via the reformation of Prince Hal, to the glorification of Henry V. Just as our view of Henry V affects our interpretation of Hal, so the way in which critics view the progress of the cycle as a whole affects their interpretation of single plays. An influential mid-century book, E. M. W. Tillyard's *Shakespeare's History Plays* (1944), argued that the cycle acts as propaganda for an orthodox Tudor version of history in which the disruptive forces of misrule and rebellion are providentially brought under control, creating civil peace at home and victory abroad.

In a structural interpretation, D. A. Traversi (1951) suggested that the play opposes public and private morality. In order to achieve political success, private feelings must be sacrificed. Hal's education as a prince involves a personally diminishing withdrawal from the pleasures of friendship and a betrayal of private loyalties: *the circumstances which demand Falstaff's banishment also involve a turning aside from life, a loss which no necessity, political or even moral, can make altogether irrelevant.* Traversi concluded however that the *loss* was justified by Hal's emergence as the supreme embodiment of political virtue and the incarnation of political competence: *the icy wind of righteous authority that will blow at Westminster . . . inhuman as the wind may seem and to some extent be, the corruption it blows away will, at least in the political order, justify it.*

Activity

Consider how disease, decay and death are presented in the imagery and characterization of the play. Do they function solely as a foil for Hal or do they also suggest anxiety about the transition of power?

Some of the most stimulating recent interpretations have come from theories which relate literary texts to their historical context, not as *reflections* of the period in which they were written but as elements that actively helped to *form* the culture of that period. Recent critics argue that the plays contain a subversive questioning of power, rule and legitimacy; that the portrait of Richard II as a weak, irritable and unstable man is a covert portrayal of Elizabeth I in her declining years; and that it requires the suppression of certain key lines in *Henry V* not to see him as a ruthless, machiavellian king whose conquests cost the lives of ordinary people.

The Merchant of Venice

Fashion moves Shakespeare's plays in and out of popularity, and none more so than *The Merchant of Venice*. It was rarely performed in the seventeenth and early eighteenth centuries, until the actor Charles Macklin revived it in 1741 after more than 150 years of neglect. It was instantly successful and has remained popular ever since. To eighteenth-century readers and audiences, Shylock was an evil miser, a harsh and grasping villain. *Ev'ry child hates Shylock*, wrote Alexander Pope in 1733, fully expecting the figure to be recognized although the play was no longer being staged. The shift in sympathy towards Shylock came with the Romantics and the nineteenth-century liberal sense of injustice at the way Jews had been treated throughout history. Walter Scott's *Ivanhoe* has saintly Jewish characters, the merchant Isaac of York and his beautiful daughter Rebecca. George Eliot created the picture of a noble, cultured Jew in *Daniel Deronda*. Dickens consciously compensated for Fagin in *Oliver Twist* by drawing an idealistic picture of a Jew in *Our Mutual Friend*.

Hazlitt was present on the opening night in 1814 of Edmund Kean's innovatory performance as Shylock, and it transformed his ideas about the play. Shylock, he wrote,

> *seems the depositary of the vengeance of his race; and though the long habit of brooding over daily insults and injuries has crusted over his temper with inveterate misanthropy, and hardened him*

against the contempt of mankind, this adds but little to the triumphant pretensions of his enemies. There is a strong, quick, and deep sense of justice mixed up with the gall and bitterness of his resentment. The constant apprehension of being burnt alive, plundered, banished, reviled, and trampled on, might be supposed to sour the most forbearing nature, and to take something from that 'milk of human kindness,' with which his persecutors contemplated his indignities. The desire of revenge is almost inseparable from the sense of wrong; and we can hardly help sympathising with the proud spirit, hid beneath his 'Jewish gaberdine,' stung to madness by repeated undeserved provocations . . . even at the last . . . we pity him, and think him hardly dealt with by his judges.

Nineteenth-century productions often dispensed with the final Act, making the trial the climax and Shylock the focus. Actors introduced incidents to soften the audience's feelings towards him. Kean, for instance, handled the harsh lines with which Shylock curses his daughter, *Would she were hearsed at my foot and the ducats in her coffin*, by pausing, then jerking backwards, and, borrowing a word from the next line, exclaiming *No, no, no*, as though he rejected in horror the imagined sight.

Irving added a new episode at the end of the elopement scene, utilizing to the full the realism of nineteenth-century sets. In a blaze of colour, music and movement, a large crowd of gay maskers revelled across the stage, sweeping away Jessica and Lorenzo in their midst. The curtain closed momentarily. When it reopened, as Ellen Terry, the great nineteenth-century actress who played Portia, recalled: *the stage was empty, desolate, with no light but a pale moon, and all sounds of life at a great distance – and then over the bridge came the weary figure of the Jew.* Slowly the curtain closed again.

Activity

> In the nineteenth century it was commonplace to end the play at the trial and omit the whole of the last Act. Henry Irving ended the trial scene with Shylock broken, stumbling out to howls of abuse from a mob off-stage. What difference does this make to the play? Once Shylock has been defeated what, if anything, remains unresolved?

As sympathy for Shylock grew, this altered perceptions of the Christian characters. The scholar Walter Raleigh wrote in 1907:

Antonio and Bassanio are pale shadows of men compared with this gaunt, tragic figure, whose love of his race is as deep as life; who pleads the cause of a common humanity against the cruelties of prejudice; whose very hatred has in it something of the nobility of patriotic passion; whose heart is stirred with tender memories even in the midst of his lament over the stolen ducats; who, in the end, is dismissed, unprotesting, to insult and oblivion.

In this interpretation the Christian characters are, at worst, insensitive, racist and uncharitable. At best they are light and shallow. The grave Antonio seems careless, a merchant who casually over-commits himself, while in her lecture notes Ellen Terry described Bassanio as *A bit of a loafer, a well-dressed handsome youth of good birth who lives on his charm.*

Twentieth-century scholars protested that such a sympathetic portrayal did not reflect the way that the Elizabethans would have viewed Shylock, but it became difficult to discuss him unsympathetically under the growing threat of Nazism in the 1930s. Either Belmont was a *fairy tale*, as H. Granville-Barker called it in 1930, or anti-Semitism had to be acknowledged as the reality of the play. Historical evidence for Elizabethan views of Jewry (for example, the crowd's joy at the execution of Elizabeth's Jewish physician Lopez in 1594) met with the counter-argument that the play voices Shakespeare's personally liberal views. Trying to deduce Shakespeare's views from his writings is extremely problematical. However, it is interesting that he wrote the play soon after riots against aliens in 1596 in Southwark, which he may have witnessed.

Shakespeare is credited with writing the following lines in the play *Sir Thomas More* (c.1595). Sir Thomas More calms a crowd of London apprentices who are rioting against *strangers* by appealing to their sympathies.

> *Imagine that you see the wretched strangers,*
> *Their babies at their backs, with their poor luggage*
> *Plodding to th'ports and coasts for transportation.*

More warns the crowd that they could find themselves in a similar plight if the king punishes their riot with banishment.

> *whither would you go?*
> *What country, by the nature of your error,*
> *Should give you harbour? . . .*
> *Why, you must needs be strangers. Would you be pleased*
> *To find a nation of such barbarous temper*
> *That breaking out in hideous violence*
> *Would not afford you an abode on earth,*
> *Whet their detested knives against your throats,*
> *Spurn you like dogs, and like as if that God*
> *Owed not nor made not you . . .*
> *what would you think*
> *To be thus used? This is the strangers' case.*

Activity

If you had to produce *The Merchant of Venice*, would you stress or soften the anti-Semitism? To what extent should productions take account of the sensibilities of contemporary audiences, and to what extent should plays be regarded as belonging to the period in which they were written?

In the twentieth century, with the reaction against realism in staging and with literary criticism turning from character analysis to structure, imagery and language, *The Merchant of Venice* was seen as symbolically opposing false, economic wealth with the true wealth of community; the love of money with the love of one's fellow beings; the value of mercantile gain with the value of good fellowship. The 'bonds' of love are more blessed than legal bonds. Liberality and the giving of oneself are signs of *the grace of God* which Portia and Bassanio possess – his feasting, masking, revelry and conviviality, and her wit, courtesy and hospitality indicate an outgoing, generous spirit. Punning on the word *gentle* and *gentile* linguistically honours the golden, aristocratic world of Belmont over the mercantile, law-bound world of Venice. Only those characters who rise above self-centredness can enter the loving world of Belmont, and this, prefigured in the casket scenes, privileges the Christians above Shylock. The grace of the giving spirit saves the Duke (and Venice) from a lawful but uncharitable and unchristian judgement. It justifies a servant leaving one master for another and bestows approval on the lovers and on Antonio, who was prepared to lay down his life for his friend.

The resolution of a play is the bringing together of a community. The harmony in the spheres described by Lorenzo in Act V is reflected in Belmont and imaged in light, the *sweet* moonlight, the *bright* stars, the distance the *little candle throws its beams*, the latter image directly linked to acts of goodness in a fallible human world. Portia brings *manna* to all *without a fee*, neatly distancing herself from the economic and legal conflicts whose language she borrows. Some late twentieth-century productions closed with the figure of Jessica or Antonio standing alone outside the house. It is a defining vision of community, which suggests that light-hearted Belmont, in its uncaring thoughtlessness, is as excluding as Venice. To W. H. Auden, Antonio, *standing alone on the darkened stage, outside the Eden from which, not by the choice of others, but by his own nature, he is excluded,* is as much an outsider as Shylock.

Psychoanalytic readings since the 1930s have suggested a homosexual interpretation of Antonio's character. Feminist criticism has pointed out the strengths of Portia, cleverly and cunningly manipulating the casket scenes to win against her dead father's patriarchal commands, and coolly outwitting all the men in the trial and ring scenes. Bringing these views together, recent interpretations have added to the obvious conflict between Antonio and Shylock a subtler conflict between Antonio and Portia for the love of Bassanio.

Activity

> There is a sense of something odd about Antonio. Why do we find it so difficult to remember that the title of the play refers to him and not to Shylock? Is he the hero of his own play?

The Jacobean era

James I ascended the English throne in 1603 believing that he was entering into great wealth, whereas the reality was that the royal income no longer provided enough to meet royal expenses. James was extravagantly generous to his family and favourites, and that intensified the competitive, envious atmosphere at Court where everything depended on having personal access to the king. His lavish entertainments were criticized at the time as luxuriously wasteful; his suspected homosexuality and partiality for male favourites was seen as dissolute. Elizabeth had assiduously projected a remote, majestical image of herself. James cared little how he appeared to his subjects, or that his Court had the reputation of being corrupt and wicked, *rotten wood*, in the words of Sir Walter Raleigh. In Elizabethan drama kings and dukes may be intemperate or mistaken but courts are rarely corrupt. In Jacobean drama, courts are usually treacherous, licentious, hypocritical and murderous.

Both Elizabeth and James exercised power over aristocratic marriages, and used it to control their nobles, who were a potential source of rebellion. Great lords had to have Elizabeth's permission for their heirs to marry. James I went further, trying to reduce friction between great families by personally arranging the intermarriage of their children. At the personal level, parents expected obedience from their children and were supported by the Church in demanding it. Elizabethan and Jacobean plays reflect this social reality. King Alonso's daughter in *The Tempest*, Juliet in *Romeo and Juliet*, the lovers in *A Midsummer Night's Dream*, Cordelia in *King Lear* and the Duchess in *The Duchess of Malfi* all need the consent of the ruler or head of the house to marry.

The independent, well-to-do heroines of the comedies are rewarded with partners of their own choosing, but they give away their power and wealth to men when they marry. The independence of tragic heroines is punished, and yet when tragic heroines obey their fathers, as Ophelia and Cordelia do, they appear innocent and their deaths unreasonable within the terms of the tragedy. 'Unruly' women were seen to threaten the patriarchal society. Feminist criticism has drawn attention to what happens to women who seek partners outside the accepted norms, breaking the bounds of race (Cleopatra, Desdemona) or rank (Goneril, Regan, the Duchess of Malfi). The female body is visibly attacked on stage. What crime or sin do women commit in sixteenth- and early seventeenth-century tragedies before they are so violently abused, raped, mutilated, tortured, strangled and murdered? In Middleton or Webster they have probably loved someone below their station. In so doing, feminist criticism suggests, women transgress the boundaries of permitted sexual relationships. Their affairs and marriages pollute the aristocratic body, which punishes them.

The women who had most opportunity of exerting power at this time were wealthy, aristocratic widows. Feminist critics like Lisa Jardine relate drama to its historical period and to the laws of wealth inheritance which, in

Elizabethan and Jacobean England, meant primarily the transfer of landed estates. They argue that the passionate love of women is perceived by male characters in the plays as lust, as a sign of depravity, unreliability and guilt. And the greater the freedom a woman exercises in her choice of partner, the more dangerously lustful she appears. The underlying messages in these plays, feminist critics suggest, support society's desire to keep women disempowered and subordinate.

Activity

> Consider the death of the heroine in any tragedy of the period. Is it peaceful or punitive, imposed or self-inflicted? Why did the heroine die, and would her death have seemed justified to any of the characters within the play? Does the death seem justified to you?

Othello

Black faces were rare in Elizabethan society, although there were envoys from Constantinople at the Court of James I. Stories about the Moors, the traditional enemies of the Christians who had conquered the Holy Land, were widespread. They appeared as exotic figures, seductive and dangerous, brave fighters but deceitful. Until *Othello,* they were always portrayed as villains in drama. The standard image of a soldier, on the other hand, was as an honest, capable, brave and loyal man. *Othello* deliberately upsets the expectations of a Jacobean audience by reversing these two typical stage characters.

Activity

> Iago's opening remarks are vengeful and angry. He boasts of his disloyalty. A contemporary audience would have been shocked by this in a soldier and would have known straight away that he was an unusually bad man. How does Othello establish himself immediately as heroic? You might like to consider in detail the effect of the single line *Keep up your bright swords, for the dew will rust 'em* (I.2.60), taking into account stage business, body language and costume, as well as the connotations of language.

The stage history of *Othello* is unusual. While most of Shakespeare's plays either dropped out of the dramatic repertory in the late seventeenth and eighteenth centuries or were grossly re-fashioned and rewritten, *Othello* remained popular. It was the Shakespearian play most often performed and its text was little altered. Until the mid-eighteenth century, actors continued to wear contemporary costumes. The frontispiece to Rowe's 1709 edition shows Othello dressed in the red uniform of an English army officer, which is how he appeared on the stage. Othello was played with nobility, decorum and sympathy, a self-controlled military hero moved to passion by jealousy and overwhelming love. His presentation as a physically beautiful black man of inherent dignity and courtesy reflected audiences' ideas of the 'noble savage'. Speeches that hinted at undignified passion (like *we say, lie on her when they belie her* and *Arise black vengeance* and *Whip me ye devils*) were cut. Othello was at the same time a romantic stranger, an English army officer and a gallant cavalier.

In every way Othello's heroism was exalted, and this included physically deforming Iago into pure evil. Samuel Sandford, who partnered the actor Betterton's Restoration Othello, was *a low and crooked Person*, according to Colley Cibber. In the early eighteenth century actors playing Iago were costumed in black and contorted their voices and bodies to present the symbolic embodiment of the moral ugliness of evil. Desdemona in contrast was purified into submissive, gentle innocence.

Dr Johnson expressed the standard eighteenth-century view of the three characters in his notes on the play (1765). His descriptions show how the interpretation of each character was heightened by contrast with the other two. His customary concern about the moral effect of literature is satisfied by his belief in the absolute evil of Iago.

> *The beauties of this play impress themselves so strongly upon the attention of the reader that they can draw no aid from critical illustration. The fiery openness of Othello, magnanimous, artless and credulous, boundless in his confidence, ardent in his affection, inflexible in his resolution and obdurate in his revenge; the cool malignity of Iago, silent in his resentment, subtle in his designs and studious at once of his interest and his vengeance; the soft simplicity of Desdemona, confident of merit and conscious of innocence, her artless perseverance in her suit and her slowness to suspect that she can be suspected are such proofs of Shakespeare's skill in human nature as, I suppose, it is vain to seek in any modern writer. The gradual progress which Iago makes in the Moor's conviction and the circumstances which he employs to inflame him are so artfully natural that, though it will perhaps not be said of him as he says of himself that he is 'a man not easily jealous', yet we cannot but pity him when at last we find him 'perplexed in the extreme'.*

> *There is always danger lest wickedness conjoined with abilities should steal upon esteem, though it misses of approbation; but the character of Iago is so conducted that he is from the first scene to the last hated and despised.*

In the mid-eighteenth century the move towards realism began, culminating in the lavishly historic scenic productions of the nineteenth century. Othello shed his English costume and appeared in Moorish dress, while at the same time the symbolism of Iago's black garb was questioned. *It is unnatural to suppose that an artful villain, like him, would chuse a dress which would stigmatise him to everyone. I think, as Cassio and he belong to one regiment, they should both retain the same regimentals*, wrote a critic in 1759. By the nineteenth century, interest in the realism of character predominated, although Iago remained resistant to this approach for longer than the other characters. Like a Vice figure from a medieval morality play he was seen as a diabolic presence, and the phrases which hint at his devilish attributes (such as *I am not what I am*, I.1.65, and *I look down towards his feet, but that's a fable*, V.2.292) were quoted to support an interpretation of the play in which it is not Iago who succeeds but the forces of evil.

Activity

> Is the tragedy solely due to Iago? Is there anything in the characters of Othello and Desdemona that aids Iago's plans? Do you think the play is a tragedy of character or a symbolic clash of good and evil?

The Victorian Othello was a romantic, mysterious figure from the Orient or Africa whose veneer of Christianity and civilization was based on a simple understanding (or misunderstanding) of Venetian manners. He was a noble gentleman: *manly and chivalrous*, the actor Macready called him (1836), and he was betrayed by Iago. By the late nineteenth century, motivations had been found for Iago's actions: he was the real intelligence in the play; he possessed an inward, intellectual delight in mastery and control. It transformed him from a 'devil' into an efficient, rational 'white' man at the very time, in the 1870s and 1880s, that Othello was coming to be seen as exotic, passionate and 'other', filled with simple 'native' emotions. In this interpretation (which some critics relate to British imperialism and Victorian ideas about the 'white man's burden'), Iago easily arouses doubts in an Othello who dwells in no firm place but is poised insecurely between civilization and barbarism. From the late nineteenth century, psychological motivations have been offered for Iago: a homosexual attraction to Othello, or a male military bonding which excludes women and pits him against Desdemona for Othello's attention.

Othello's natural nobility and simplicity could be read as truly civilized, and Venetian sophistication, in the character of a super-subtle Iago, as barbaric. In *Shakespearean Tragedy* (1904) A. C. Bradley gave us the romantic, Victorian Othello.

> *He does not belong to our world, and he seems to enter it we know not whence – almost as if from wonderland. There is something mysterious in his descent from men of royal siege; in his wanderings in vast deserts and among marvellous peoples; in his tales of magic handkerchiefs and prophetic Sibyls; in the sudden vague glimpses we get of numberless battles and sieges in which he has played the hero and has borne a charmed life; even in his chance references to his baptism, his being sold to slavery, his sojourn in Aleppo . . . So he comes before us, dark and grand, with a light upon him from the sun where he was born; but no longer young, and now grave, self-controlled, steeled by the experience of countless perils, hardships and vicissitudes, at once simple and stately in bearing and in speech, a great man naturally modest but fully conscious of his worth, proud of his services to the state, unawed by dignitaries and unelated by honours, secure, it would seem, against all dangers from without and all rebellion from within. And he comes to have his life crowned with the final glory of love.*

Bradley claimed that Othello causes his own downfall. *Othello's mind . . . is very simple . . . Emotion excites his imagination, but it confuses and dulls his intellect . . . he is by nature full of the most vehement passion.* Iago by contrast has *exceptional powers of will and intellect.* By contrasting the two men in this way, Bradley produced a structural interpretation of the play that balanced a cool, rational, intelligent Iago with a passionate, emotional Othello who gradually loses his reason. Reason versus Passion.

There are other obvious structural pairings: evil and good, Christian and pagan, insiders and outsider, black and white. A diabolical Iago can be paired with a patient, suffering, Christ-like Desdemona; the Christian Venetians can be contrasted with Othello retreating into paganism; the securely based Venetian society with a *wheeling stranger*; the white Venetians with black Othello. Roderigo and Brabantio both use language that indicates they are racist, and what of the Duke's apparently complimentary remark, *Your son-in-law is far more fair than black* (I.3.289)? The compliment depends on a shared understanding of the terms of a comparison in which fair equates with good and handsome and black with bad and ugly, and it reveals the unconscious racism of Venice. Othello, courteously treated by the state whose need of his military prowess is extreme, may not have faced the possibilities of subconscious racism, even in Desdemona, until Iago betrays him into the idea.

Activity

> Paul Robeson's performance as Othello in London (1930) and America (1943) tested the public reaction to a black man embracing a white woman on stage. This is, of course, essentially the plot of *Othello*, but at the time the casting of a black actor and a white actress challenged colour taboos. Nowadays questions are more likely to be asked when a white actor plays the role, as Laurence Olivier did for the National Theatre in 1964 and Antony Hopkins for the BBC in 1981. You might like to investigate the circumstances and audience reaction to these or other productions. What is the relationship, if any, between the casting of Othello and the racial perceptions of the audience?

In the twentieth century the concept of the 'noble' Othello came under pressure. Those who chose to portray him as 'ignoble' pointed to his egotistical, self-dramatizing speeches, in which he weaves romantic stories about himself as hero. T. S. Eliot criticized him for *endeavouring to escape reality.* Of his suicide speech, Eliot wrote: *I have always felt that I have never read a more terrible exposure of human weakness.* If the fault lay in a less-than-noble Othello, the power of Iago was diminished. No longer the symbol of evil, he dwindled in some critics' eyes into a sordid little man, spouting nonsense about devils in order to boost his low self-esteem. The most radical character reassessment, however, was of Desdemona.

To the Victorians, Desdemona was pure, modest, dependent and powerless. Hazlitt spoke of her *resignation and angelic sweetness of temper.* Actresses spent much of their time on stage kneeling: before the Senate, Brabantio,

Iago, Othello, and at prayer. Yet Desdemona is the embodiment of power when she first appears on stage. The Jacobean audience would have regarded her as strongly and wilfully rebellious for marrying without her father's consent and for speaking directly to the Duke instead of through a male petitioner. Why does she become so obedient and passive in Cyprus?

Feminist criticism has opened the question further by asking how male and female codes affect all the women in the play. Emilia and Bianca are marginalized by their subservient positions in a male sub-group, the army. Some critics go so far as to suggest that Emilia is a battered wife. Bianca is despised and disbelieved because of her profession. Desdemona emerges in feminist views as a strong, open, confident woman at the start of the play, so why is there such a radical change in her behaviour and why so quickly? Iago and Othello are bonded through shared military experiences and are more at ease with one another than either is with his wife. A recent feminist argument, based on the only major event which happens to Desdemona in Cyprus, her marriage night, suggests that she is ardently sexual and that this shocks Othello who has lived until his marriage with a male, military code that treats women with contempt.

Activity

> Compare the presentation of Desdemona in productions you have seen in the theatre and on film. The innocent, passive reading is surprisingly persistent (you might like to watch the Orson Welles film or look at stills from it). Have you seen, or can you conceive of seeing, a portrayal of Desdemona that shows her remaining strong throughout the play?

The Duchess of Malfi

The heroine of *The Duchess of Malfi* (1613) is another strong woman who defies her family to marry a man of her own choice. She is widowed when the play opens, and has to manoeuvre secretly against a dangerously corrupt Italian Court full of male intriguers. Webster's characters inhabit a bleak, morbid world. His plots present scenes of planned and accidental killings, and his poetry is suffused with references to death, decay, and the grave. Secrets contribute to the dark, distrustful atmosphere. Characters flatter and deceive, while desperately trying to discover the truth about each other. The Duchess is isolated by her secret life and although Bosola comes to know and admire her, he changes too slowly to protect her.

Activity

> In any Webster play, honest characters and relationships of trust are few. Who do you think is honest, and how central are they to the plot?

Bosola is one of the most interesting characters in *The Duchess of Malfi*. He tells Julia he is a *blount soldier* but he acts as an *intelligencer* or spy. In himself he becomes a man divided. Is he the melancholic whom the brothers use to carry out their revenge, or is he an agent of fate, the hammer of justice who kills the Duchess's murderers? Or is he an agent of God, the means of bringing the Duchess on a spiritual journey from pride and wilfulness through self-pity and suicidal despair to resignation, composure and humility? The plot of Marlowe's Elizabethan tragedy *Dr Faustus* turns on an absolute belief in God. Jacobean tragedies show a more questioning attitude, and characters seem puzzled about the life to come, while the slaughter of innocent and guilty alike questions our sense of justice. Is God's presence evident in *The Duchess of Malfi,* or is the world of the play ruled by retributive fate or arbitrary chance? It depends on whether you read the play as purely and simply a revenge tragedy, or as a play about fate, or as an allegory.

Activity

> Gather together quotations from *The Duchess of Malfi* in which the characters refer to the cosmic background and the life to come. What do the quotations reveal about the play's attitude to these concepts?

Critical debate on the play has centred on the Duchess. She is a great lady, known only by her title, who possesses palaces, forests and meads. As she is a Renaissance grandee, marrying below her rank is a grave offence. She argues movingly and wittily in Act III Scene 5 that a man's *owne actions* should count more than rank, but she is aware of the rules she is breaking. Her brothers condemn her in language that echoes the sexual disgust of male characters in Jacobean tragedies towards widows who remarry (*lust; whore; a notorious Strumpet*).

She is condemned within the play as intemperate, proud, lustful, rash and headstrong, yet presented as warm, teasing, affectionate, stoical, capable and quick-thinking when danger strikes. *I am Duchess of Malfi still* is her most famous line, and it can be acted proudly, defiantly, ironically, stoically or self-deceivingly. Some critics see her as a self-determined individualist. Protestant doctrine did not approve of self-determination. Calvin's *Institutes* stated:

> We are not our own; therefore, let us not make it our end to seek what may be agreeable to our carnal natures. We are not our own; therefore, as far as possible, let us forget ourselves and the things that are ours. On the other hand, we are God's; let us, therefore, live and die to Him.

Activity

> Are we to judge the Duchess as God-defying and self-determined, as embodying the Renaissance claim for individuality? Is she a victim of her brothers' resolve to protect the family's lands, wealth and social status, or a Christian soul travelling from sinful pride to spiritual resignation? Any consideration of her character needs to take into account the power of the poetry she speaks and her behaviour on stage in the scenes of torment and death. What evidence would you choose to support your own view of the Duchess?

Ben Jonson

Ben Jonson wrote plays for the public theatres as well as creating masques, with the designer Inigo Jones, for the Court of James I. His emergence as the leading writer of Court masques owes much to Queen Anne's delight in performing in them, and it was she who gave him his first Court appointment in 1604. He was rewarded with a pension in 1616, but Jonson had an uneasy relationship with the Court. He hated its hypocrisy, intrigue and corruption. A satirical attack in the play *Eastward Ho!* (1606) on James's large gifts of money and land to his Scottish friends landed Jonson and his co-authors in prison. Jonson had an aggressive personality and a history of falling out with his co-authors, other writers and finally with Inigo Jones. His combative nature often landed him in trouble.

His writings are based on classical models. He prided himself on classical correctness in poetic style and in following the conventions of the dramatic unities. Although he left Westminster School at a young age to join his step-father's bricklaying trade, Jonson was well grounded in the classics and he continued to read them, becoming, through self-education, deeply knowledgeable. The close study of any of his plays reveals how much he draws on classical sources.

Volpone

In the complexity and moral ambiguity of *Volpone* (1605), Jonson gave satiric voice to the attraction and repulsion he felt for the Court and for worldly success. On the surface, the moral position of the comedy appears simple – we are asked to condemn greed. The characters are not individuals, but types or 'humours'. Their names link them directly with the predatory natures of the animals and birds they represent. The vulture, the crow and the raven are eaters of dead flesh. The fox, a sly creature in folk fables, is the master of trickery. The fly darts around, annoying but apparently harmless, until everyone is forced to recognize that he too feeds off dead and decaying flesh. It is difficult to see how the characters of Voltore, Corbaccio and Corvino can be other than utterly condemned. Greed drives them to risk and waste the very thing they seek: wealth. Greed drives them to betray the relationships that should separate humans from animals, whether it is protecting a wife's honour or a son's inheritance.

It is when we consider the examples of good behaviour, Celia and Bonario (Bonario meaning 'good' man, and Celia meaning 'heavenly') that the play seems less simple. Does Celia instigate her own difficulties when she allows herself to be attracted by Volpone's mountebank performance? Dropping her handkerchief could be a sign that she is seducible – it is certainly read that way by Volpone. She remains firm in the face of her husband's betrayal and resists his commands, but the situation is questionable. We cannot wish Volpone to succeed, but given her husband's behaviour do we want her to remain faithful? The plot's solution appears to lie in her saviour, the young and handsome Bonario, but here too things are far from simple. For all his good intentions, Celia and he are saved in the end by Volpone's self-unmasking, not by their own honesty and virtue, and not by the just intervention of God, fate or the law. With the conspirators in disarray, we expect Celia and Bonario to unite. Instead, we are left with a weak presentation of goodness and moral virtue, lacking the validation of the accustomed romantic ending to a comedy.

Activity

> What is your impression of Celia and Bonario? Do you find them attractive as characters? What would the play gain by pairing them off at the end? What would it lose?

With the character of Volpone, the moral world of the play becomes even more ambiguous. The attack on greed is its essence and the play opens realistically and symbolically with the blasphemous deification of wealth. But is it gold that Volpone worships, or its *cunning purchase* and the opportunity to exercise his delight in acting? For he is an excellent actor, flipping from role to role with aplomb and panache, revelling in his success. He makes the decision to throw off his disguises in order to bring down Mosca – no one else saw through his game. Nor is he the traditional, ascetic miser; he is a sensualist. Language and music, poetry and invention pour out of him, evidence of the pleasure he takes in the beauty of life, whether it be a lovely woman or the sensual delights he describes in his seduction speech to Celia. Jonson gives him the imagery and the vitality of a poet.

Activity

> Can you find lines or images in the speeches of Volpone that, were they not given to the villain in the play, could have been spoken by a heroic character?

As a stage play *Volpone* is powerful. Partly this comes from the stage business of Volpone and Mosca, and partly from their obvious enjoyment of their own plots and performances. Both characters indulge in a gleeful self-congratulation which is infectious, and our enjoyment of their zestful activities can mitigate our condemnation. Volpone's vigour is striking since he is not young – the illness he feigns could become a reality at any moment.

Activity

> Do you feel that Volpone shows a fierce determination to wrest pleasure from life while he can? What of his three 'children', the dwarf, the hermaphrodite and the eunuch? What does it reveal of him that he keeps these three in his house? Does Volpone appal you, or do you find him an attractive stage character?

The Epistle that preceded the published version of the play shows Jonson to be defensive on several points, one of which was that the ending or *going-out,* as he called it, of his comedy is *not joyful.* He claims that he punishes his characters severely in order *to put the snaffle in their mouths that cry out, we never punish vice in our interludes,* but he seems to feel this might not suffice as a defence and goes on to argue that it is *the office of a comic poet to imitate justice and instruct to life*. The Epistle reveals anxiety that the audience may be disappointed in the play's conclusion, finding it insufficiently amusing.

Activity

> Consider the end of the play; the lack of resolution in the Bonario–Celia relationship, the class-based difference in the severity of Volpone's and Mosca's punishments, the situation in which Voltore, Corvino and Corbaccio are left. Do you find the ending just and instructive, or are the unresolved situations disturbing?

The Tempest

In the Prologue to *Volpone*, Jonson implicitly criticizes Elizabethan comedies for not following the classical rules of the unities of *time, place, persons*. Early Shakespearian comedies range widely across space and time, but in his final comedy Shakespeare chose to work within the classical unities. The action of *The Tempest* occurs in one place, an island, and Prospero feels impelled to hasten his plan to completion in a single day. *The Tempest*, probably Shakespeare's last solo composition, falls into the group of late plays that do not fit comfortably into the three genres of the Folio: histories, comedies and tragedies.

The Tempest is unique in another way. It is the only play Shakespeare wrote for an indoor theatre, the Blackfriars. It was performed also at the Globe and on more than one occasion at Court, in 1611 and in 1613 when it was part of the festivities at the wedding of King James's daughter Elizabeth to the Elector Palatine. We can see the effect of the masque tradition on the play, which uses spectacle and *quaint device*. Prospero's magic works through music, illusion, dance and masque. The illusions may have been designed as a compliment to James, who loved masques and book-learning. They have more commonly been seen as a metaphor for the shaping, illusioning power of art, so much so that the play has been read bio-graphically as Shakespeare's conscious farewell to the stage. Current criticism is sceptical of biographical interpretations but there is no doubt that Prospero exerts a control over the events and people within the play that mirrors the artist's control over the play itself.

Shakespeare based his plot on accounts of a real incident. The Virginia Company was set up in 1606 and established its first American colony in 1607. In 1609 one of a small fleet of ships bound for the new colony was shipwrecked in a *dreadfull storme*. With considerable luck and deter-mination, the colonists made landfall in the Bermudas, discovering to their surprise that the islands were not *given over to Devils and wicked Spirits* but were *contenting* and *habitable* and *commodious*. Scholars are convinced that Shakespeare read the eyewitness account from which these quotations are taken. Current readings of the play consider that it shows Shakespeare's troubled analysis of colonial adventures in the New World.

An alternative current interpretation, which also relates the play to its original production and historical period, points out that New World readings ignore the fact that the play is set in the Old World. Milan, Naples and Tunis were Renaissance states in the Mediterranean. The reason for the Neapolitan Court being at sea is a royal wedding in Tunis. The play reflects, this interpretation argues, the hopes and anxieties of the Jacobean Court and James's concerns to make diplomatic, dynastic alliances. Gonzalo's prayer, *Look down, you gods / And on this couple drop a blessed crown* (V.1.201–2) would have been spoken in front of James's daughter and her new husband.

Activity

> Look into the historical circumstances of Court productions of the play and James's diplomatic endeavours to secure suitable spouses for his children. What evidence can you find in the play of a similar concern with dynastic marriage? How important do you feel this theme is to the play as a whole?

In the seventeenth and eighteenth centuries, Caliban was presented as a monster. Prospero fitted the Enlightenment ideal of man as God's supreme creation, the pinnacle of reason, so Caliban was relegated to the bottom of creation – physically and spiritually. He *personified malice*, wrote the critic Maurice Morgann in 1777, a *character kneaded up of three distinct natures, the diabolical, the human, and the brute*. It was the Romantics with their interest in the imagination and the poetry of the play who first believed that Caliban had human qualities. Hazlitt, in his 1811–12 lecture, called him:

> *one of the wildest and most abstracted of all Shakespeare's characters, whose deformity whether of body or mind is redeemed by the power and truth of the imagination displayed in it . . . Shakespeare has described the brutal mind of Caliban in contact with the pure and original forms of nature; the character grows out of the soil where it is rooted, uncontrolled, uncouth, and wild . . . The Poet here shows us the savage with the simplicity of a child, and makes the strange monster amiable.*

Hazlitt also pointed out that Caliban was, through inheritance from his mother, the legitimate ruler of the island, ushering in a perception that was picked up in twentieth-century political interpretations.

In the late nineteenth century, Caliban became associated with Darwinian theories of evolution and the 'missing link'. Emphasizing his half-human, half-bestial qualities, the actor Herbert Beerbohm Tree wrote: *in his love of music and his affinity with the unseen world, we discern in the soul which inhabits the brutish body of this elemental man the germs of a sense of beauty.* Although his costume was animalistic, shaggy and dripping with seaweed, Beerbohm Tree ended his portrayal with a moment of human emotion. The retreating ship was seen on the horizon. Caliban stretched his arms after it in mute despair. As the stage lights dimmed to night, Caliban was *left on the lonely rock. He is king once more.* Frank Benson, his wife recalled, *spent many hours watching monkeys and baboons in the Zoo,* and he *delighted in swarming up a tree on the stage and hanging from the branches head downwards.* Edward Gordon Craig records that he even entered *with a fish between his teeth.*

Herbert Beerbohm Tree as Caliban, painted by Charles A. Buchel

Activity

> Look at the illustration above and at further illustrations of nineteenth-century productions of *The Tempest* and consider the costume of Caliban. What ideas are conveyed by his appearance?

Nineteenth-century stage settings may have been realistic, but nineteenth- and early twentieth-century interpretations tended to be allegorical, with Prospero in benign control. What it was that he was in control of altered according to different allegorical interpretations. If Caliban was humanity at the dawn of civilization trying to raise itself out of the mud, Prospero was civilization at its height, nurturing and educating him towards enlightenment. If the usurping and murderous courtiers were fallen men, Prospero was the agent of change, purgation, reconciliation and divine forgiveness. If the island represented fruitful and unregenerate nature, Prospero personified the transforming power of art. If Prospero played at being God, he concluded as a penitent Christian, dismissing his *rough magic* and the *vanity* of the masque. He calls for *heavenly music.* In the Epilogue he humbles himself, using the language of Christianity: *despair, prayer, mercy, faults, pardoned, indulgence.*

A Victorian allegorical interpretation that continued throughout the twentieth century was a political one: Prospero as coloniser, and Caliban as underdeveloped native. This interpretation began in response to Victorian imperialism. In 1892 Andrew Lang put the argument in terms which sympathized with the oppressed Caliban:

> *He was introduced to the benefits of civilisation. He was instructed.*
> *The resources of his island were developed. He was like the red men*
> *in America, the blacks in Australia, the tribes of Hispaniola. Then*
> *he committed an offence, an unpardonable offence, but one that*
> *Caliban was fated to commit. Then he was punished. Do we not*
> *'punish the natives' all over the world, all we civilised powers?*

The Tempest was seen as defining the moment when the Old World encountered the New, when the powerful met the powerless, took over their lands and imposed on them the language of the conqueror. Prospero ceased to be the benevolent, reconciling magician, restoring what had been lost and unselfishly shouldering the burdensome duties of good government. Instead he was seen as irritable and vengeful, blind both to his usurpation of the island and to its parallels with his brother's usurpation of Milan. In readings kind to Prospero, he learns forgiveness and moves in the course of the play from arrogant control to releasing humility. In darker readings, sympathy sides with Caliban and Ariel as natives disturbed, controlled and finally abandoned by a power that no longer requires their services. In the late twentieth century the idea of Caliban as the symbol of natives under colonial rule was widened to include any victimized or excluded group, third-world struggles for liberation and the fight against apartheid.

Recent criticism, in the words of David Kastan, has:

> *wrested the play from the idealisations of romance . . . in which*
> *the hand of a 'great creating nature' can be felt organising the*
> *turbulence of earthly existence, re-establishing love and human*
> *continuance. No longer is* The Tempest *a play of social reconcilia-*
> *tion and moral renewal, of benevolent artistry and providential*
> *design; it now appears as a telling document of the first phase of*
> *English imperialism, implicated in the will to power of the Jacobean*
> *court, even as an 'instrument of empire' itself.*

Activity

> A clear indication of thematic and allegorical readings of the play is whether directors add stage business after Prospero's Epilogue. Have you seen productions in which Prospero's exit or Epilogue is not the final moment in the play? How does the ending relate to the director's interpretation of the play as a whole?

3 Seventeenth-Century Contexts

Central to the history of the seventeenth century is the Civil War of 1640–49 and its revolutionary outcome, the trial and execution of King Charles I. For the first and only time, England embarked on a republican form of government. It was a brief experiment, lasting from 1649 to 1653, at which point Oliver Cromwell dismissed Parliament (as irritated by its behaviour as Charles I had been), and took control as Lord Protector. The Commonwealth became the Protectorate. Cromwell had risen from modest origins through his successful generalship of the victorious parliamentary army to become absolute ruler of England. His strong personality and his conviction that he was carrying out God's work helped the country to achieve peace but, as an experiment, republicanism failed. After Cromwell's death, Parliament restored Charles II to his father's throne.

The argument between Charles I and Parliament was a struggle to define the scope and boundaries of each other's powers. On the king's side this was called his prerogatives, and on Parliament's side, its privileges. At the start of Charles's reign in 1626, the royal prerogatives were much the same as James I had enjoyed. The king chose his own counsellors, including civil, religious and military leaders, summoned and dismissed Parliament at will, could declare war and negotiated foreign policy. The crown revenues were exclusively his to spend. Parliament had the right to vote over additional taxes, make laws and discuss grievances but the last two rights were weak since they traditionally agreed to the crown's initiatives. However, during the seventeenth century the monarch's growing financial dependence on Parliament gave it a power which it had not previously possessed.

The financial problems that pressed hard upon the Stuart monarchs were part of the country's larger economic difficulties. Since the early sixteenth century, the population had been rising inexorably – so more food was needed. The seventeenth century saw the cultivation of royal forests, fens, commons and waste land, but this did not prevent serious price inflation and food shortages from the 1620s to the 1640s. England's developing colonies – which were to be so richly profitable to the state in the eighteenth century – were, in the early years of the seventeenth century, still risky, private ventures. All the Stuart kings had financial difficulties. The throne was about £400,000 in debt when James I ascended, and the crown revenues were no longer adequate. Charles I, a less cautious man than his father, became exasperated by Parliament's reluctance to vote him sufficient money. From 1629 to 1639 he ruled without it, raising money by dubiously legal means which were widely resented.

In an effort to achieve uniformity of worship, he tried to impose the Book of Common Prayer on Scotland. It was resisted. He invaded un-successfully, and the cost of the war forced him to summon Parliament in 1640. After a long wait of eleven years, Parliament was determined to assert itself. One of its first acts was to make it illegal to dissolve Parliament without its own consent. It was not Parliament's intention to abolish the monarchy; what parliamentarians wished to do was to restore the balance between prerogatives and privileges which they believed had existed in the mythically 'golden' reign of Elizabeth I. Charles I never wavered in his belief that he was answerable only to God. Parliament argued that the king's powers were subject to *fundamental laws* which had been ignored by *evil counsellors*. John Pym, in a speech in 1641, claimed:

> *The law is the boundary, the measure betwixt the King's prerogative and the people's liberty . . . If the prerogative of the King overwhelm the liberty of the people, it will be turned into tyranny; if liberty undermine the prerogative, it will grow into anarchy.*

In the seventeenth century there was no comfortable consensus of beliefs, either religious or political. Individual decisions were made amidst passionate arguments, and people were prepared to die for their beliefs about true religion and government. That there was a 'right' answer seemed obvious, so one only needed to find it – the right answer would bring peace and salvation.

Unfortunately, if one answer was right all who got it wrong would be damned in the next life. People agonized about what was 'right' religious belief. The English Protestant church established under Elizabeth I was a careful amalgam of Puritan creeds and Catholic practices, and it had been accepted by the majority of her subjects. A substantial minority, legislated against but tolerated, remained faithful to the old church in spite of the anti-Catholic feelings that surfaced whenever the Stuart monarchy appeared to be returning the country to Catholicism. At the other extreme were Puritan sects inspired by Calvin's theology, who wanted stricter forms of Protestant-ism. Unlike the Catholics, they were not united. Small groups would form around particular leaders or localities, adhering to their own interpretation of the Bible.

What these disunited Protestant sects had in common was a belief in the authority of the Bible as the Word of God, and in the truth of personal inspiration. The Bible had been translated into English in the previous century and made available to all who could read. Men were beginning to demand evidence on which to base belief, in the same way as they were beginning to seek scientific proofs about the natural world. Instead of accepting the 'official' view from the pulpit, literate people could read and reach their own conclusions about the Bible's teachings. Many problems of interpretation gave rise to heated disagreements, and these overflowed into politics. Charles I drew upon the Bible to defend his royal prerogative and, at the other extreme, the Levellers used the Bible to support their call for equality for all.

Puritans shared a love of plain living and a hostility to ritual, which smacked to them of 'popery'. They questioned the divine right of kings and some rejected the Church of England. Small communities emigrated to the Continent or risked the dangers of the Atlantic crossing to found colonies in America, which they hoped would be models of godly living and an inspiration to the old world. *We shall be as a city upon a hill. And the eyes of the world are upon us*, preached John Winthrop on board the Arabella as it sailed for New England in 1630, following the Pilgrim Fathers who had led the way in 1620.

The metaphysical poets

The name 'metaphysical poets', which was given to John Donne (1572–1631) and the poets who were influenced by him, gives the impression that these poets are very philosophical and write on some 'higher plane', but they were all very much men of the world they lived in. They were not professional writers but educated men who gave expression to their deepest feelings in poetry which was written for themselves and a few friends. Donne started writing in the 1590s and his influence is still to be found in the work of Andrew Marvell (1621–78).

Their poems were usually circulated in manuscript, and when they were printed their audience was small. There is no sense of lines written with a wide public in mind. These poets were writing for people who shared their type of background, education and knowledge of the world. They belonged to an age that valued versatility, and most of the metaphysical poets led lives in which, at various times, they were soldiers, diplomats, courtiers, politicians, and clerics, while writing their poetry. Donne's *Canonisation* tells the man who interrupts the poet and his love to *take you a course, get you a place, / Observe his Honour or his Grace, / Or the King's real or his stamped face* – either study, take a government office, become a lawyer or a churchman, turn courtier or merchant. That was any educated man's choice. The metaphysical poets were educated in the classics, took an interest in astronomy, astrology, mathematics, cosmography, cartography, mathematics, medicine and travel, and were well read in the Bible.

The poets drew on their wide-ranging knowledge in their imagery. Cartography, for instance, began to redraw the world in the late fifteenth century to illustrate the discovery that the world was round, not a flat rectangle with winds at the four corners and edges over which one could fall. Early maps were large and hand-made, marks of social status as well as sources of information, because only the very wealthy had rooms of a sufficient size to display them. The advent of printing changed the way maps were presented. In 1570, one of the great cartographers of the sixteenth century, Abraham Ortelius, published maps in book form. He was congratulated by another of the century's great cartographers, Gerardus Mercator.

> *You deserve no small praise, for you have selected the best descriptions of each region and have digested them in a single manual which without diminishing or impairing the work of any, may be bought for a low price, kept in a small place, and even carried about wherever we wish.*

Mercator's *low price* was a relative comment. Books of maps were still expensive items, but they allowed educated people access to the new knowledge. Donne's sonnet *At the round earth's imagined corners* plays with ideas from both old and new cartography in its opening line, placing angels in the corners where the winds were often drawn. In *A Hymn to God my God in my sickness* he uses the image of himself as a flat map in an extended metaphysical 'conceit'.

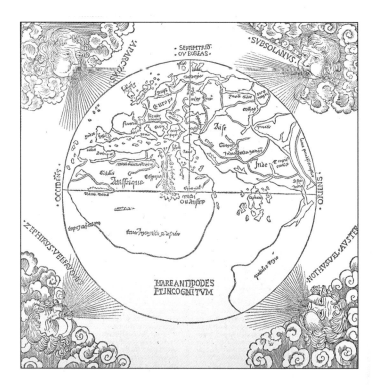

A world map drawn in 1522, showing the winds at the four corners of the earth

Activity

In a selection of metaphysical poems of your own choice, consider the types of learning and experience they reflect. You might like to concentrate on one poet, or follow a single theme, such as seventeenth-century cosmography, cartography, mathematics or geography, in more than one poet. Often these poets mix old and new learning in their imagery. Look at Donne's poetry in particular and think about what this suggests about the place of new learning in his thinking.

John Donne

A metaphysical 'conceit' was a comparison so far fetched, between things so remote, that it needed to be thoroughly explained. John Dryden wrote of Donne in 1693 that he *affects the metaphysics,* and Samuel Johnson picked up on Dryden's phrase, naming the group *a race of writers that may be termed the metaphysical poets.* He criticized them for:

> *a combination of dissimilar images, or discovery of occult resemblances in things apparently unlike . . . The most hetero-geneous ideas are yoked by violence together; nature and art are ransacked for illustrations, comparisons, and allusions . . . but the reader . . . though he sometimes admires, is seldom pleased.*

A famous example of a metaphysical 'conceit' is one that Donne used in a poem to his wife. Written in 1611 when he was about to take a young nobleman on a tour of Europe, the *Valediction: Forbidding Mourning* compares their relationship during his absence to a pair of compasses. He will be the moving leg, making a circle, while she is the fixed leg, her steadiness making his circle perfect, so he can *end, where I begun.* As the *fixed foot* which *makes my circle just* she remains at home, her steadfastness showing the depth of their love and guaranteeing that he will return with nothing altered. There is a hint of cartography in the choice of compasses, suggesting that she is the point of origin from which his journey is measured and mapped. A circle is the image of perfection. Their union is perfect through their love, and should be exemplified by the perfect circle. The poet turns a conventional poem begging the beloved not to grieve at his absence into a powerful assertion of their unchangeable union.

Activity

Consider Dr Johnson's explanation and criticism of the metaphysical 'conceit'. Work with a partner, one finding evidence for and one against his view, basing your argument on at least two poems.

The metaphysicals wanted to convey their passionate feelings in forceful language, using vivid analogies to explore ideas. They did not consider any type of language or subject to be unsuitable to poetry. They used analogies from domestic life as well as from the new learning, and their metaphors juxtapose very contrasting ideas. If you look at their dates, you will see that most of them are close to the time when Shakespeare was writing. Their language is closer to the rhythms and vigour of everyday speech used in the drama than to the poetic conventions of earlier and later periods. They use idiomatic phrases and dramatic monologue, as in Donne's *The Canonisation,* which opens with a curse – *For God's sake hold your tongue* – though by the end of the poem it has become a holy invocation. This new kind of private poetry was suited not only to expressions of profane but of divine love. Donne and George Herbert both used 'conceits' to analyse their personal religious doubts and convictions.

The early metaphysical poets were writing in the aftermath of the Reformation, and their poetry expresses religious struggle. Donne's theological content concentrates upon sin and salvation. Donne was born into a recusant Catholic family, that is, a family who remained faithful to the old church when it was no longer politically expedient to do so. He was raised a Catholic but at some time in the 1590s became an Anglican, without which advancement at Court would have been impossible. After a time at Court and years of exile from it after an imprudent marriage to his master's daughter, he became an Anglican priest. Critics have seen in his work a constant concern with fidelity and falseness, an unease and anxiety about loyalty and deceit, which they attribute to his change of religion. One way of approaching his work is to see its paradoxical nature as a tension between Catholic imagery, as in *The Canonisation* and *The Relic*, and the individualism of a Protestant voice, seeking salvation.

George Herbert

Like Donne, George Herbert (1593–1633) was an Anglican priest. Even more than Donne's, his poetry is embedded in religious imagery that draws on earlier symbolic uses. In *A Reading of George Herbert* (1952), Rosemond Tuve responded to the critic William Empson's claims for Herbert's originality by pointing out how much the poet owes to the older Catholic tradition. Herbert wrote poetry expressing his search for God's true way, and voices his struggle with human frailty. His own health was poor and he died relatively young. *Sorrow was all my soul: I scarce believed, / Till grief did tell me roundly, that I lived*, he wrote in *Affliction*. But he has a strong conviction of Christ's redeeming love. He never loses his basic assurance of the love of God or his constant belief, and despair always gives way to trust. A struggle ending in resolution can be found in several of his poems.

Activity

> Choose one of Herbert's poems which moves from spiritual disquiet to peace. What disturbs and distresses the poet? What brings him peace in the end?

The personal and private character of metaphysical poetry means that religious and secular ideas interlock in many of the poems. This is particularly true of Donne. Herbert's *The Temple*, by contrast, is a construct of religious meditations, all recorded as experiences from his past as he strove to gain the confidence that he has achieved through his experience of God. Donne's poems are more inward, and mix the religious with the secular. Many of his love poems use the idea of death as a metaphor for lovers parting, or he imagines his own death as a context for his relationship with his beloved. In *The Expiration* he even puns on the word.

Henry Vaughan

George Herbert and Henry Vaughan (1622–95) were both born on the Welsh borders, to important landowning families. Herbert spent almost all his life in England, and his boyhood exposure to Welsh is not evident in his poetry. Vaughan, on the other hand, was brought up in Wales. After a time as a student at Oxford and service on the royalist side in the Civil War he returned to Wales to live as a doctor for the rest of his life. It appears to have been a sanctuary to him from the horrors of war. In this sanctuary he wrote poems as a record of his personal struggle to find God. He described himself as a 'Silurist', taking the name from an early warlike Welsh tribe in the Brecon area. This seems to indicate that he saw himself writing as a Welshman. To be a doctor he needed fluent Welsh, and in his poem *Daphnis* he writes of listening to bardic poetry in boyhood: *Here, where the careless world did sleep, have I / . . . The visions of our black but brightest bard / . . . full often heard.* The magazine of the Usk Valley Vaughan Society, *Scintilla*, contains articles discussing, among other points, Vaughan's Welsh background.

Activity

In his life of Vaughan, F. E. Hutchinson writes: *There is something more essential and valuable – the Welshman's imaginative vision, both intense and daring, his sensitiveness to the beauty of nature in all her moods, and his wistful yearning for lost youth, for friends departed, and for peace beyond the grave.* Do you feel Vaughan's poetry contrasts his youth and Civil War experiences with his religious ones? What tensions does this set up? Those of you who have knowledge of Welsh might like to investigate the Welsh linguistic and literary influences in his poetry.

Critical responses

In the eighteenth century, Dr Johnson described the metaphysicals in rather dismissive tones: *they endeavoured to be singular in their thoughts, and were careless of their diction . . . Their thoughts are often new, but seldom natural . . . Their attempts were always analytick: they broke every image into fragments.* Metaphysical poets were little read in the eighteenth and nineteenth centuries. Vaughan seems to have been forgotten completely until his poems were republished in 1847. Early in the twentieth century, a new collection of their work was edited by Grierson with notes to help the reader, and this did much to make them more widely known.

The forceful juxtaposition of complex ideas and the idiomatic language found in the major metaphysical poets appealed to T. S. Eliot, who was seeking a new poetic voice after the First World War. His essay (1921) helped to draw attention to them, although he did not 're-discover' them as has sometimes been claimed. Since his influential essay, the metaphysicals have been held in high esteem, reflecting their relevance to modern ways of thinking. Richard Gill, in *John Donne: Selected Poems* wrote: *his unusual language expresses the tensions of human feeling and . . . his intellectual ingenuity serves to show our richly complex yet unified world in which even apparently unrelated things . . . are related.*

Civil War and its Aftermath

Although the seventeenth century was a time of intense debate about the freedom of worship, political liberty and the power of the monarchy, few expected a civil war. Fighting was started by a small group of militant men driven by the conviction that they were doing the Lord's work, and a king equally convinced that he ruled by divine right. The disloyalty implicit in a civil war brought many parliamentarians back to the king's side, so that, in the early stages, it seemed probable that Charles I would win. It took the New Model Army created by Cromwell to swing the victory. Only a handful of men in the Commons voted for the king's trial and execution; most Englishmen viewed regicide with horror.

> *At the later end of the year 1648 I had leave given mee to goe to london to see my Father & during my stay there at that time at Whitehal it was that I saw the Beheading of King Charles the first . . . On the day of his execution, which was Tuesday, Jan. 30, I stood amongst the crowd in the street before Whitehal gate, where the scaffold was erected, and saw what was done, but was not so near as to hear any thing. The Blow I saw given, & can truly say with a sad heart; at the instant whereof, I remember wel, there was such a Grone by the Thousands then present, as I never heard before & desire I may never hear again.*

> *Philip Henry* Diaries and Letters

The patient behaviour of Charles I at his trial and execution excited sympathy. The publication of *Eikon Basilike* portraying him as a martyr was widely, if erroneously, believed to have been written by the king himself while in prison. It stirred guilt and remorse, even amongst parliamentarians. The Commonwealth, with its Puritan ban on ceremonies, plays and customary festivals like Christmas, lost popular support. At Cromwell's death there was a confused political hiatus and then Parliament, led by the army, reinstated the monarchy. The return of Charles II was greeted with joy, as John Evelyn recorded in his diary.

> *This day came in his Majestie Charles the 2^d to London after a sad, & long Exile . . . with a Triumph of above 20000 horse & foote, brandishing their swords and shouting with unexpressable joy.*

For committed Puritans it was a despairing moment: the loss of their hopes and the defeat of republican ideals. The bodies of the rebellion's leaders were dug up and the heads were displayed at Westminster. Cromwell's head stayed there for many years. Samuel Pepys, whose diary also records the *Great joy* of the Restoration, wrote in the same entry that the Commons *voted that all books whatever that are out against the government of King, Lords and Commons should be brought into the House and burned.* Among the writings ordered to be burnt were pamphlets written by the Commonwealth's chief propagandist, John Milton.

John Milton

John Milton (1608–74) was born into a Puritan family. His father converted to Protestantism, for which he was disinherited by Milton's grandfather, who remained firmly Catholic. He moved to London where he became a scrivener (a combination of lawyer and money-lender) and where Milton was born and educated until he went to university. Milton's father supported his clever, academic son at Cambridge University until he was 30 years of age. Milton spent his time acquiring a formidable classical education, writing lyric poetry and masques, and travelling on the Continent from which he returned in 1639 to help the revolution. From 1649 to the mid 1650s when he lost his sight, Milton was at the centre of political affairs and chief propagandist for the government. As late as 1660 he wrote *The Ready and Easie Way to Establish a Free Commonwealth*, hoping to influence men against the Restoration.

This was dangerously late to be publishing for the republican cause. He was imprisoned for a short while after the Restoration, and spared execution probably because he was judged to have been sufficiently punished by poverty and blindness. In the isolation of his enforced retirement, Milton returned to poetry and produced his finest work. He began *Paradise Lost* in the last years of the Protectorate when he was losing heart under the semi-regal rule of Cromwell. He completed it in 1667, and in 1671 he published his two final poems, *Paradise Regained* and *Samson Agonistes.* At the same time another disappointed Puritan, John Bunyan, was writing *Pilgrim's Progress* in prison.

Paradise Lost is an epic. It opens dramatically in the middle of the story with the rebellious angels falling from heaven. In the middle books Raphael shifts the narrative back in time as he tells Adam and Eve about Satan's initial revolt, the War in Heaven and the Creation. The final books move the narrative forward in time to the fall of Adam and Eve and their expulsion from Paradise. The double fall of angels and of man, from a state of grace and place of bliss to punitive torment and outcast solitude, imposes a melancholy mood on the narrative. Many critics feel this mirrors Milton's feelings of despair as his great hopes of the republic for which he had worked came to nothing.

It is hardly surprising that a poem conceived in turbulent times is per-vaded by the consciousness of war. Book 1 plunges into a military metaphor at line 44. *Him the Almighty Power / Hurld headlong flaming from th'Ethereal Skie / With hideous ruin and combustion down / To bottomless perdition.* Critics have used the description of Satan's fall as an example of Milton's grand style, magniloquent-sounding phrases which cannot be concretely visualized. But if we place the poem in the context of the Civil War, we can see the image as a flaming cannonball, similar to the image Marvell used in *To his Coy Mistress* of a cannon attacking the gates of a city, as a metaphor for the pleasure and urgency of love. *Let us roll all our Strength and all / Our sweetness, up into one Ball / And tear our Pleasures with rough strife / Thorough the Iron gates of Life.* Satan's defiant speech at 1.663–4 is that of a general rousing his battered troops for a renewed assault. *He spake: and to confirm his words, out-flew / Millions of flaming swords.*

Activity

> It is not only Satan and the rebel angels who are associated with the vocabulary of war. In the first fifteen lines of God's opening speech (2.80–95) how many words can you find that carry military connotations?

For twenty years in the prime of his life, Milton wrote political pamphlets about power and rule, freedom and obedience. The discourse of *Paradise Lost* reflects the debates that were going on around him. The gathering of the fallen angels is called a *solemn Councel* (1.755) in which they *expatiate and conforr / Thir State affairs* (1.774–5). Satan chairs the discussion, the angels speak in turn, formally and at length, respond to each other's points, and reach decision by vote.

Activity

> We must not base our view of modern debate on the quick ripostes we see in television coverage of 'Prime Minister's question time'. Try listening to some of the fuller exchanges in the Lords or Commons, or to a current affairs programme that discusses controversial issues. What in the manner of the fallen angels' debate seems familiar? What has changed over the centuries? How does the consultation in *Pandemonium* arrive at its decision? What arguments are put forward, and how does Satan sway the fallen angels to support him? Consideration of these points should alert you to the manipulative oratory of Satan and the political rhetoric of the debate in hell. If possible, read this section of the poem aloud in a group, sharing the roles.

Milton had hoped to persuade men of the rightness of the parliamentary cause through reason. Satan and God embody the arguments of his prose writings. Milton's God is a God of reason, a God who explains his actions, not a God of mystery – which to the Puritans was a Catholic concept. Pym spoke for the parliamentarians when he said that law was the protection of liberty. *Paradise Lost* argues that *Libertie . . . which always with right Reason dwells* (12.83–4) consists in a willing and rational obedience to law. Milton's God is neither above the law nor subject to it. He is the law, the *high Decree / Unchangeable, Eternal* (3.126–7). To disobey the law is to reject God.

Satan personifies Milton's attack on the monarchy. Kings were false, they were tyrants when they claimed to be above the law. Satan talks much of freedom, but to Milton he was like Charles I, *Rebel to all Law* (10.83). The freedom he claims is the freedom to act without restraint, without law. He even complains that it is *Flatly unjust, to binde with Laws the free* (5.819). Satan's language draws upon revolutionary phrases, and his words ring with courage and passion. *What though the field be lost? / All is not lost* (1.105–6). *Know ye not mee? Ye knew me once no mate / For you, there sitting where ye durst not soare* (4.828–9). But the heroic figure portrayed in the early books gradually changes and is revealed in his true form.

The seventeenth century saw the beginning of England's colonization of America, Bermuda and the West Indies. Elizabethans called these lands the 'New World'. Sixteenth-century explorers like Sir John Hawkins, Sir Francis Drake and Sir Walter Raleigh boasted of riches there for the taking: gold, pearls and trading *commodities*. More thoughtful men saw opportunities for spreading Christianity amongst the natives and settling England's unemployed. By the seventeenth century, promotional literature about the colonies was widespread. A typical pamphlet enthuses about Virginia in 1616:

> *The country yeeldeth abundance of wood, as Oake, Wainscot, Walnut trees, Bay trees, Ashe, Sarsafrase, Live Oake, greene all the yeare . . . there are incredible variety of sweet woods, especially of the Balsamum tree, which distilleth a pretious gum; that there are innumerable White Mulberry trees, which in so warme a climate may cherish and feede millions of silke wormes . . . the river swarmeth with Sturgeon; the land aboundeth with Vines, the woodes doe harbor exceeding store of Beavers, Foxes and Squirrils, the waters doe nourish a great encrease of Otters . . . the Orenges which have beene planted did prosper in the winter . . . it is one of the goodliest countries under the sunne.*

John Smith describes New England in 1616 from a more moral point of view but in an equally encouraging manner.

> *Who can desire more content . . . then to tread, and plant that ground hee hath purchased by the hazard of his life? If he have but the taste of virtue, and magnanimitie, what to such a minde can bee more pleasant, then planting and building a foundation for his Posteritie, gotte from the rude earth, by Gods blessing and his owne industrie?*

Visions of the 'happy isles' of the 'New World' appear in literature. Shakespeare's *The Tempest* of 1610 (see page 41) is one example. Marvell's *The Bermudas* (1653) is another. Milton's Eden draws on pamphlet descriptions of the luxuriant fruitfulness of the colonies, and Satan journeys to paradise like a voyager bent on discovery and profit.

Activity

> Read descriptions of Satan's journeys (2.1010–22, 2.1034–55, 4.131–83, 9.99–118). How are both the dangers and delights of discovering a new world conveyed? What parallels might there be with trading expeditions and colonial expectations?

Critical responses

Paradise Lost was published in 1667 to little immediate acclaim. The part Milton played in the revolution was not forgiven by royalists. In 1687, William Winstanley wrote:

> *John Milton was one, whose natural parts might deservedly give him a place amongst the principal of our English Poets . . . But his Fame is gone out like a Candle in a Snuff, and his Memory will always stink, which might have ever lived in honourable Repute, had not he been a notorious Traytor, and most impiously and villanously bely'd that blessed King Charles the First.*

Fellow poets, however, recognized Milton's achievement. Marvell and Dryden both eulogized him.

In the eighteenth century *Paradise Lost* became hugely popular, helped by a series of essays by Joseph Addison published in *The Spectator* in 1712 praising its religious content. Dr Johnson, a royalist and devout Anglican, wrote in 1779 in the period immediately following successful revolutions in America and Europe. He too reacted warmly to Milton's religious theme: *Of his moral sentiments it is hardly praise to affirm that they excel those of all other poets . . . In Milton every line breathes sanctity of thought.* But he was troubled by the revolutionary messages. *Milton's republicanism was, I am afraid, founded in an envious hatred of greatness, and a sullen desire of independence; in petulance impatient of controul, and pride disdainful of superiority. He hated monarchs in the state and prelates in the church; for he hated all whom he was required to obey.* Dr Johnson's even-handed conclusion shows both admiration and reservations:

> *In reading* Paradise Lost *we read a book of universal knowledge. But original deficience cannot be supplied. The want of human interest is always felt.* Paradise Lost *is one of the books which the reader admires and lays down, and forgets to take up again. None ever wished it longer than it is. Its perusal is a duty rather than a pleasure. We read Milton for instruction, retire harassed and overburdened, and look elsewhere for recreation; we desert our master and seek companions.*

The nineteenth-century Romantics appropriated Milton for the revolutionary cause. Satan became a voice for freedom. Blake wrote a lengthy poem called *Milton*, whose introductory stanzas *And did those feet in ancient time / Walk upon England's mountains green?* have been adopted as a hymn. Few who sing it realize that the lines were written in praise of Milton. A Jacobin and a radical, Blake insisted: *The reason Milton wrote in fetters when he wrote of Angels & God, and at liberty when of Devils & Hell, is because he was a true Poet and of the Devil's party without knowing it.*

Hazlitt hailed Satan as a hero in his 1818 Lectures.

> *Satan is the most heroic subject that ever was chosen for a poem; and the execution is as perfect as the design is lofty. He was the first of created beings, who, for endeavouring to be equal with the highest, and to divide the empire of heaven with the Almighty, was hurled down to hell. . . . His ambition was the greatest, and his punishment was the greatest; but not so his despair, for his fortitude was as great as his sufferings . . . He was baffled, not confounded. He stood like a tower . . . His love of power and contempt for suffering are never once relaxed from the highest pitch of intensity. His thoughts burn like a hell within him; but the power of thought holds dominion in his mind over every other consideration . . . After such a conflict as his, and such a defeat, to retreat in order, to rally, to make terms, to exist at all, is something; but he does more than this – he founds a new empire in hell, and from it conquers this new world, whither he bends his undaunted flight.*

P. B. Shelley, who was expelled from Oxford University for writing an atheistic pamphlet *On Liberty*, decided God was the villain and even denied that Satan was evil.

> *Nothing can exceed the energy and magnificence of the character of Satan as expressed in* Paradise Lost. *It is a mistake to suppose that he could ever have been intended for the popular personi-fication of evil. Implacable hate, patient cunning, and a sleepless refinement of device to inflict the extremest anguish on an enemy, these things are evil . . . Milton's Devil as a moral being is as far superior to his God as one who perseveres in some purpose which he has conceived to be excellent in spite of adversity and torture is to one who in the cold security of undoubted triumph inflicts the most horrible revenge upon his enemy, not from any mistaken notion of inducing him to repent of a perseverance in enmity but with the alleged design of exasperating him to deserve new torments.*

The nineteenth century saw the beginnings of the attack on Milton by women. The American Sarah Grimké's comment is symptomatic of a Victorian feminist reaction to Eve:

> *If man is constituted the governor of woman, he must be her God; and the sentiment expressed to me lately, by a married man, is*

*perfectly correct: 'In my opinion,' said he, 'the greatest excellence
to which a married woman can attain, is to worship her husband.'
He was a professor of religion – his wife a lovely and intelligent
woman. He only spoke out what thousands think and act. Women
are indebted to Milton for giving to this false notion, 'confirmation
strong as holy writ.' His Eve is embellished with every personal
grace, to gratify the eye of her husband; but he seems to have
furnished the mother of mankind with just intelligence enough to
comprehend her supposed inferiority to Adam, and to yield
unresisting submission to her lord and master.*

Twentieth-century critics, responding to the nineteenth-century scientific
doubts about the literal truth of the book of Genesis, were divided between
those who defended Christianity in the poem and those who attacked it. C. S.
Lewis suggested that readers' antipathy to the poem lay in their own
declining faith. *Many of those who say they dislike Milton's God only mean
that they dislike God.* William Empson led the attack for non-believers. *I
think the traditional God of Christianity very wicked and have done so ever
since I was at school.* He argued for a humanist Milton, a man of *civilised
conscience* whose puritan belief in the literal truth of the Bible and the
justice of God landed him in difficulties when he attempted to justify that
justice. *The reason why the poem is so good is that it makes God so bad.*
Empson's approach was based on a close and sensitive reading of the text,
and by the mid-century, modernist criticism was focussing attention on
matters of style. Christopher Ricks, building on Empson's methods in
Milton's Grand Style (1963), wrote one of the best of the modernist critiques
of the poem and helped to retrieve Milton's reputation as one of the masters
of style.

Recent criticism has tried to place *Paradise Lost* in the context of its creation.
A leading historian of the seventeenth century, Christopher Hill, looked in
detail at the historical setting of the poem. In his *Milton and the English
Revolution* (1977), he wrote:

*But we have to work a little to grasp Milton's relevance. We cannot
just let the poetry speak for itself. Some of it will, most of the ideas
will not; and Milton is nothing if not a poet of ideas. To understand
his relevance we must see him as a man of total political
commitment. Like Wordsworth, he started out with extravagantly
high hopes: unlike Wordsworth, he strove to cling on to them.*

Hill's thesis is that, since Milton believed that the revolution was God's cause
and that the men who fought for it were godly, he needed to explain its
failure. The reason must lie with human agents. The only way to explain evil
and human sin was that it arose from the original Fall. Milton's intellect
told him that he must accept God's will *but his submission to the
events of 1655–60 was highly reluctant . . . how could a free and rational
individual accept what God had done to his servants in England?* Hill

concludes that *Milton expressed through Satan (of whom he disapproved) the dissatisfaction which he felt with the Father (whom intellectually he accepted).*

Of the many critics who have continued to explore the context of the poem, one of the fullest accounts is David Norbrook's *Writing the English Republic* (1999):

> *The closer we bring* Paradise Lost *to its original context . . . the harder it becomes to square a blandly apolitical or defeatist reading of the epic with its author's values . . . The imagery of heavenly kingship helped to pose the question of heavenly justice in the sharpest and most provocative way to a republican reader.*

4 Restoration and Eighteenth-Century Contexts

● ●

All sorts of Silk Gowns, being a parcel of Rich Brocades, Venetian, Japan'd, and Thread Sattins, Tissues, Damasks, and a variety of other Silks, bought great Pennyworths, of People that have failed, and to be Sold so by Mrs. Attaway, who lives in Devereux Court, in the Passage from the Temple to Essex buildings.

Fine Brazil SNUFF . . . may be had at SAM's Coffee-House, Ludgate Street; or at his Sister's Shop, two Doors on this side the King's Head in Epsome, where she can supply any gentleman or lady with the same; as also Tea, Coffee, and Chocolate at reasonable Rates.

Advertisements in The Spectator *April 17 and March 31, 1711*

The Restoration

Charles II, the Stuart king whose return was greeted with such joy (see page 52), was a man of easy affability, and he proved to be a tolerant ruler. In the Declaration of Breda, issued prior to his Restoration, he promised amnesty and conciliation: *We do declare a liberty to tender consciences, and that no man shall be disquieted or called in question for differences of opinion in matter of religion.* Louis XIV of France hoped Charles would return England to the old faith, and secretly financed him during his reign. Personally, Charles probably preferred the Catholic religion but his dominant interests were neither religion nor power – he was happy to pass his time in court festivities and multiple love affairs. He had dealings with both Protestant and Catholic countries in Europe and tried not to offend Parliament. Constitutional problems were delayed until the accession of his brother James II, who was openly Roman Catholic.

When James came to the throne, a group of leading Whigs and Tories who were determined to maintain a Protestant succession urged William of Orange (husband of James's daughter Mary) to claim the throne in Mary's name. He invaded England in 1688 in the Glorious Revolution, so called because James II fled into exile without bloodshed. The change of regime was followed by the Declaration of Rights, later converted into the Act of Settlement in 1701, which limited royal privileges. No future king could be a Roman Catholic, or suspend the laws, or maintain a standing army. Parliament's powers increased and the two-party system of government and opposition developed. The struggle for political power was no longer between King and Parliament, but between the Tories (the country party representing 'landed' interests and sympathetic to the Stuarts) and the Whigs (the mercantile and business party, the 'moneyed' interest). Although the transition from James II to William and Mary was peaceful, for many years there was a possibility that James II or his son (the 'Old Pretender') or grandson (the 'Young Pretender', Bonnie Prince Charlie) might regain the throne. People were suspicious of those with passionate political allegiances. For most, the aim was to avoid another civil war and, although neither dissenters nor Catholics were given equal civil rights, there was greater toleration of political and religious differences in the eighteenth century than in the seventeenth century.

A major incentive for William to invade Britain had been his fear that Charles II was about to make an alliance with France, the enemy of the Netherlands. Once in power, William brought England into the war against France, a war that continued intermittently until 1713. From 1689–97 war cost England £5.5 million a year, and from 1702–12, £8.5 million. William needed funds. New forms of custom and excise duties and taxation were introduced, including a tax on windows and a tax on land that was so successful it raised around £2 million annually. The Government began to borrow through lotteries, bond issues and the Bank of England. Paper credit had been used since the 1650s by goldsmiths, but the establishment of the Bank of England in 1694 marks the true beginning of modern banking methods: the free movement of capital, secure international payments, assured savings, interest rates and the institution of the National Debt. Coinage gave way to paper money in the form of banknotes and promissory notes, greatly easing the conduct of trade, which needed liquidity and credit.

Wealth and prosperity

By contrasting two play scenes, one from the seventeenth century and one from the eighteenth, we can see the change in the nature of private wealth. Jonson's *Volpone* (1605) opens with the miser gloating over his treasure – a mass of gold coins, plate and jewels. The climax of Congreve's *The Way of the World* (1700) centres on a black box which contains a legal deed of conveyance. The evidence of wealth has shifted from the possession of tangible treasure to documents – paper assurances and legal promises of credit.

In spite of the unease occasioned by the possibility of a second Restoration of a Stuart king, the end of the seventeenth century and the opening decades of the eighteenth century were years of political stability and economic progress. Britain's mercantile trade prospered. Raw materials were imported and manufactured goods were exported, sometimes back to their country of origin. Cotton from India returned as cloth. Sugar and molasses from Barbados and the West Indies returned as rum. Tea, coffee, spices, indigo, silk and porcelain were imported for home consumption from the east; from the west and the Baltic came sugar, tobacco, fish, timber and furs. The colonies had to import manufactured articles and the balance of trade was to Britain's advantage. A particularly profitable section of the Atlantic trade triangle consisted of slaves brought from Africa to the West Indies and southern states of America. By the mid-eighteenth century, London was the financial and trading centre of the world.

Daniel Defoe, in *The Complete English Tradesman* (1726) comments upon the growth of England's trade and the prosperity it brought to individuals and to the State.

> As to the wealth of the nation, that undoubtedly lies chiefly among the trading part of the people; and tho' there are a great many families rais'd within few years, in the late war by great employments, and by great actions abroad, to the honour of the English gentry; yet how many more families among the tradesmen have been rais'd to immense estates, even during the same time, by the attending circumstances of the war? such as the cloathing, the paying, the victualling and furnishing, etc. both army and navy? And by whom have the prodigious taxes been paid, the loans supplied, and money advanced upon all occasions? . . . Has not the trade and tradesmen born the burthen of the war? . . . Is not trade the inexhausted fund of all funds, and upon which all the rest depend?

Prosperity changed the face of London. After the Great Fire of 1666, St Paul's Cathedral and the Royal Exchange were rebuilt and new churches were designed by Wren and Hawksmoor. Housing expanded westward, creating the West End with its great squares: Hanover, Grosvenor, Cavendish, Portman. Wealth was not confined to London. Cities like Bristol and Edinburgh acquired impressive Georgian buildings, while Bath and Tunbridge Wells became elegant leisure resorts.

Social life was transformed by new types of attractive public spaces – parks and pleasure gardens, malls, exchanges, theatres and, later in the century, assembly rooms and medicinal baths. Newspapers, gentlemen's clubs and coffee shops all appeared after the Restoration, as well as shops trading in luxury items like chinaware, silks and satins, coffee, tea, and 'toys' – the eighteenth-century word for fashionable articles like bracelets, buckles and snuff-boxes. Daniel Defoe complained of the triviality of shops' wares and the lavishness of their fittings:

> in painting and gilding, fine shelves, shutters, boxes, glass doors, sashes and the like, in which they tell us now, 'tis a small matter to lay out two or three hundred pounds, nay, five hundred pounds, to fit up a pastry cook's, or a toy shop . . . We find the most noble shops in the city taken up with the valuable utensils of the tea table.

Activity

> Look in detail at the settings of Restoration and eighteenth-century comedies. How do they reflect the lives of the well-to-do in England? You might like to compare the geographical range of the settings in Restoration drama with the settings of Shakespeare's plays.

Luxury goods eased the lives of those who could afford them, predominantly a London and court-based society. In Pope's *The Rape of the Lock* (1711) Belinda is cossetted in her comfortable life by exotic and precious commodities: gems from India, perfumes from Arabia, tortoise-shell combs, silks, brocades, porcelain jars and Indian screens. Coffee is served at court in china cups, filled from a silver urn on a Japanese lacquered table.

> *For lo! the Board with Cups and Spoons is crown'd,*
> *The Berries crackle, and the Mill turns round.*
> *On shining Altars of Japan they raise*
> *The silver Lamp; the fiery Spirits blaze.*
> *From silver Spouts the grateful Liquors glide,*
> *While China's Earth receives the smoking Tyde.*

In *The Way of the World* Millamant insists, in her terms of marriage, on remaining *sole Empress of my Tea-table.* (Mirabell insists on restricting her drinking to tea, coffee and chocolate, banning gin-based tipples like the cherry brandy to which Lady Wishfort is addicted.) In Restoration drama, an invitation to dine is a common way of getting characters off stage and one of the standard town–country jibes is about the differing times of dinner. In *The Way of the World*, when Sir Wilfull Witwoud arrives at his aunt's he is scornful to find her still dressing at an hour when he would have finished dining: *Dressing! What, it's but Morning here, I warrant with you, in London; we shou'd count it towards Afternoon in our Parts, down in Shropshire. Why then, belike my Aunt han't dined yet.* In Pope's *Epistle to Miss Blount, on her leaving the Town, after the Coronation*, he pities her because of her *solitary tea* and having to *dine exact at noon.*

Consumables, merchandise and luxury novelties became a medium of expression in the literature of the period. In *The Country Wife* (1675) oranges and china are deliberately used to indicate illicit sexual desire. Luxury and immorality are linked, but are either condemned? The figure of the fop, who features so prominently in Restoration comedy, from Etherege's Sir Fopling Flutter to Vanbrugh's Lord Foppington, is ridiculed for taking fashion to extremes. The outsized periwig and outrageous tailoring, always of the newest style, express the fop's self-absorption, as do the over-punctilious courtesies and meaningless good manners. Pope uses stained brocade and cracked china jars in *The Rape of the Lock* to symbolize a young woman's delicacy and vulnerability. With any Restoration text it is worth considering the extent to which the presence of commodities produced by the mercantile trade creates the setting and atmosphere, and the extent to which such articles carry deeper meanings.

Activity

> In a Restoration or early eighteenth-century text, list the commodities mentioned and how often they are referred to. It will become evident that articles associated with dress and appearance, or with dining and entertainment, establish a character's way of life as modish and moneyed. Trade may not be directly mentioned, but it is the essential basis of the society portrayed in these texts. Are deeper symbolic purposes being expressed through the use of commodities?

Landed gentry invested in trade, and the wealth it brought gave them the opportunity of enlarging and enhancing their estates. The eighteenth century is the period when many of the great English houses laid out their grounds to plans inspired by designers Humphrey Repton, William Kent and Capability Brown. New plants and trees entered the country in abundance. The great eighteenth-century discoverer Captain Cook was accompanied on his first voyage by the botanist Sir Joseph Banks, whose mission it was to bring back new botanical specimens from the Pacific. One of the main pastimes of a gentleman became the improvement of his estate.

Alexander Pope did not own his modest five-acre garden at Twickenham, he rented it. Yet he laid it out with the same enthusiasm as the great lords whose estates he delighted to visit, to watch them changing the English landscape. In *Moral Essay IV: Of the Use of Riches*, he ridicules Timon whose grandiose improvements were for show, not use. Pope's image of the morally good life, public and private, is Lord Burlington's estate at Stowe. The well-managed, great estate is a recurring literary symbol throughout the eighteenth century, until swept away by the Romantic passion for untamed nature. In the early nineteenth century Jane Austen is still using the great estates of Pemberley and Mansfield Park to symbolize the ideal life, although she reveals, albeit discreetly, the economic realities. The owner of Mansfield Park, Sir Thomas Bertram, and his eldest son are absent in the West Indies for much of the novel, overseeing the source of their wealth – the sugar and slave trade.

In *The Country Wife* Pinchwife calculates a man's wealth by his land. While weighing up his preference for Horner as a husband for Alithea, he says: *His estate is equal to Sparkish.* Two decades later, Congreve was using the language of trade, finance and banking. Money, often in the form of bonds, deeds and documents, drives the action of *The Way of the World*. If you wish to follow the intricacies of the plot, keep your eye on the money. Who possesses it, who needs it, who stands to inherit or to lose it?

Activity

> Even in small exchanges, the importance of money is revealed in *The Way of the World*. Read the passage between Lady Wishfort and Foible (Act III Scene 1) from *Ods my Life, I'll have him, I'll have him murder'd . . .* to *. . . Ay dear Foible; thank thee for that dear Foible.* List the forms of punishment devised for Mirabell. In what ways do these reflect the importance of money in society? If you wish to investigate further telling moments, you could look at

Marwood's outburst against Foible later in the same scene. Her strongest fury is caused by the fact that Foible is *a very Master-Key to everybody's strong-Box.* Sir Wilfull reveals near the end of the scene that his travelling funds depend on the degree to which his income, based on land, is taxed, and that in turn depends on whether Britain needs to continue financing a war in Europe. Consider also the punishment Lady Wishfort threatens upon Foible in Act V. What does this reveal about life in London for the poor?

Personal relationships are described in the language of commerce. Pinchwife refers to his wife as his *freehold* (Act II Scene 1); Harcourt denies he made love to Alithea at a play, saying: *I see all women are like these of the Exchange, who, to enhance the price of their commodities, report to their fond customers offers which were never made 'em* (Act III Scene 2). Horner, the master operator, explicitly makes the connection between sexual and commercial transactions:

> *Ladies, I know, like great men in offices, you seem to exact flattery and attendance only from your followers, but you have receivers about you, and such fees to pay, a man is afraid to pass your grants. Besides, we must let you win at cards, or we lose your hearts. And if you make an assignation, 'tis at a goldsmith's, jeweller's, or china house, where, for your honour you deposit to him, he must pawn his to the punctual cit, and so paying for what you take up, pays for what he takes up.* (Act V Scene 4)

Activity

In *The Way of the World* (Act III Scene 1) Millamant requests the song *Love's but the frailty of the Mind.* Contrast this lyric with one of Shakespeare's, such as *O mistress mine! Where are you roaming?* and note the competitive element in the Restoration definition of love. How is this created? What light does it throw on Millamant's conquest of Mirabell? Her final acceptance uses the vocabulary of acquisition: *Well, you ridiculous thing you, I'll have you.* Do you find this a joke or have mercantile values coloured relationships?

Individualism

The entrepreneurial spirit of the eighteenth century saw a loosening of guild and apprenticeship rules. Whereas in Shakespeare loyalty in master-servant relationships is a reliable sign of virtue (such as Kent and Lear or Orlando and old Adam), in eighteenth-century literature self-reliance becomes heroic. Consider the independent sufficiency of those isolated heroes Robinson Crusoe and Gulliver, both literary creations of the early eighteenth century. In 1651 Thomas Hobbes had published a treatise, *Leviathan*, written while he was in exile as the tutor to Charles II. The premise of *Leviathan* is that people are naturally selfish and in pursuit of their own individual ends; that life, in what became a famous quotation, is *nasty, brutish, and short*, and that far from being endowed with basic Christian instincts of charity, benevolence and gregariousness, individuals and societies would be continually at war were it not for absolute rulers who could enforce obedience and peaceful cooperation.

By the start of the eighteenth century the idea that there might be a social value in selfishness was being openly expressed. A popular essay by Bernard Mandeville shows how attitudes to personal enterprise and labour relationships were changing. Mandeville started life as a writer of light pieces for coffee-house magazines, translating La Fontaine's animal fables into comic English verse. In 1705 he published *The Grumbling Hive*, which he developed in 1714 into *The Fable of the Bees: Or, Private Vices, Publick Benefits*, adding an Introduction, Inquiry and Remarks to later editions as its fame grew. In *The Grumbling Hive* we recognize a political picture of Restoration Britain:

> *They were not Slaves to Tyranny,*
> *Nor rul'd by wild Democracy;*
> *But Kings, that could not wrong, because*
> *Their Power was circumscrib'd by Laws.*

Mandeville's argument is that personal greed, far from being evil, creates general prosperity.

> *Thus Vice nurs'd Ingenuity,*
> *Which joined with Time and Industry,*
> *Had carry'd Life's conveniencies,*
> *It's real Pleasures, Comforts, Ease,*
> *To such a Height, the very Poor*
> *Liv'd better than the Rich before.*

Cheating, avarice and corruption are rife in the hive. It is a society where everyone is out for themselves and, far from being chaotic, it is a comfortable world: *every Part was full of Vice, / Yet the whole Mass a Paradise.* The bees complain to Jove and he grants their prayers for a Reformation of Manners. Mandeville has a low opinion of 'Reformation'. With Reformation, the basis of the hive's commercial economy disappears. The bees lose their wealth and retreat, poverty-stricken, to the simple life in a hollow tree. Mandeville is not a theoretical economist of the stature of Adam Smith, whose enquiry into *The Wealth of Nations* (1776) was one of the founding texts of economic theory, but his phrase *private vices, publick benefits* became a sound-bite of the eighteenth century in defence of mercantile politics and unrestrained individualism.

Activity

An example of the selfish core of individualism, unrestrained by Christian ideals, is Horner in Wycherley's *The Country Wife*. Horner's character has always troubled critics. Is he a monster of sexual depravity who ought to be punished? Is he a charmer whose cleverness we are meant to approve? Is he a liberated Restoration Cavalier freed from the years of Puritan restraint? Is he a ruthless, self-interested Hobbesian man, pursuing his *nasty, brutish* ends in a natural way? Does he deserve the milder Mandeville tag of *private vices, publick benefits* because his selfish ways give pleasure to many ladies?

What if we consider him as a self-interested entrepreneur? He plans his campaign in a meticulously businesslike way; focuses on his goal, works hard, suffers indignities, lies and cheats to achieve his ends. He is charming and considerate, able to persuade others to his will and loved by his 'victims'. These are the virtues of the self-made man in an entrepreneurial world. How should we judge, indeed should we judge, the ends he pursues?

Attitudes to women

In the Marxist reading above, sex has become a commodity and Horner is the image of an acquisitive, materialist society. An alternative, feminist reading sees Horner helping married women to assert power in one of the few ways available to them. The ideal of wedded bliss faded in Restoration comedy. Marriages are often portrayed as unhappy alliances and wives take revenge through sexual infidelity.

Restoration actresses were regarded as loose women (see Unit 8, *Theatres and Playing Spaces*). Many were mistresses to aristocrats, suggesting that the professionalism of an actress may well have increased her commodity value.

Frontispiece engraving to
Amboyna *from John Dryden's*
Dramatick Works, *1735, showing*
Ysabinda being untied
just after her rape

Restoration audiences were as interested in actresses' private lives as their public performances. The line between the two was blurred and a female role was an opportunity for displaying the physical attractions of the actress, especially in scenes of near-'rape' (see page 68) and in 'breeches' roles.

Activity

> Consider the opportunities for displaying the female body in *The Country Wife*, *The Rover* and *The Relapse*. Does voyeurism explain the cynical attitude towards sexual relationships in Restoration drama?

In the comedies women appear equal to men in wit and cunning. Heroines may 'dwindle into a wife', but not without having held their own verbally against the men. In reality, women were no more liberated in eighteenth-century England than they had been in previous centuries, but in Restoration plays (many of them written by women) there is an open voicing of women's position and women's complaints. It has been suggested that the innovation of allowing actresses to appear on the stage strengthened the female viewpoint. Some of the explanation must lie in the intellectual freedom to question all institutions which was encouraged by the Civil War, but sexual relationships in Restoration comedy do tend to emphasize unresolved conflict rather than the harmony evident in Shakespearian comedy.

Activity

> What power do female characters have? Heroines like Helena, Hoyden and Millamant appear independent, vocal and quick-witted. Do you feel they gain or lose by marriage? Can you sense in their words and actions any concern about the married state? What does the epilogue to *The Country Wife* reveal about the power, or powerlessness, of women? You might like to think about who, in play and epilogue, is *cozening* whom?

Society and law

An interest in how societies operate, in their economies and labour relationships, is present in many eighteenth-century texts, such as Defoe's *Robinson Crusoe* (1719) and *Moll Flanders* (1722), Swift's *Gulliver's Travels* (1726) and *A Modest Proposal* (1729). Independent, individual effort in the making of livelihoods is valued, and there is a reluctance to condemn. Defoe's Moll Flanders lives on what she can glean, pluck, charm and thieve from wealthy folk. What she 'earns' by dubious and illegal means are the portable commodities of eighteenth-century trade and the financial security of advantageous marriages. Defoe remains morally neutral towards her trade. Indeed, he appears to sympathize with her in her worst moments, awaiting execution for theft in Newgate prison, because the plot allows her to escape. For all its happy ending, *Moll Flanders* shows the dark side of eighteenth-century prosperity: poverty and the punitive legal system.

The number of laws to protect ownership increased during this period, as did the severity of punishment. Those who had possessions defended their property with judicial savagery. Hanging was the penalty for trivial thefts, and public executions were not only common but hugely popular events. In 1688 about fifty crimes carried the death penalty, but by 1800 there were nearly two hundred. In Charles II's time transportation was an alternative to the death penalty. By the eighteenth century it had become a punishment for petty offences. The rapacious and savage side of eighteenth-century life is glossed over in some texts by wit and satire, but every now and then awareness surfaces, as in *The Rape of the Lock* with Pope's famous couplet: *The hungry Judges soon the Sentence sign, / And Wretches hang that Jury-men may Dine* (Canto III lines 21–2).

Activity

> Consider, in a Restoration play of your choice, which characters require or are actively seeking money. What is their fate likely to be if they fail to secure it?

The savagery of individualism is overlaid in Restoration drama by polite manners. Controlled behaviour is a virtue. The open expression of passion, whether of anger, hostility or love, is considered ill-mannered. Lord Foppington in *The Relapse*, having lost the wealthy heiress to his younger brother, says: *I think the wisest thing a man can do with an aching heart is to put on a serene countenance, for a philosophical air is the most becoming thing in the world to the face of a person of quality.*

Memories of the civil war may have encouraged men to confine themselves to a war of words rather than swords, and to use language to control, conceal and deflect differences of opinion. At the Restoration there was a growing interest in the improvement of manners. A Society for the Reformation of Manners was formed, and *The Tatler* and *The Spectator* published essays on gentlemanly behaviour. In *The Rover*, set in pre-Restoration times in Spain, the financially stretched, drinking, whoring gallants, constantly breaking out into sword-fights, are a recognizable picture of the cavalier followers of King Charles in exile. After the Restoration, drunkenness, swearing and fighting were disapproved of in polite society. In *The Rivals* (1775), Bob Acres claims *Damns have had their day* as he practises the new, genteel, *sentimental swearing*. Captain Absolute, on the way to a duel, has to hide his sword under his greatcoat, aware that: *A sword seen in the streets of Bath would raise as great an alarm as a mad dog.*

Activity

> In a play of your choice, are there characters who are drunk on stage or occasions when one character draws his sword on another? How does the author show he condemns this behaviour and what does it reveal of the character that he resorts to it?

Eloquence and wit

Restoration wit springs from a conscious desire on the part of characters to speak elegantly. Fluent, well-turned conversation is a sign of the well-bred gentleman and there is amused contempt for country characters who behave roughly and speak bluntly. *It is from the frequent conversations in Cities, that the Humour, and Wit, and Variety, and Elegance of Language, are chiefly to be fetch'd*, wrote Bishop Sprat in his *History of the Royal Society*. London was considered the place where manners were learned and conversation was sharpened, in contrast to the social isolation of the countryside.

The courteous tone, however, can mask irritation, deceit, disdain and downright hostility. There is a harsh competitive edge to much of the raillery. Consider the exchange between Mirabell and Fainall in the opening lines of *The Way of the World*, where Fainall cleverly avoids allowing Mirabell the opportunity of retrieving the money he has won from him; or the initial loving encounter between Fainall and his wife which is followed, after her exit, by his outburst of hatred. In *The Country Wife*, Margery's inability to use the dissembling language of the town shows her innocence. Her insistence on speaking the truth is part of the fun of the plot and of her charm for an audience, but is it a virtue? Critics disagree about whether Wycherley is using her outspoken language to castigate hypocrisy or to hint at the value of sophisticated lying.

Activity

> Consider the closing scene of *The Country Wife*, including the epilogue. Horner carries the day. Margery is forced to return to her boorish husband and the boredom of the countryside. Has Margery gained or lost by learning to lie? What, if anything, has Horner won? What value does the epilogue place on dissembling? Is hypocrisy the price of toleration? What do you think are the virtues, if any, in the world of Wycherley's play?

Country characters in the comedies are lampooned for their lack of eloquence and their boorishness (although there is great regard for the value of their estates). Hoyden in Vanbrugh's *The Relapse* (1696) is a character similar to Margery Pinchwife. Her father, Sir Tunbelly Clumsey, welcomes visitors to his gates with a blunderbuss, lets loose the dogs and locks up his daughter. Hoyden's bursting sexuality and vitality are conveyed by her frankness of speech and directness of manner. Her opening remark, *It's well I have a husband a-coming, or, ecod, I'd marry the baker, I would so*, continues the joke of the rough, linguistic energy of the countryside. Many Restoration comedies pit the sophisticated manners of the town against the uncouth manners of the country.

Changing values

Farquhar's *The Recruiting Officer* (1706) is unusual by being set in Shrewsbury and in treating country characters with respect and dignity. The heroine Silvia's boldness and intelligence transform her rakish lover into an honourable, loving husband, happy to settle to life in the country. Moreover, she manages to do this without breaking her word to her father not to marry without his consent. By the late eighteenth century, comedies were more likely to be set in the countryside and, however rough and ready their manners, the characters are no longer figures of fun. In Goldsmith's *She Stoops to Conquer* (1773) it is the town hero who lacks language skills. Stammering and inarticulate with shyness, he cuts a poor figure beside the country heroine Kate, who has to pretend to be a serving girl to release him from his inhibitions. Like Silvia, she is respectful and affectionate towards her father, whose down-to-earth, practical, *old-fashioned* style of living is portrayed as sensible and virtuous.

Between early and late eighteenth-century comedies, we see a change in the way that characters value each other. In Restoration drama, people are isolated. Social politeness conceals personal differences and emotional distance. Dissembling is an approved art. Late eighteenth-century senti-mental drama, however, shows affectionate relationships: obedient sons, warm-hearted daughters, loving fathers, loyal and supportive friends. The harsh emphasis on financial matters softens to an ideal of love validated by the lack of monetary motives. In *She Stoops to Conquer* young Marlow can only win Kate by overcoming his class inhibitions against marrying a poor servant girl, and in Sheridan's *The Rivals* (1775) Captain Absolute has to pretend to be a penniless ensign to win the affections of Lydia Languish. His relationship with his irascible, overbearing father may appear courteous and dutiful rather than affectionate, but there are clues in the text that reveal the love and pride both men feel for each other.

Activity

> How could an actor reveal in performance the affection which Sir Anthony Absolute feels for his son, and what phrases in the text would support such an interpretation? Similarly, what evidence is there in the text of Captain Absolute's affection and respect for his father?

Lydia's fortune is described in the mercantile imagery of the time:

> *I believe she owns half the stocks! Zounds! Thomas, she could pay the national debt as easily as I could my washerwoman! She has a lap-dog that eats out of gold, – she feeds her parrot with small pearls, – and all her thread-papers are made of bank-notes!*

A romantic, she wishes to renounce her fortune to prove the sincerity of her lover. Captain Absolute is only pretending to be poor and his love is more truly tested when his father tries to force him into an arranged marriage. Meanwhile in the sub-plot, Faulkland tests Julia's sincerity by pretending he has to fly the country, and he nearly loses her when he reveals the subterfuge. Marriages are still underwritten by fortunes which are not relinquished at the ends of plays, but the emphasis on truth in personal relationships points forward to the nineteenth-century idealization of poverty as a sign of honesty and virtue.

A common theme behind the pretences of sentimental drama is the wish to test the truth of appearances, and to uncover any differences between face value and real value. In Restoration comedy it is a positive achievement to dissemble, to disguise passion and feelings with graceful wit and easy eloquence. In late eighteenth-century drama good manners are taken for granted. The hero and heroine's goal is now to discover what lies behind protestations of love and the facade of polite behaviour.

Activity

> Consider the words 'sincere' and 'sincerity' in *The Rivals*. What ideals and anxieties does their use reveal?

The pairs of lovers in *The Rivals* are opposed. Lydia is romantic and sentimental; Julia practical and sensible. She calls Lydia's attitude to financial matters a *caprice*, and displays a calm, rational ability to cope with Faulkland's neurosis. With the men, it is Captain Absolute who is rational and in control, compared to Faulkland's emotional dithering. Faulkland's testing of Julia's love is an extreme version of Lydia's romanticism, which believes that poverty, mental anguish and defying social norms are necessary proofs of true love. Absolute knows that Lydia's sentimental romanticism is *damned absurd* and he calls Faulkland's imagined worries *whimsical*, but his own rational approach begins to break down when Lydia rejects him. He enters irrationally into a dangerous duel with Sir Lucius. (There is no reason not to take the duel seriously. Sheridan eloped with his young wife and subsequently fought two duels over her.) Julia's control is pushed beyond the limit by Faulkland's final test.

The conclusion condemns *the errors of an ill-directed imagination* and the epilogue places *sense* and *merit* above beauty, revealing a striking contrast with Restoration comedy. The earlier admiration for cavalier rakes and the cynical belittling of husbands has changed to a middle-class ethos that promotes the virtues of domesticity in marriage. *Man's social happiness* rests not on mistresses, but on wisely chosen wives.

Critical responses

Critical attacks on Restoration drama started early, with Collier's famous assaults in 1698 on its immorality and flouting of neo-classical rules: *Being convinc'd that nothing has gone farther in Debauching the Age than the Stage Poets, and Play-House, I thought I could not employ my time better than in writing against them.*

Edmund Burke in 1748 praised Congreve's *lively Wit, solid Judgement and rich Invention*, but complained that he *added such Obscenity, as none can, without the greatest Danger to Virtue, listen to; the very texture and ground-work of some of his Play is Lewdness.* Dr Johnson enjoyed Congreve's *quick and sparkling* wit but he registered concern about his moral influence: *The perusal of his works will make no man better . . . their ultimate effect is to represent pleasure in alliance with vice, and to relax those obligations by which life ought to be regulated.*

Restoration comedy fell out of favour in the late eighteenth century and disappeared from the stage altogether in the nineteenth. The absence of performances for nearly a hundred years is the clearest sign that Victorian morality devalued the plays, in spite of the enthusiasm of some literary critics. In 1822 Charles Lamb confessed that he enjoyed the plays and regretted their declining popularity. He argued that they should not be judged on moral grounds, claiming (with dubious logic) that they did not relate to real life:

> *The artificial Comedy, or Comedy of manners, is quite extinct on our stage. Congreve and Farquhar show their heads once in seven years only, to be exploded and put down instantly. The times cannot bear them. Is it for a few wild speeches, an occasional licence of dialogue? I think not altogether. The business of their dramatic characters will not stand the moral test. We screw everything up to that . . . I do not know how it is with others, but I feel the better for the perusal of one of Congreve's – nay, why should I not add even of Wycherley's – comedies. I am the gayer at least for it; and I could never connect these sports of a witty fancy in any shape with any result to be drawn from them to imitation in real life. They are a world of themselves almost as much as fairy-land.*

But when Leight Hunt produced an edition of Restoration drama in 1840, it provoked an outraged review by Lord Macaulay, who forcibly spelt out Victorian objections to the plays. His reaction to the female characters and his defence of marriage is revealing:

> *This part of our literature is a disgrace to our language and our national character. It is clever, indeed, and very entertaining; but it is, in the most emphatic sense of the words, 'earthly, sensual, devilish'. Its indecency, though perpetually such as is condemned not less by the rules of good taste than by those of morality, is not, in our opinion, so disgraceful a fault as its singularly inhuman spirit . . . We find ourselves in a world, in which the ladies are like very profligate, impudent and unfeeling men, and in which the men are too bad for any place but Pandaemonium or Norfolk Island . . . during the forty years which followed the Restoration, the whole body of the dramatists invariably represent adultery, we do not say as a peccadillo, we do not say as an error which the violence of passion may excuse, but as the calling of a fine gentleman, as a grace without which his character would be imperfect. It is as essential to his breeding and to his place in society that he should make love to the wives of his neighbours as that he should know French, or that he should have a sword at his side. In all this there is no passion, and scarcely anything that can be called preference. The hero intrigues just as he wears a wig; because, if he did not, he would be a queer fellow, a city prig, perhaps a Puritan. All the*

> *agreeable qualities are always given to the gallant. All the contempt*
> *and aversion are the portion of the unfortunate husband.*

Critical disapproval continued in the early twentieth century. L. C. Knights wrote an essay in 1937 comparing the plays unfavourably with Tudor and Jacobean drama. The grounds for his objections were no longer their sexuality or morality but their triviality:

> *The criticism that defenders of Restoration comedy need to answer*
> *is not that the comedies are 'immoral', but that they are trivial, gross*
> *and dull . . . although Congreve recognises, at times, the triviality*
> *of his characters, it is to the world whose confines were the Court,*
> *the drawing-room, the play-house and the park – a world completely*
> *lacking the real sophistication and self-knowledge that might, in*
> *some measure, have redeemed it – that he limits his appeal. It is,*
> *indeed, hard to resist the conclusion that 'society' – the smart town*
> *society that sought entertainment at the theatres – was funda-*
> *mentally bored.*

Writing in *English Social History* (1944) G. M. Trevelyan was as offended by the plays as Lord Macaulay had been a hundred years previously:

> *A hard disbelief in virtue of any kind was characteristic of the*
> *restored leaders of politics and fashion, and was reflected in the*
> *early Restoration drama which depended on their patronage.*
> *One of the most successful pieces was Wycherley's* Country Wife;
> *the hero, by pretending to be a eunuch, secures admission to*
> *privacies which enable him to seduce women; one is expected to*
> *admire his character and proceedings. In no other age, before or*
> *after, would such a plot-motive have appealed to any English*
> *audience.*

There were attempts in the first half of the twentieth century to defend Restoration drama (Bonamy Dobrée, 1924; Virginia Woolf, 1937) and there were occasional and successful productions. As society's mores became more uninhibited in the flower-power years of the 1950s and 1960s, the plays were performed more regularly and critical attitudes changed, partly in response to performance. It is notable that recent admirers of Restoration comedies appreciate their effectiveness on stage. Harold Love wrote in 1974:

> *It is in the theatre that we are going to find the clearest evidence*
> *for Congreve's stature, not merely as an inspirer of splendid and*
> *occasionally not so splendid evenings, but, along with Pope and*
> *Swift, as one of the three supreme masters of language of his*
> *generation. . . . He presents us with characters who, while lacking*
> *a Shakespearian fullness of life, possess an authentic dramatic*
> *individuality and who are placed in relationships with each other*
> *which, as the dramatist matures, are increasingly informed with*

the ambiguities, indeterminacies and conflicting perspectives of real life . . . The real nature of the social relationships will only be understood when we have penetrated beyond the public surface, beyond the language of deportment, to the appetites and vulnerabilities which that language, and the code of behaviour of which it is a part, are expressedly designed to conceal . . . it is possible in performance to generate a sense of society, a sense that what is happening between the characters is just as important as what is happening in them, and that there is not just one but a number of personal perspectives involved, each suggesting its own interpretations and evaluations. . . . To this extent, at least, the best of Congreve is inexhaustible.

A Cultural History of Drama, by Shepherd and Womack (1996) notes the

conspicuous presentness of Restoration theatre, its lack or refusal of mechanisms for distancing the performers and confining them within the scene where they would appear as mere embodiments of imaginary characters. By appearing in social space, explicitly performing in front of a crowd which is conscious of its own presence, the actor accepts the relations with a spectator as an open social transaction. She – or he – is not just an image in an ethical mirror, but is really being looked at and enjoyed. In all theatre there is perhaps an implicit voyeurism; but this particular theatre makes it ingeniously and scandalously explicit. One trace of this awareness is the coarse and recurring joke, in prologues and epilogues, about the sexual availability of the actresses. Some actresses literally were prostitutes, but the joke is not so much recording a social fact as expressing a cultural attitude: that to make a living by exhibiting one's body in public is a kind of prostitution in itself. In this context, Jeremy Collier begins to look as if he does not altogether deserve the patronising footnotes he usually gets from the twentieth-century admirers of Vanbrugh or Congreve.

Alastair Fowler, in *A History of English Literature*, asks the question:

How are we to estimate Restoration comedy? From Macaulay onwards, opinion has alternated between moral disapproval, on the one hand, and, on the other, something like Charles Lamb's (and Bonamy Dobrée's) view that the form is unreal, artificial and therefore immune from moral considerations – which has given rise, in turn, to charges of triviality and emptiness. But the point of the comedy begins to be seen as lying more in display of manners expressing scepticism, or exploring ambiguous moral concepts . . . there are things to learn from presentations of intelligent vice in full swing (if sharply observed), which could not be learnt from virtuous precepts. They may not exactly be lessons of virtue; but they feed the moral life none the less.

5 Romantic Contexts

• •

In the late eighteenth century, Europe was rocked by revolutions which were inspired, in part, by the success of the American Revolution. Commercially and politically the American colonies were bound to Britain, and the colonists' desire for more control of their affairs turned to anger when Britain imposed new stamp and import duties in 1765 and 1767. Slowly, and for the most part reluctantly, both sides embarked on the American War of Independence. There were those in Britain, radicals and dissenting reformers, who supported the colonists' 'right' to independence and welcomed their victory in 1783.

The French Revolution and its aftermath

When revolution broke out in France in 1789 it was greeted enthusiastically by many in England, including the early Romantic poets William Blake, William Wordsworth and Samuel Coleridge. Wordsworth was in France at the time, awaiting the birth of his illegitimate daughter and hoping, in vain, to be allowed to marry the mother, Annette Vallon. Memories of his first love and first child influenced his later description of those days, but he summed up a general feeling when he wrote: *Bliss was it in that dawn to be alive, / But to be young was very Heaven!* (*The Prelude*, 1805, X.693–4).

The euphoria was short-lived. With the September Massacres in 1792, the execution of the King and Queen in 1793 and Robespierre's Reign of Terror, British enthusiasm for the ideals of the French Revolution wavered. Edmund Burke published *Reflections on the Revolution in France* (1790) denouncing the Revolution, arguing that men were not naturally equal and that long-established institutions should be respected. He was answered by Thomas Paine in *The Rights of Man* (1791), who protested that no generation should feel bound by the past and that political power should be given to the will of the majority:

> *Every age and generation must be as free to act for itself, in all cases, as the ages and generations which preceded it. The vanity and presumption of governing beyond the grave, is the most ridiculous and insolent of all tyrannies. Man has no property in man.*

The Rights of Man was enormously popular; it brought about pressure for universal male suffrage which ultimately led to the widening of the franchise in the nineteenth century. (Women did not receive the vote until the twentieth century.) But the government's immediate reaction was to suppress reforming movements. Many people who were originally sympathetic to the Revolution were horrified by the executions and massacres in France. Blake wrote the poems in *Songs of Experience* in revolutionary disillusionment, and Wordsworth and Coleridge also changed their attitudes. In the central books of *The Prelude*, Wordsworth recounts how his early enthusiasm gave way to a sense of betrayal.

By 1793 Britain was at war with revolutionary France. At first Napoleon's military genius inspired French victories, and Britain was close to defeat by 1797. Then Nelson's successes at sea and Wellington's on land began to turn the war in Britain's favour, and in 1815 Wellington decisively defeated Napoleon at Waterloo. The cost to Britain was great. Food prices soared as the war disrupted trade, and it was a time of great hardship for the urban poor. Life was even worse for the poor in rural areas. The enclosures of the eighteenth century and the development of agricultural and spinning machinery reduced employment in the countryside. The rural poor left the countryside to seek work in the growing industries in the northern towns or in London, where there was an unending need for domestic servants. There was widespread rural distress and numerous unemployed and homeless people. Dorothy Wordsworth's *Journals* have almost weekly entries about men, women and children begging at her door or on the highways, and many of the solitary, elderly wanderers of Wordsworth's poems are retired or injured soldiers and sailors, the rejected, homeless, unemployed flotsam of the Napoleonic wars.

The Government's attitude towards the lower classes in their distress was harsh and punitive. Worried by what had happened in France, those in authority were fearful of the power of the mob. Twice in the 1790s Prime Minister Pitt suspended *habeas corpus* (the right to appear before a judge or a court when arrested), and in 1799 he introduced Combination Acts which forbade working men from combining into clubs and societies. Any large working-class meeting was considered potentially dangerous. Radical leaders were arrested, tried and transported to Australia. In the notorious 'Peterloo' incident in 1819, an open-air meeting at Manchester of handloom weavers protesting about their economic conditions was dispersed with such force that eleven people died and hundreds were injured.

The condition of the poor

On the whole the middle class feared mob violence and were not sympathetic to working-class agitation, but many individuals were stirred to action by the condition of the poor. Often it was members of the evangelical church who led the way, like William Wilberforce, parliamentary leader of the movement to abolish slavery. Slaves had been brought to America and the West Indies in large numbers during the eighteenth century. Between the 1680s and 1780, over two million were transported from Africa. There were far fewer in Britain, perhaps ten thousand at the most, and it was in Britain that the movement had its first success. Slavery was made illegal in 1772 and in 1807 the slave trade was abolished.

Besides slavery, the plight of the chimney-sweepers aroused public concern in the late eighteenth century, although it took far longer to ban the practice – nearly a hundred years of repeated efforts. Boys as young as five or six years of age were sold to master sweeps. They were made to climb naked up twisting, narrow, soot-filled chimneys, forced on by burning fires or prodding sticks. They cried their trade in the streets when not at work and slept, unwashed, on their soot-filled sacks.

One reason why the French Revolution was initially welcomed by many liberals and why there was growing public anxiety about the treatment of young children was the extent to which the ideas of the eighteenth-century Enlightenment had become accepted. Enlightenment philosophers started from a conviction that a human being was a creature of reason, born in freedom and equality. If people were given choice and the freedom to develop their individual faculties, they would rise to their highest potential. In 1690 John Locke published *An Essay Concerning Human Understanding*, arguing that the human mind was a blank at birth, like a piece of empty paper, and that ideas were imprinted on the mind by experience. It followed therefore that the kind of upbringing and education a child received was the basis of his or her moral development. In 1762 Jean-Jacques Rousseau in France opened his book *Social Contract* with the famous sentence which influenced the French Revolution: *Man was born free and everywhere he is in chains*. In *Emile*, he argued that children were born good and innocent – it was society that corrupted them, perverting their natural instincts. If left to develop naturally, children would acquire moral consciences and a correct sense of right and wrong from their own experiences.

The Romantic movement

The early Romantic poets were attentive to the upbringing and education of children and their writing shows concern, sometimes anger, about the conditions of the most vulnerable members of society. Blake's sympathy for slaves, chimney sweeps, and for any young child sold into harsh labour is evident in his *Songs*. A black boy, slave or sweep, is a figure who symbolizes a victimized labour force. Many of Wordsworth's and Coleridge's poems are about children or solitary, dispossessed adults. Revolution and social protest underlie their writings and those of the later Romantic poets, Byron, Keats and Shelley, even though their subject matter differs. All six poets are now called Romantic. It was not a word used at the time, but a label attached later to the change in sensibility that occurred around the late eighteenth and early nineteenth centuries.

Besides revolutionary fervour, what did Romantic poets share in common? Technically, there was a turning away from the earlier neoclassical, formal 'rules' of composition, and a move to simpler, more conversational vocabulary and freer poetic forms. The early Romantic poets wrote in the unsophisticated genres familiar to illiterate people (see Unit 11, Approaches to Poetry), as in Blake's *Songs* and Wordsworth and Coleridge's *Lyrical*

Ballads. Wordsworth and Coleridge became close friends in 1797 when both were living frugally in the Quantock Hills in Somerset. Together they published *Lyrical Ballads*, pooling their poems to raise money for a joint trip to Germany. The poems were startlingly new in subject matter and in style. Wordsworth called them *experiments* because they used *the language of conversation in the middle and lower classes.* The poems were in simple ballad form and the tone was, as they intended, conversational.

In content too there was a clear shift in taste. The Romantics fell out of love with the mercantile world, the silks and fripperies, the material possessions of the earlier eighteenth century. They fell in love with nature and the innocence, simplicity and spontaneity which they thought uncorrupted children and 'primitive' people possessed. The early Romantics wrote about the dispossessed and outcasts on the margins of society – the very young or the very old, the infirm and the mad. Above all, they wrote about themselves. Strong, impassioned feelings were valued, as testifying to the truth of individual experience at a time when the institutions of church and state were being questioned and direct experience was hailed as the basis of moral development. The strength of personal experience carried its own moral authority, particularly if it took the form of a dream or vision in which the poet was transported beyond himself, guided by a greater force.

The Romantic movement may have rejected neoclassical techniques, but it was deeply influenced by the Enlightenment belief that all people were created *equal and independent*, as Jefferson wrote in his draft for the American Declaration of Independence, with a right to *life, and liberty and the pursuit of happiness.* Individualism is a strong presence in Romantic poetry. The persona of the poet is often the sole voice and hero of the poem. An isolated figure, he is not guided by the religious and moral teachings of church or state institutions – he is his own moral authority. He makes his lonely way in quest of something he cannot define, impelled to wander, apparently randomly, by breezes, clouds, stars or his own impulses, trusting completely in the truth of his sensations and believing that his private feelings are ratified by visionary glimpses of a greater reality.

Activity

Can you identify a Romantic poem that centres on a solitary figure, either as the speaker or the hero of the poem? Think about his or her experiences and select one that moved him or her deeply. What, if anything, appears to give moral weight to the experience? Is there any sense of an external moral authority? If so, is it the voice of church or state, or does the guiding presence communicate directly with the poem's speaker? If there is no external moral authority, is the poem's speaker trusting entirely to intensity of feeling to confirm the importance of the experience?

Insight and inspiration

The Romantics believed that poets felt and saw more deeply and more clearly than ordinary people. To Wordsworth a poet was a *dedicated* spirit. Insight came in moments inspired by imagination, the creative power revered by the Romantics, who valued their inner experiences above all – the subjective spirit should prevail over the objective rules of reason. Inspired moments could not be summoned at will. They came unbidden, but the presence of nature was generally important, especially for Wordsworth and Coleridge, and the approach of inspiration is indicated by a shift in the natural scene, by breezes, by water, by a change in the light, or by something that foregrounds the poet's awareness of a natural object which, until then, had been perceived only vaguely as background, like the water-snakes in *The Ancient Mariner* or the high uprearing rock in Book I of *The Prelude*. With Keats it is usually an art object that releases his vision, and Blake can have visions at any moment, in any place.

Activity

> Select a visionary experience in a poem you are studying. Can you identify a particular cause of the vision – an object, scene or incident that activated it? How does the poet recognize the visionary moment? How does he or she feel after it has passed? Can you see a relationship between the initiating cause and the nature of the visionary experience?

Romantics who lost their political fervour did not abandon their revolutionary desire to transform the world. Romantic writing is full of symbolic narratives of destruction and construction, of visions of a better future, reflecting the impulse towards change that was strong in Europe at the time. Mary Shelley's *Frankenstein*, Coleridge's *Christabel*, and Keats's *Lamia* show one kind of frightening transformation, the uncanny, half-human creatures of the Gothic tradition. But poets were more concerned about improving the lives of ordinary people. Blake's children leap and play in the sun, free from the restraints of Nurse or work. For the weakest and most victimized, the sun shines only after death, and one cannot miss the urgency of Blake's vision of a society where children may play in this life, as well as the next one. Coleridge's Ancient Mariner is a changed personality by the end of his story, and the wedding guest is *a sadder and a wiser man* for listening to it. Coleridge predicts a transforming upbringing for his own child in *Frost at Midnight*. The babe will learn *far other lore*, through nature's *ministry* and the *Great Universal Teacher*. Wordsworth felt himself transformed by nature's influence at heightened moments, moments that form the climaxes of incidents he describes in many of his best poems. In *Ode on a Grecian Urn* and *Ode to a Nightingale* Keats describes a sense of losing his identity and dissolving into a finer entity.

The Romantic vision, in which the poet passes into knowledge beyond his conscious boundaries, is an isolating state. The poet is both the voice and the subject of his poem. In *The Prelude*, *Ode on Immortality* and *Tintern Abbey*, Wordsworth records the long passage of time he required before a sense experience became an illuminating vision. Coleridge and Keats describe the moment as it occurs, and for them the vision remains baffling, unresolved and unclear. Coleridge's *Kubla Khan* breaks off before the poet wakes from his dream, and Keats is left unsure at the end of his *Odes* whether he dreams or is awake. This can happen to Wordsworth also. In *Resolution and Independence*, he encounters the lonely, wandering Leech Gatherer who, like Coleridge's Ancient Mariner, seems to possess superhuman qualities.

Activity

Choose a Romantic poem which describes an inexplicable vision. How does the poet create a sense that the revelation is not fully grasped? Why does he feel that the vision, although not understood, is precious? (You could consider vocabulary, imagery, the use of questions, the mood of the poet.)

William Blake

The social status of the Romantic poets ranged from the aristocratic Lord Byron and the well-to-do Shelley to those who were lower middle-class in origin and financially insecure. Wordsworth (1770–1850), Coleridge (1772–1834) and Keats (1795–1821) were orphaned at an early age and supported in life by patrons and friends. Blake (1757–1827) was the son of a London hosier. He was apprenticed at fourteen to an engraver, the only Romantic poet to complete a craft apprenticeship. (Keats abandoned his medical training.) Blake practised the trade of engraving all his life. It was not a trade that brought him prosperity and, like many other artists and poets at the time, he was befriended by a wealthy patron. But Blake did not enjoy dependency, and after three years of living with his patron in Sussex (1800–1803), he returned to London and a life of obscurity and poverty.

In 1789 Blake published *Songs of Innocence* in small books, illustrated, printed and coloured by himself. In 1794 he added *Songs of Experience*, issuing the two books together as *Shewing the Two Contrary States of the Human Soul*. At the same time he was writing long celebratory poems on the French and American Revolutions. In 1791 Joseph Johnson, a radical publisher, printed the first part of his *French Revolution*, but it was never published. Whether Blake and Johnson were frightened of being arrested as Prime Minister Pitt cracked down on suspected revolutionaries, or Blake destroyed it himself as his views changed, we can never know. He remained a radical all his life, but there is no doubt that he passed through a political crisis at the time he was finishing *Innocence* and starting *Experience*.

Scholars have pointed out how closely the rhyme, rhythm and language of some of the *Songs of Innocence* echo the hymns and little moral poems being written for children at the time, for example Isaac Watts's *Divine Songs for the Use of Children*. This suggests that Blake may originally have designed *Innocence* to sell in the market of early readers for children. Look at the illustration on the title page. It could be a picture of children learning to read at their mother's knee. But if *Innocence* started as a reader for children, *Experience* seems to reflect Blake's anxiety and anger at adult behaviour.

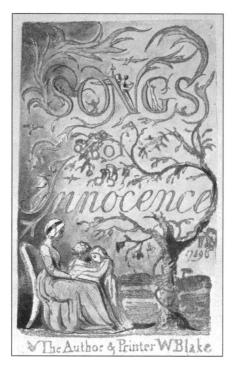

Blake's title page for his Songs of Innocence, *published in 1789*

Poems which can be read in isolation as nursery rhymes in the context of the combined books represent one side of a debate Blake is conducting over society, its organization and government.

Activity

Consider *Songs of Innocence* on its own. What signs can you find that some poems might have been written for children? You might like to look at *The Shepherd, Infant Joy, On Another's Sorrow, Divine Image, A Cradle Song, Spring,* or *The Lamb.* You should consider content: who is speaking, to whom, and in what mood? You should consider technique: choice of vocabulary, use of repetition, rhythm and rhyme, stanza form, and syntax. What is the effect of the biblical language? If you had bought the book in 1789, before *Songs of Experience* was published, would any poems have alerted you to the possibility that Blake was moving towards a contrary view?

There are songs in *Innocence* where Blake, unlike Isaac Watts, refuses to give the reader a comforting moral conclusion, or where the content of the poem throws into question whether a concluding moral tag is to be taken seriously or ironically. Add to this degree of uncertainty the later linking of *Songs of Innocence* with the 'contrary' songs in *Experience*, and the burden of moral judgement is placed on each reader's individual response. Blake gives no overt guidance within the poems, no sympathetic or protesting comment that might point towards an attitude he wishes us to adopt. Rather, he leaves us with questions. Questions abound in the texts of the poems, and in *Experience* they are left unanswered except in *Holy Thursday*, which closes with emphatically absolute statements.

How, for example, should we read *The Chimney Sweeper* in *Songs of Innocence*? The social conditions referred to in the poem are historically accurate. Is that sufficient to move us to sympathy or anger? The cry that the child could scarcely utter was the street cry of the boys calling for customers, yet the word looks uncommonly like weeping. Is Blake setting the scene realistically, or subtly appealing to the reader's emotions? Is the promise of heaven after suffering on earth ample reward or comfort, or does Blake intend us to read the poem (especially the moral tags and the final line) ironically? Should we feel happy that Tom has some reassurance – he is happier for the dream – or angry that anyone should try to suggest that *doing his duty* and being *a good boy* are acceptable in those circumstances?

Different answers are given to these questions by different schools of criticism (see pages 86–87). A symbolic reading, particularly if it included the illustration, might interpret the children's release from the black coffins as souls released from bodies, freed from the black dross of earthly pain into joy. *An earthly darkness of the flesh is finally escaped spiritually*, wrote Wicksteed in 1928. The children are associated with whiteness and lambs, language that expresses their innocence, and the biblical phrases (about washing in rivers and rising on clouds to God the Father) support a symbolic reading of their spirituality.

An alternative, Marxist interpretation sees Tom's dream as a way of reconciling children to their oppression, using words like 'duty' and 'pity' from the discourse of religious and moral teaching in order to establish and reinforce submission. There is evidence of determination to sustain these conditions in the contrast between the relative speed with which slavery was made illegal after agitation began, and the blocking by the House of Lords on numerous occasions in the nineteenth century of bills aimed at reforming conditions for chimney sweeps. Heather Glen writes:

> In Songs of Innocence *'pity' is always operative within the world.* . . .
> *It is not, as in 'The Human Abstract', a reified abstraction, apparently
> displaced from human agency. Its object is another seen with more
> than usual vividness and clarity – little Tom Dacre; the emmet, the
> charity children; not a generalized 'somebody' whose only attribute
> is poverty. And in giving it the name of one of the most central of
> polite moral virtues – a virtue whose underside he was later to
> expose – Blake is confronting his reader with an inescapable
> question. What is the relationship between the mode of experience
> presented in these poems and the official moral language of the
> society they depict?*

Activity

> The children in *The Chimney Sweeper*, especially Tom, are innocent. Is the poem? Is the speaker? Who is the speaker, an adult or a child? Even if the speaker is an adult who knows she or he is glossing over reality, she could be doing it kindly, helping Tom to accept intolerable and probably deadly conditions. Do you find the closing line, with its maternal, caring, religious phraseology, reassuring? Or do you find that your sympathy for the children makes you want to reject the message of the last line?

The endings of many *Songs* are ambiguous, and a useful way into the poems might be to consider the implications of the final lines. Even when we know something of Blake's political and moral views, his poems remain enigmatic. We know, for example, that Blake was well aware of the horrors of the slave trade. In 1791 Joseph Johnson employed him to engrave sketches illustrating an account by Captain Stedman of an expedition to Surinam in South America. Stedman had been appalled by the brutality inflicted on African slaves, and some of the sketches Blake engraved depict sickening scenes of torture. How does *The Little Black Boy* in *Songs of Innocence* reveal Blake's abhorrence of slavery?

Activity

> The simple religious language of white and black, lambs and God, places the poem in the tradition of hymns and moral tracts for children. The reassuring, loving tone of the mother creates a comforting mood as she tries to reconcile her son to his earthly fate with promises of heavenly bliss. How do you respond to the final phrase, *and he will then love me*? Is it possible to ignore the note of longing in the little boy's awareness of his rejection?

When we turn to *Songs of Experience* Blake's anger is easier to detect, but the songs are no easier to interpret. By calling attention to the pairing of the poems in the *Songs*, Blake forces us to make comparisons.

Activity

> The two *Holy Thursday* poems refer to the same event, the service in St Paul's Cathedral on Ascension Day for charity-school children and their guardians. We cannot miss the savagery of *Experience*. Should this make us look again at *Innocence*? If the children's singing is a *trembling cry*, does this detract from its earlier description as *harmonious thunderings*? Are we meant to hold both 'contrary' descriptions in our minds and come to a conclusion not expressed directly in either poem? Should we applaud the guardians for their social charity or condemn them for ignoring the fundamental wrongs of the political situation?

The Chimney Sweeper *from* *Blake's* Songs of Innocence and Experience

Critical responses

Blake's *Songs* sold very poorly, although he continued to print them to order throughout his life, altering the colour and arrangement of each new book. He remained relatively unknown in the nineteenth century. Until the mid-twentieth century, critics saw him as a mystic, a man 'slightly touched', who *saw all things under the form of eternity*, as Symons wrote in 1907. To Northrop Frye, writing in 1947, his vision is Christian:

> *Childhood to Blake is a state or phase of imaginative existence, the phase in which the world of imagination is still a brave new world and yet reassuring and intelligible. In the protection which the child feels from his parents and his evening prayer against darkness there is the image of a cosmos far more intelligently controlled than ours . . . it was to the same vision that Jesus was appealing when he put a child in the midst of his disciples . . . The reader needs no commentary to help him understand the terrible indictment . . . in the* Songs of Experience. *Contempt and horror have never spoken more clearly in English poetry. But Blake never forgets to see behind all the cruelty of man the fact of his fall.*

As editions which reproduced the original illustrated texts became available, critics began to look closely at the integration of language and design, and produced symbolic readings – some of which drew attention to the possibility of sexual rather than religious interpretations for poems like *The Sick Rose, My Pretty Rose Tree, The Blossom, Infant Joy,* and *The Garden of Love.* Such readings have been contested by later critics like Heather Glen (quoted above), who are more interested in Blake's context and how his 'mystic' symbols are rooted in historical events. The sparseness of Blake's language, the ambiguity of his imagery, the power of his brief lyrics and the suggestiveness of his illustrations mean that close readings of text and illustration are always worthwhile.

Samuel Coleridge

For Coleridge, proximity to Wordsworth in 1797–8 was inspiring, and his best poetry was written in those years. The friends went to Germany in 1798 and in 1799 the Wordsworths, William and his sister Dorothy, returned to the Lake District where they made their permanent home. Coleridge went to live near them in 1800, and at that time wrote the last of his major poems, *Dejection: an Ode.* His addiction to opium, his unhappy relationship with his wife and his personal unreliability strained and, to his sorrow, broke the friendship.

Both men shared an intense love of the countryside, and until Coleridge's health gave way they were active walkers, covering many miles on most days. Nature, which Blake treats symbolically, is a reality in their poetry. Both men composed poetry while out of doors, declaiming their words as they walked. *The Idiot Boy*, a favourite of Wordsworth's, was *composed in the groves of Alfoxden, almost extempore.*

Activity

> Read a passage from Wordsworth or Coleridge aloud. Note how conversational Coleridge sounds (*Kubla Khan* is an exception). *The Prelude* is dependent for its effects on ordinary words, and key terms accrue weight by repetition. (You might like to study Wordsworth's use of the following word clusters: *breeze, breath; sense, sensation, sensibility; form, forms, forming*; and *being, Being, presence.*) The simplest words are potent. Listen for Wordsworth's placing of *I, but, if, is* and *and*, which carry surprising power in his syntax.

Coleridge believed that God's influence worked through the natural world where everything shared in One Life. To love nature was to recognize God's presence. In his poetry these moments of recognition occur in isolation. Wordsworth's visionary moments are followed by solitary reflection or troubled dreams. With Coleridge, always the more sociable of the two poets, the persona in his poems rejoins human society – even if only in the imagination as in *This Lime-Tree Bower my Prison*, or as a wandering stranger, as in *The Rime of the Ancient Mariner.*

Critical responses

The Rime of the Ancient Mariner, Coleridge's most famous poem, is the essential Romantic poem, with its solitary wandering hero, its foregrounding of nature, its individual quest for morality, and its moments of inspired vision. It was recognized as a great poem from its first publication. Hazlitt, a severe critic of Coleridge, wrote: *Let whatever other objections be made to it, it is unquestionably a work of genius – of wild, irregular, overwhelming imagination.* Coleridge had not been to sea when he wrote the poem, but he was immensely well-read in travel literature and his poem draws on accounts of pioneering voyagers in the Pacific (*We were the first that ever burst / Into that silent sea*) and the Antarctic (*ice, mast-high, came floating by / As green as emerald*) like Captain Cook, Captain Bligh, and John Davis. His borrowings, meticulously researched by Livingston Lowes in *The Road to Xanadu* (1927), give the supernatural poem fantastic yet credible settings. Livingston Lowes traced many of the poem's phrases to quotations from books by travellers.

The simple story of the sailor who shot an albatross is potently suggestive and open to as many interpretations as a *Song* by Blake. Focusing on Coleridge's belief that all living creatures share One Life, some critics have interpreted the poem as depicting a justified punishment for an inhospitable and murderous act, in Humphry House's phrase *a ghastly violation of a great sanctity*. The poem has also been read as a myth of redemption: the sinning soul, punished and penitent, finds God's forgiveness. W. H. Auden (1951) interpreted the poem as a Christian allegory. He related the albatross

> to the Dove of the Holy Spirit, and through him to the innocent victim, Christ, the water-snakes which are that in nature, whether outside man or within himself, for which he feels aversion because he cannot understand them aesthetically or intellectually and despises because he cannot make use of them. But for the Fall (the shooting of the Albatross), Adam (The Ancient Mariner) would never have consciously learned through suffering the meaning of Agape, i.e., to love one's neighbour as oneself without comparisons or greed (the blessing of the snakes), so that the Ancient Mariner might well say in the end, O felix culpa.

The Latin phrase is the one by which medieval Christianity taught that eating the apple in Eden was a 'happy' sin, since it brought Mary and Christ into the world.

William Empson attacked these readings in an influential essay in *Critical Quarterly* (1964) on the grounds that shooting the albatross does not deserve the scale of punishment inflicted on the Mariner and crew. He used lines (later cut) from the first version of the poem as evidence for his claim that the practical Mariner shot the bird for food. Linking the poem to the unfinished *Wanderings of Cain*, which Coleridge was writing around the same time, Empson argued: *What Coleridge wanted to write about was uncaused guilt.* The poem symbolized guilt, both the psychological guilt that was a feature of Coleridge's personality and the collective sense of guilt which underlay European maritime expansion as it penetrated previously unknown lands and subjugated alien peoples in search of mercantile profit. Readings influenced by Empson and extending his view suggested that the boat that carries Death and Life-in-Death could be a slave trader.

In another interpretation, the poem has been read as imaging the mental journey of the creative poet. Along with *Kubla Khan* and Keats's *Odes*, *The Ancient Mariner* represents the imagination and symbolizes creativity. The Romantics held the creative artist in high esteem. In the *Preface* to the 1800 edition of *Lyrical Ballads*, in which *The Ancient Mariner* appeared, Wordsworth defined a Poet (he used the capital letter) as: *a man, it is true, endowed with a more lively sensibility, more enthusiasm and tenderness, who has a greater knowledge of human nature, and a more comprehensive soul*. Shelley claimed poets were *the unacknowledged legislators of the world*. The first part of *Kubla Khan*, with its man-created pleasure-dome, a *miracle of rare device*, a *Paradise*, is read as symbolizing the achievement of the poet's imaginative and creative power. Its second part, like so many of Coleridge's poems, is read as describing the very process of creativity, visionary, inspired by delight and awe, and deeply embedded in Nature.

William Wordsworth

In September 1799 Coleridge wrote to Wordsworth: *I wish you would write a poem, in blank verse, addressed to those who, in consequence of the complete failure of the French Revolution, have thrown up all hopes of the amelioration of mankind . . . It would do great good and might even form part of 'The Recluse'*. This was the title of the epic poem that Wordsworth tried to write and never completed. As part of his project for this *magnum opus*, he planned to prefix some lines to explain how he became a poet. This preface was referred to among his family and friends as 'the poem to Coleridge'. Wordsworth never published it or gave it a name. He composed the poem we now know as *The Prelude* in fits and starts over more than fifty years. Two books were written quickly in 1798–9, incorporating lines previously published in *Lyrical Ballads*, and this material formed the bulk of Books I and II in later versions. By 1804 he had completed a five-book version, and in 1805 he extended this to thirteen books, on which he continued to work all his life. His widow published his final version, and it was the family who entitled it *The Prelude*.

Activity

> Compare parallel texts for Books I and II of the 1799 and 1805 versions, noting which passages Wordsworth removed from the earlier version to use in later books in the 1805 version. What is the effect of removing these passages? Which version do you prefer?

In Book I of *The Prelude* he explains that he sought in vain for a grand subject. It never occurred to him that he had already found one because, as he wrote to Coleridge, it was *unprecedented in literary history that a man should talk so much about himself*. Wordsworth actively remembers his past, the precious *spots of time* as he calls them (XI. 257) in order to reflect on visionary moments. As he recollects past experiences, the emotions he felt at the time are re-created in his verse and enter into his state of being in the present. In the meditative and celebratory lines that follow his descriptions of these incidents, he arrives at a deeper understanding of past events, even as he feels them anew in the present. Past and present merge.

Activity

> Read Book IV.247–64, where Wordsworth compares revisiting *past time* to looking from a slow-moving boat into still water. He cannot separate the weeds, fish and pebbles that he sees in the depths from the reflections of sky, mountains and clouds. Occasionally his own reflection, or the sun glancing or the wind ruffling the water, complicates the scene still further. What does this imply about the way memory and reflection work for Wordsworth?

The *spots of time* are not always moments of heightened pleasure and excitement, like the skating episode in Book I. They can be unsettling, admonitory moments of fear, bordering on terror. In every case, whether rapturous or disturbing, the poet is made aware of the natural world. What had been the background of his activities is propelled into his consciousness, and nature is foregrounded, as in the boat-stealing incident. Note how the *rocky steep* is at first a natural landmark for his rowing, then it reveals a *huge cliff* which first passively *rose up* and then actively *strode* after him, and seemed the cause of his troubled dreams.

Activity

> Choose a passage where Wordsworth describes a memorable incident from his childhood. What role does nature play in it? Is nature in the background or foreground? At what point is it brought into the forefront of his consciousness, and how does language show this shift occurring?

In the early books of *The Prelude*, the full meaning of the *spots of time* is hidden from the boy Wordsworth, but in later books he is conscious of the visionary gift. You might like to look at the moment when he realizes he is a dedicated spirit (VI.324–45) or his ascent of Snowden (XIII.1–119). The first two books are often read on their own as a vivid evocation of boyhood, but they are part of a larger whole, the first stage in the growth of the poet's mind which is the theme of *The Prelude*.

Critical responses

In 1843 Wordsworth became Poet Laureate. To nineteenth-century readers, he was a mystic, a Christian moralist and a Romantic poet of 'the sublime'. A. C. Bradley, in his 1909 *Oxford Lectures on Poetry*, said:

> *However much Wordsworth was the poet of small and humble things, and the poet who saw his ideal realized, not in Utopia, but here and*

> *now before his eyes, he was, quite as much, what some would call a*
> *mystic . . . we may prefer the Wordsworth of the daffodils to the*
> *Wordsworth of the yew-trees, and we may even believe the poet's*
> *mysticism to be moonshine; but it is certain that to neglect or throw*
> *into the shade this aspect of his poetry is neither to take Wordsworth*
> *as he really was nor to judge his poetry truly, since this aspect*
> *appears in much of it that we cannot deny to be first-rate.*

Since the beginning of the twentieth century, *The Prelude* has been read as charting the growth of self-consciousness, showing the importance of memory in forming the human identity. Guided by nature, the mind journeys from sense experience in youth to self-conscious adulthood, but it is memory and imagination that transform *the blank misgivings* and *shadowy recollections of first affections* into visionary glimpses of the *immortal sea* described in his *Immortality Ode*.

Recent criticism has placed Wordsworth in the context of his times. Nicholas Roe (1997) writes:

> *Wordsworth's insistence on the poet's unique humanity arose out*
> *of the intellectual crisis which accompanied the faltering of*
> *revolutionary progress in the mid–1790s . . . Wordsworth's repre-*
> *sentation of this conflict was a 'bar', or a court of law, at which he*
> *brought his own mind to trial,*
>
> > *Now believing,*
> > *Now disbelieving, endlessly perplexed*
> > *With impulse, motive, right and wrong, (X.892–4)*
>
> *a figure which in* The Prelude Book X *corresponds to the 'ghastly*
> *visions' of 'unjust tribunals' (X.374, 377) which ruled in Paris during*
> *the heyday of Robespierre's Terror. The contrarieties of*
> *Wordsworth's inner life are thus made to correspond to a dreadful*
> *fracture in contemporary political life . . . Amid the intellectual*
> *contradictions and confusions produced by the collapse of the*
> *French Revolution, Wordsworth refashioned himself as the poet of*
> *'Lyrical Ballads', advocating a receptivity to 'the lore which nature*
> *brings' against the partial learning of 'sages' and the deadly*
> *machinations of the 'meddling intellect'.*

John Keats

Keats, who died of tuberculosis at 25, seems less politically and socially involved than the older poets who lived through the French Revolution. Like them, his poetry depicts a baffled sense of yearning after ideal, elusive states of existence, but his desire to be free of mortality, to escape into a world of pure art and beauty, looks forward to the Victorian fascination with death, with medieval times and with idealized fairy lands. Some critics feel that Keats's poetry is a response to industrialism rather than to the failure of revolution. Catherine Belsey (1980) argues:

> *One of the main thrusts of Romanticism is the rejection of an alien world of industrial capitalism, recurrently signified in images of death, disease and decay. Poetry claims to create a living world, fostered by nature but springing essentially from the subjectivity of the poet, from what Coleridge calls the Imagination, a mode of perception which endows the phenomenal world with a vitality and an intensity issuing ultimately from the soul itself: 'Oh Lady! We receive but what we give, / And in our life alone does Nature live'* (Dejection: an Ode). *The Romantic vision, though it needs the phenomenal world for its realization, transcends and transforms the material and the mortal . . . But . . . the higher knowledge proves to be a dream or a reversion to the very reality whose antithesis it was to represent. . . . Much of the poetry of the nineteenth and early twentieth centuries constitutes a record of increasing despair as the contradictions in the Romantic rejection of the world become increasingly manifest.*

Activity

> For Keats, the visionary dream never lasts. The nightingale's song *fades*, the Greek urn turns into a *cold pastoral*, the knight awakes on a *cold hillside*. How does the persona in the poem feel when he cannot sustain the vision? In which world do you feel the persona lives – reality, dream, or both? Could the vision reflect a desire to escape from political and social anxieties, or a way of coming to terms with them?

Critical responses

Keats's reputation suffered initially from critics who fastened on his youth and his lower-class origins. He was attacked as a 'cockney' writer in *Blackwood's Magazine* in 1818 and his poems were criticized as sensual, immature, adolescent erotic fantasies. Byron called them 'mental masturbation'. The general nineteenth-century view, whether hostile or adulatory, saw him as rather feminine and a dreamer. In his memorial ode, *Adonais*, Shelley compared him to *a pale flower by some sad maiden cherished*, and Gerard Manley Hopkins described Keats as *one of the beginners of the Romantic movement, with all the extravagance and ignorance of his youth . . . His contemporaries, as Wordsworth, Byron, Shelley, and even Leigh Hunt, right or wrong, still concerned themselves with great causes, as liberty and religion; but he lived in mythology and fairyland the life of a dreamer.*

Recently critics have questioned the nineteenth-century view of Keats's poetry as unworldly and unreal. By considering the circumstances of his life (the dissenting school where he had his education, his early admiration for radicals like Leigh Hunt and Hazlitt, the oppositional journals widely read in his circle), they interpret Keats's dreams of unobtainable ideal worlds as a need to distance himself from harsh and repressive social conditions. His escapism into fairyland, goes the argument, is a glimpse of an ideal 'vision' or dream-world which contrasted with the industrial and political conditions of the time which made the Romantics despair.

Nicholas Roe (1997) re-interpreted *To Autumn*, long regarded as a tribute to Ceres, goddess of the harvest, as an expression of Keats's liberal political beliefs. Keats composed it at the end of the week (18 September 1819) in which Henry Hunt, the main speaker at the Peterloo meeting, had entered London to mass acclaim. Like the other Peterloo organizers tried in England for conspiracy and sedition, Hunt was acquitted, whereas those unfortunate enough to be tried in Scotland were sentenced to transportation. The English sentences were seen as the triumph of justice and liberalism, and Keats joined the large, rejoicing crowd who lined the streets to welcome Hunt to the capital. Roe argues that *To Autumn* reflected Keats's feelings at this politically charged time. Roe reads further significance into the Ceres figure in the poem:

> *Ceres presides over land originally 'common to all men'; over food, farming, cultivation, and prosperity; and over the laws determining 'rights and properties' among contentious humankind. She represents nature's abundance, and also the rights and laws that determine a just distribution of that plenty . . . Certainly, the mythical associations of the goddess, uniting fruitfulness and justice, would have garnered further significance at a season when killings, trumped-up prosecutions, and rumoured conspiracies seemed likely to provoke a revolution.*

6 Victorian Contexts

• •

Manchester
The town itself is peculiarly built, so that a person may live in it for
years, and go in and out daily without coming into contact with a
working-people's quarter or even with workers, that is, so long as he
confines himself to his business or to pleasure walks. This arises
chiefly from the fact, that by unconscious tacit agreement, as well
as with outspoken conscious determination, the working-people's
quarters are sharply separated from the sections of the city reserved
for the middle-class . . . stretching like a girdle, averaging a mile
and a half in breadth, around the commercial district. Outside,
beyond this girdle, lives the upper and middle bourgeoisie, the
middle bourgeoisie in regularly laid out streets in the vicinity of the
working quarters . . . the upper bourgeoisie in remoter villas with
gardens . . . in free, wholesome country air, in fine comfortable
homes, passed once every half or quarter hour by omnibuses going
into the city. And the finest part of the arrangement is this, that the
members of this money aristocracy can take the shortest road
through the middle of all the labouring districts to their places of
business, without ever seeing that they are in the midst of the grimy
misery that lurks to the right and the left . . . Right and left a multitude
of covered passages lead from the main street into numerous courts,
and he who turns in thither gets into a filth and disgusting grime,
the equal of which is not to be found – especially in the courts which
lead down to the Irk, and which contain unqualifiedly the most
horrible dwellings which I have yet beheld. In one of these courts
there stands directly at the entrance, at the end of the covered
passage, a privy without a door, so dirty that the inhabitants can
pass into and out of the court only by passing through foul pools of
stagnant urine and excrement. This is the first court on the Irk above
Dulcie Bridge – in case any one should care to look into it. Below it
on the river there are several tanneries which fill the whole
neighbourhood with the stench of animal putrefaction.

Frederich Engels: The Condition of the Working Class in England, *1844–5*

The Industrial Revolution

The first stage of Britain's Industrial Revolution, around 1780–1840, was
based on the cotton trade. Raw cotton from the West Indies and America
entered England chiefly through the port of Liverpool, although Bristol and

Glasgow were also important ports for the Atlantic and colonial trade. The bulk of the manufactured cotton textiles were re-exported. In the 1830s and 1840s over half of all Britain's export trade was cotton. The increase in textile production was possible because of improvements in weaving (the flying shuttle) and inventions in spinning. The spinning 'jenny' of the 1760s allowed more than one thread to be spun at a time, and in the 1780s the spinning 'mule' harnessed this breakthrough to steam power. Weaving continued as a cottage and home industry but the water-based, steam-powered spinning 'mule' required a factory and in time weaving too was brought into the factory system. Cotton spinning transformed Manchester into the first of the great nineteenth-century industrial cities. Its population increased ten-fold between 1760 and 1830, by which time Manchester and Salford possessed three times the steam power of Birmingham.

In the second stage of the industrial revolution, around 1840–1895, coal, iron and railways replaced water, cotton and canals as the major sources of power, raw materials and transport, but the pattern of factory and city growth which transformed Britain from a predominantly rural into an industrial and city economy was set in the early years of the century. The rural poor, suffering from unemployment and a rising population, poured into the swelling cities of the Midlands and the North to work in factories. In the mid-eighteenth century only London and Edinburgh had populations over 50,000. By 1801 eight cities had grown to this size and by 1851, when the first census was taken, there were 29, with Manchester's population at 338,000; Glasgow at 375,000; Liverpool at 395,000; Dublin at 405,000 and London at 2,239,000. By 1881 many cities had doubled again in size and London, now over four million, was the largest city in the world. More revealing of the way Britain was being transformed from a pastoral to an urban society were the figures in the 1851 census which showed that, for the first time, just over half the population lived in urban developments. By 1881 the proportion of urban population was over seventy per cent.

The cities that attracted workers in such numbers from the countryside lacked the facilities to house them, and in an unregulated, *laissez-faire*, profit-seeking environment the shoddiest of dwellings were rapidly built close to the factories, which were themselves close to the polluted rivers which powered the machines in the first stage of the Industrial Revolution. The desperately crowded, dirty and disease-ridden conditions appalled inquiring foreigners like Engels (quoted above) and De Tocqueville, who wrote a similar description of Manchester in his *Journeys to England and Ireland* (1835). When machinery changed from water to coal power, blackening smoke from factory chimneys added to the terrible appearance of industrial areas. Engels was pointedly ironic about the way in which the rising, affluent middle classes physically separated their homes and averted their eyes from the poverty of the working class, but the danger of these insanitary areas, especially after cholera arrived in Britain in 1831, was a matter of concern to the authorities. It led to a parliamentary enquiry, the Chadwick *Report on the Sanitary Condition of the Labouring Population*

(1842). Chadwick's diagnosis of the disease was mistaken. It was not, as he believed, air-borne but carried in polluted water. However, the utilitarian reforms his report instigated, including underground sewerage systems and the provision of clean water, did attack the main causes of infection.

The factory system was perceived by contemporary critics to bear harshly on the working class because, unlike agricultural work, it was immune to seasonal or daily variety. Gas-lit factories worked on through darkness, and the working day was extended to twelve or thirteen hours. The work was mechanical and repetitive. The very name used to designate factory workers, 'hands', suggested that they were not regarded as people but as parts in a mechanical process. Factory owners were seen as driven by the profit motive, uncaring as to the welfare of their workers or the greater good of their country. *It is the Age of Machinery*, thundered Carlyle in *Signs of the Times* (1829):

> *On every hand, the living artisan is driven from his workshop, to make room for a speedier, inanimate one. The shuttle drops from the fingers of the weaver, and falls into iron fingers that ply it faster. The sailor furls his sail, and lays down his oar; and bids a strong, unwearied servant, on vaporous wings, bear him through the waters . . . Men are grown mechanical in head and in heart, as well as in hand.*

Carlyle's hostility was not only to industrialization but to the Utilitarian philosophy which supported it. Jeremy Bentham (1748–1842), who formulated utilitarian ideas, believed that human behaviour acted on rational principles and could be influenced by appealing to a person's enlightened self-interest. Feelings (a Romantic concept against which he reacted) and sympathy were no basis for morality. Nor were Christian teachings. The only valid basis for Utilitarianism was an educated self-interest which, if universally applied, would result in 'the greatest happiness of the greatest number'. It was a philosophy to which Dickens, like Carlyle, took exception. The novel *Hard Times*, Dickens's plea for sympathetic feeling and creative imagination as the best 'education', was dedicated to Carlyle.

The slow march of reform

Parliament, which had begun to reform itself with the Reform Act of 1832, slowly legislated for improvements. The Factory Act of 1833 prohibited the employment of children under nine years of age in textile factories. In 1842 children under ten were forbidden to work in the mines. The 1830s and 1840s were times of economic distress in England, and of devastating hunger in Ireland where over a million died of starvation, but by 1851 – the time of the first census – Britain was a prosperous nation. The pressure for reform in housing, labour conditions, public order, education, prison and women's rights increased, not only in Parliament but from the growing body of social reformers; concerned, active individuals and religious, evangelical groups.

The Second Reform Act of 1867 widened the franchise to all male urban householders owning or renting a building to the value of £10 annually, opening up the likelihood of universal male suffrage in the future. It became important, in the emerging democratic state, to educate the electorate, and in 1870 elementary schooling for all children became compulsory.

For women, improvements came slowly. Working-class women were treated, as were children, as a source of cheap labour in the early nineteenth century, and their working conditions had to wait upon parliamentary legislation for improvement. The middle-class woman was idealized as *the angel in the house* and confined, by this concept of her role, to the domestic sphere where she was expected to exude sweetness and light, moral rectitude and unfailing fidelity in support of her husband – who alone could enter the public world. The law held women of all classes to be inferior to men, and the pressure on them to remain virgin until marriage and 'pure' thereafter was reinforced by the socially imposed bogey of the 'fallen' or 'ruined' woman, a scorned and despised alternative role into which women were cast. Deprived of the vote, of access to professional work, public office or higher education, and financially dependent upon men, middle-class women led restricted lives. Leading women began to campaign against these restrictions. Some reforms occurred in the nineteenth century, for example in the right of married women to retain ownership of their property and in the treatment of prostitutes, but the 'Women Question', as it was termed, was still being strongly argued in the twentieth century when many of the main issues, for example female suffrage, began to be addressed.

'Heaven helps those who help themselves' was the theme of Samuel Smiles's enthusiastic and encouraging book *Self-Help* (1859) which was a collection of potted biographies of men who won their way to wealth and social status from the poorest of beginnings, by dint of their own efforts. Every example was a success story. Smiles's overt message is a confident assertion that any working-class man can better himself, socially and financially. The underlying message, however, reinforces the Victorian work ethic. Just as Victorian ideology required women to be pure, it motivated men to be industrious. The nineteenth-century class system, where class was signalled by accent, manners, dress, housing, culture and employment, was rigid and powerfully divisive but even more ideologically important was the division between 'respectable' and 'unrespectable'. Poor but honest men and women were classed as respectable, indeed were encouraged to make respectability their goal since it kept them passive and non-rebellious. Victorian anxiety centred on the unrespectable groups, especially the criminal underclass which the middle classes feared might turn into a revolutionary mob. The weakest members of the working class, children, women, the elderly and the infirm, found themselves crushed between the pressure to be respectable and the need to make a living wage. It is salutary to read Smiles's book alongside Henry Mayhew's *London Labour and the London Poor* (1851), a series of interviews first published in the *Morning Chronicle* which he carried out among the working population of London. As far as possible, he let working-class people speak for themselves, adding little by way of comment and passing no judgement. The authentic tone of the accounts of their working lives and living conditions made a great impact at the time and still makes moving reading today. This is his interview with a needlewoman:

> *I had no idea of the intensity of the privation suffered by the needlewomen of London until I came to inquire into this part of the subject. But the poor creatures shall speak for themselves . . . The first case is that of a good-looking girl. Her story is as follows:*

> *'I make moleskin trowsers. I get 7d. and 8d. per pair. I can do two pairs in a day . . . but some weeks I have no work at all. I work from six in the morning to ten at night; that is what I call my day's work. When I am fully employed I get from 7s. to 8s. a week. My expenses out of that for twist, thread, and candles are about 1s 6d. a week, leaving me about 6s. per week clear. But there's coals to pay for out of this, and that's at the least 6d. more; so 5s. 6d. is the very outside what I earn when I'm in full work. Lately I have been dreadfully slack; so we are every winter, all of us 'sloppers', and that's the time when we wants the most money . . . My father died when I was five years of age. My mother is a widow, upwards of 66 years of age, and seldom has a day's work . . . I am 20 years of age . . . We earn together, to keep the two of us, from 4s. 6d. to 5s. each week . . . I was virtuous when I first went to work . . . I struggled very hard to keep myself chaste, but I found that I couldn't get food and clothing for myself and my mother, so I took to live with a young man . . . He did promise to marry me, but his sister made mischief between me and him, so that parted us . . . I am now pregnant by him . . . I was very fond of him, and had known him for two years before he seduced me . . . Could I have honestly earnt enough to have subsisted upon . . . I should not have gone astray, no, never – As it was I fought against it as long as I could – that I did – to the last . . . My child will only increase my burdens, and if my young man won't support my child I must go on the streets altogether. I know how horrible all this is. It would have been much better for me to have subsisted upon a dry crust and water rather than be as I am now. But no one knows the temptations of us poor girls in want. Gentlefolks can never understand it.*

In the depressed decades of the 1830s and 1840s, the poverty of the working class and their growing numbers in conurbations fed a middle-class fear of mob violence. Across the Channel, the European revolutions of 1848 were a warning of what might happen should the 'many' rise up against the 'few'. In these circumstances, the peaceful, respectable behaviour of the lower classes who attended the Great Exhibition of 1851was taken as a hopeful sign that Britain, by the middle of the century the world's most prosperous

Wentworth Street,
Whitechapel *by Gustave
Dore, 1872: poverty and
overcrowding for the
working people*

Women on Morning
Ride *by Gustave Dore,
1872: leisure and
privileges for
the rich*

trading nation, was exempt from the social unrest that threatened other European countries. Lord Macaulay's diary for the opening day of the Great Exhibition says: *I saw none of the men of action with whom the Socialists were threatening us . . . There is just as much chance of a revolution in England as of the falling of the moon.*

The decline of religious faith

Macaulay's confidence was not generally shared. Contributing to the mid-Victorian fear that the working-class might rebel was the fact that attendance at church was declining, since it was felt that any turning away from the Christian virtues of duty, obedience and humility that the churches preached was *fraught with grievous danger to property and the State.* To provide for the religious needs of people displaced from the countryside into the burgeoning cities, Parliament had passed funds as early as 1818 to build new, urban churches. But Victorians were shocked when the 1851 census revealed that only half the population attended church and of those who did attend, half worshipped at Nonconformist churches. There were many reasons for declining church attendance, among them class divisions which alienated the poor. In an Anglican church in a town, the middle class paid for family pews and the working class were confined to free benches at the back. Long working hours discouraged church attendance on the only day of rest. More fundamental, however, was a growing climate of doubt about the truth of religion, partly in response to scientific advances which shook belief in the literal truth of the Bible. Geological discoveries (Lyell's *Principles of Geology* was published in 1830–33) showed that the world had not been created in seven days but had been formed over aeons. The evolutionary theory of Darwin's *Origin of Species* (1859) and *The Descent of Man* (1871) challenged the biblical claim that man was created in one day, 'a little lower than the angels'.

Compared to the present day, the Victorian era was deeply religious, and social practices were embedded in religion. Sunday observance meant that nearly all commercial and leisure activities were closed on that day, and ritually all important public occasions began with a Christian prayer. Many new churches, Anglican and Nonconformist, were built. There were numerous missionary and evangelical movements which spread the gospel abroad and worked for social reform at home. But scientific discoveries suggested that physical matter, including human beings, operated and developed according to discoverable, mechanical laws. This cast doubt on the existence of God, which created great anxiety for the Victorians. Charles Kingsley summed up a general mood when he preached in 1866:

> *Science frees us in many ways . . . from the bodily terror which the savage feels. But she replaces that, in the minds of many, by a moral terror which is far more overwhelming. Am I – a man is driven to ask – am I, and all I love, the victims of an organized tyranny . . . Are we only helpless particles, at best separate parts of the wheels of a vast machine?*

The shock of religious doubt helps to account for the elegiac tone of many mid-Victorian poems, even when it is not as overt as it is in Matthew Arnold's *Dover Beach*:

> *The sea of faith*
> *Was once, too, at the full, and round earth's shore*
> *Lay like the folds of a bright girdle furled.*
> *But now I only hear*
> *Its melancholy, long, withdrawing roar,*
> *Retreating, to the breath*
> *Of the night-wind, down the vast edges drear*
> *And naked shingles of the world.*

Although Darwin's evolutionary theories were disturbing at the time and prompted furious public debate as well as hostile cartoons based on the 'missing link', the basic message – that humans advanced and improved through evolution – chimed with the Victorian belief in progress. Nineteenth-century literature displays a strange mixture of melancholy and confidence, which mirrors Victorian anxiety about social inequalities and loss of religious faith, and Victorian optimism that their economic, scientific and industrial achievements promised continuing progress. This progress also seemed to impose a duty on Victorians to colonize and improve the undeveloped world, the 'lesser breeds without the law'. Imperialist conquest

Charles Darwin satirized as A Venerable Orang Outang *in* The Hornet, *22 March 1871*

and colonial settlement created the British Empire, with its monopoly of colonial and underdeveloped countries' markets which produced so much of Britain's nineteenth-century wealth. At its height, in the last decades of the nineteenth century, nearly a quarter of the globe was ruled from Westminster, and the pressure of a rapidly rising population was relieved by large-scale emigration to the under-populated colonies.

The nineteenth-century novel

The social conditions of the times are meticulously reflected in the realist novel, which developed as a new genre in the nineteenth century out of the eighteenth-century novel, itself an innovatory literary genre. The realist novel has a forward-moving, morally progressive plot in which individuals face the shock of social and historical change. Nineteenth-century novels were long, with an abundance of characters, because they attempted to span large sections of society. From Jane Austen at the start of the century to Thomas Hardy at the end, writers created fictional worlds which were recognizable pictures of real life. The writers' passion for reform tended to sanitize and sanctify working-class characters, and demonize wealthy ones.

Mary Shelley

Mary Shelley's *Frankenstein* (1818) is outside the mainstream development of the realist novel. It is almost in a class of its own. Although it was conceived as a ghost story, it has no ghosts; and although it was classed as a gothic novel, it dispenses with the usual mysterious, gothic, medieval settings and supernatural plot. Shelley made her story contemporary, and instead of gloomy castles, monasteries and dungeons, she placed Frankenstein in a nineteenth-century laboratory. But features of the gothic horror tradition are present. The laboratory has a threatening air of seclusion and mystery; a major character is the supernatural monster who terrorizes the other characters; and the pursuit of knowledge drives Frankenstein into melodramatic madness and despair.

Unlike the gothic genre, which was short-lived, *Frankenstein* has remained a popular novel, perhaps because – in spite of its fantastic plot – it speaks to real anxieties. Numerous interpretations have been suggested: it is a warning about the uncontrollable nature of scientific discovery and the dangers inherent in 'progress'; it is a revision of *Paradise Lost*. Frankenstein, driven by Faustian curiosity, creates life and then refuses to take responsibility for his creation. In the absence of God, the moral battle in the novel is between the monster and Frankenstein, between the former's complaint that his maker is unjust, and the latter's horror at the forces he has unleashed. The novel's language echoes *Paradise Lost* at several points. Frankenstein likens himself *to the archangel who aspired to omnipotence* and now is *chained in eternal hell*. The monster also recognizes the Miltonic parallels, but cannot decide whether he has been cast as Adam or Satan.

Frankenstein evokes in readers a degree of sympathy with the monster's complaint, and he is not the only creature who suffers. A deep sense of injustice runs through the novel, much of it perpetrated by the monster himself, who, like Frankenstein, is both abuser and victim. Some critics regard the monster as reflecting the liberal reaction to the emergence of the industrial working-class as a political and social force, and to the unrest in the early years of the nineteenth century. The Shelleys were politically radical. Mary's husband, the poet Percy Bysshe Shelley, wrote *The Masque of Anarchy*, with its refrain 'Ye are many – they are few', in protest at the Peterloo massacres. But memories of the French Revolution were stirred by the Luddite attacks, and this disturbed liberals, most of whom shared the middle-class fear of an uneducated mob rising against them and attacking their property. Pity and fear, sympathy and revulsion were mixed in their attitude to the working class, much as they are in the portrait of the monster.

Yet another reading argues that the novel is a myth of birth. The death of Mary's children (only one survived infancy), the competitive atmosphere in which she wrote alongside Byron and her husband, and the Romantic tendency to emphasize the act of creativity in writing, are all held to be evidence that her anxieties about pregnancy and maternity merged with her struggle to write a successful story. It is a reading that draws attention to the question of whose story is told in the novel's unusual narrative structure. The framing structure is a series of letters to Walton's sister relating the monster's story as told to Frankenstein, and Frankenstein's story as told to Walton. But the reader comes at the narrative in the opposite direction, through the viewpoint of Walton (who feels sympathetic kinship with Frankenstein), then through the viewpoint of Frankenstein (who hates the monster) and only last through the viewpoint of the monster himself, who lives at the heart of the story. In each instance, the reader's sympathy is focused on the immediate narrator. Omnipotent authorial comment is absent. Multiple stories are offered.

Each narrator explains himself in terms of his childhood education, and again and again the novel describes the process by which individuals' characters are formed. The most detailed explanation of the growth of human consciousness and conscience is the monster's account of his own development from the moment of his waking awareness. Abandoned by Frankenstein, he is entirely self-educated and thus provides a case study for Rousseau's theory of self-directed education. He learns by experience the benefits and dangers of fire. Learning from sensory experience, however, gives the monster only the knowledge necessary for physical survival. Observing the De Lacey family stirs his desire to be a social creature. He becomes aware that he is lonely, and he supports the family with kindly acts. As he learns language, first spoken and then written, he acquires sensibility and a sense of morality. The books Shelley picks for him illustrate her ideas about the process of education. From reading Goethe's *Sorrows of Werther*, the monster gains the Romantic high regard for affective feelings; from Plutarch's *Lives* he learns republican values; and from *Paradise Lost* he acquires concepts of good and evil. He learns that the nineteenth-century obsession with class and money condemns anyone who lacks them to be *a vagabond and a slave.* He is brought to the ultimate Romantic question, What was I? The monster's education appeared to be forming a physically capable, morally sensitive, social being until he was rejected. Injustice, rejection, brutality and isolation turn him into an anti-social murderer.

Activity

> You may prefer to do this as a group activity. Re-read Chapter 11 and make a list of what the monster learns. Against each item, identify the process by which the monster is educated: sensory perception, observation, example, language, experience or reflection. To what extent do you feel the monster's character is formed by 'education' in the widest sense, including both good and bad experiences? He ends by seeking Frankenstein's pardon. Where do you think he learned remorse and guilt?

Brontë and Dickens

Many later nineteenth-century novelists shared the Romantic interest in the moral growth of human consciousness. Schools, on the whole, are depicted unsympathetically. Think of Lowood in *Jane Eyre* or Mr Gradgrind's school in *Hard Times*. We know that Lowood was based on Charlotte Brontë's own experiences at Cowan Bridge, and there is historical evidence that the schools in Victorian novels are reasonably faithful pictures of reality. In criticizing the schooling system, Brontë and Charles Dickens were not showing lack of faith in education. Moral development is crucial in the formation of heroes and heroines, and how this development takes place, how people are educated to be morally good, is a question addressed in many novels. Jane Austen's heroines learn from their mistakes. It is a personal transformation in which the character comes to share the moral viewpoint which the author has already imposed on the reader, taking our agreement for granted. With later nineteenth-century writers, moral judgements are more open to question; the church no longer offers sure guidance. Brontë's Lowood was a charitable school, and its Christian rituals are bitterly attacked. Dickens's Coketown is stuffed with churches affiliated to competing branches of the Christian faith, all condemned for offering nothing that meets working-class needs. Neither author is irreligious – the death scenes of Helen Burns and Stephen Blackpool both use religious vocabulary. *Jane Eyre* closes in total religious commitment and *Hard Times* uses biblical language in its chapter and section headings. 'Sowing', 'Reaping', and 'Garnering' contrast the mechanical, utilitarian approach to time in Coketown with an alternative way of measuring time, which is natural, seasonal, and religious in language and implication – that 'as ye sow so shall ye reap'.

Activity

> Consider, in a nineteenth-century novel of your choice, the author's interest in the acquisition of moral consciousness. Are we presented with characters whose moral character was formed before the novel opened, or are we shown the effects of childhood on adult development? Do characters face moral dilemmas, and if so are they tests of an unchanging morality or an education into a new moral understanding? (It can be as interesting to consider a 'bad' character as the hero or heroine.)

Victorian novels featured the full range of class and gender and reflected their inequalities, but fictional heroes and heroines tended to be middle-class, appealing to the readers who were the novels' main consumers. Jane Austen's Emma has to be 'educated' to behave kindly towards the poor-but-respectable Miss Bates, but she also has to learn that Harriet Smith, though respectable, is not of her own class. More revealing of Jane Austen's acute registering of class differences is the near invisibility of servants in her novels. Mrs Bennet, in *Pride and Prejudice,* may be affronted when Mr Collins inquires which of her daughters cooked the dinner, but the cook herself makes no appearance in the novel. In *Wuthering Heights* Heathcliff loses Cathy to Edgar solely because of class. Pip in *Great Expectations* learns late that his entry into the middle class and the rank of gentleman has been paid for by a convict, and that his 'expectations' were based on false assumptions. He reacts with humanity to the revelation, but class divisions are central to Dickens's approval of his actions.

Activity

> How does the author signal to the reader the class of any character in a nineteenth-century novel you are studying? You should consider speech, dress, manners, occupation and way of life. Does the character's class have a bearing on what happens to him or her in the novel?

Hard Times is unusual in having a working-class hero, Stephen Blackpool. You may even feel that he is not the hero of the novel compared to the middle-class women, Sissy Jupe and Louisa Gradgrind for, though Dickens makes Stephen Blackpool heroic, he is also a victim of the system. It is the circus folk who escape the limitations imposed by class.

Activity

> You may wish to divide this activity across a group. For each major character in *Hard Times*, locate their place of residence. What does the type of dwelling and area in which the character resides tell you about class divisions in Victorian society? How do the living quarters of the circus folk break free from the rigid class patterns of Victorian society?

Class is about more than wealth, but characters are significantly affected by money issues. In *Great Expectations*, money cannot save Magwitch and it destroys Estella, but it buys the education and lifestyle that lift Pip from the working class into the middle class. Money distracts Mrs Bennet in *Pride and Prejudice* and its acquisition rewards her two elder daughters. Money can both raise and lower characters in the social scale. Oliver Twist moves between the lowest strata of society and the comfort of a middle-class home with Mr Brownlow. For Fagin and the Artful Dodger, the options are less promising. The irony of the Dodger's performance before the court which sentences him – he puts on a middle-class air but continues to speak with a lower-class accent – serves to drive home Dickens's message that it is class, as well as criminal activity, that condemns him. Dickens was no radical. His conservatism and fear of the mob (revealed in his description of the revolutionary mob in *A Tale of Two Cities* and his attitude to the strike in *Hard Times*) prevent him from suggesting that class determines character. His novels are peopled with poor, respectable characters for whom he has great sympathy, but whom he judges to be morally better by remaining working class. In *Hard Times* Mr Bounderby is a 'self-help' member of the working class who has all the middle-class trappings of success (a house in town and a house in the country, servants and a middle-class wife). He is condemned, while his mother – patiently travelling once a year to catch a glimpse of her son – is honoured by these adjectives: *honest, simple, self-reliant, cheerful.*

Activity

> Consider the importance of money in the plot of any nineteenth-century novel. Are characters constrained by their financial situation? In similar circumstances in the present day, would the characters you are considering have more options open to them?

Poverty was especially harsh on women. The limited avenues open to respectable, educated women condemn Jane Eyre to the job of governess, and her frustration breaks out in Chapter 12 where she addresses the reader with a passionate plea for equality of opportunity with men. The reaction of the Rivers's servant indicates the starvation to which she would have been abandoned if she had not landed on the doorstep of relatives in her hour of greatest need. The plot requires her to become an heiress. To Brontë, class is less important than wealth when making her heroine equal to her hero. For younger women, prostitution or the socially outcast state of 'kept woman' were alternatives to unemployment, but for ageing women the dreaded workhouse loomed. Mrs Sparsit in *Hard Times* is a wonderfully dramatic villainess but her punishment, to become the companion to Lady Scadgers whose own income is insufficient to maintain her social status comfortably, shows how a lack of earning power and the pursuit of respectability bore down on middle-class women. This explains Mrs Sparsit's coddling of Mr Bounderby and her obsession with the downfall of his wife.

Distress among rural workers increased in the 1870s when cheaper food began to be imported from the Americas and Australasia. Rural unemployment was a major cause of emigration in the last decades of the century, and Thomas Hardy's novels show its effects on rural populations. His minor female characters are the ones who reveal the economic pressures most starkly. If you track the fates of Izz, Marian and Retty in *Tess of the*

D'Urbervilles you will see the destructive effects that occasional, poorly paid employment had on women.

Activity

> Consider the economic position of women in a nineteenth-century novel of your choice. In what ways are their opportunities more restricted than the men's? What effect does this have on them?

Illness and death are common in Victorian novels, and this is not surprising at a time when infectious diseases were widespread and antibiotic medicines had yet to be discovered. Many children died young and many women died in childbirth. Infant mortality was 154 per thousand births in 1840, and the figures had not improved in 1890. The Victorians could not escape the daily, visible reminders of death. People died at home, not in hospitals, and mourning rituals connected with dress and social behaviour were strictly observed. Because the air was believed to carry disease, in the literature of the period images of fog, dust, smoke and the blackening of buildings all carry implications of pollution, both physical and moral. Climaxes in the novels are often death-bed scenes, lingered over as characters die slowly and vocally, expressing 'truth' with their final words. The good die peacefully, the wicked horribly, and the author is sometimes moved to add his or her own commentary on the death of loved characters.

Activity

> Do any major characters die in a novel you are reading? Does the author make their deaths an important moment in the novel?

Tennyson

The poem that most appealed to Victorian sensibilities was a powerful poem of grief, *In Memoriam* by Alfred Tennyson (1809–1892). No one expressed more keenly than he the clash of optimism and pessimism which the 'shock' (John Stuart Mill's term) of change created in society. His poetry registers belief in a triumphant progress towards a better future: *Forward, forward let us range, / Let the great world spin for ever down the ringing grooves of change (Locksley Hall,* 181–2). Often in his verse there is a summons to a *noble* cause (consider the end of *Maud* and of *Ulysses*). He uses the imperative voice and the vocabulary of striving effort: *Follow, Forward, Strive, Come, Hark, Seek.* But an elegiac tone is also present, and the lasting effect of reading Tennyson is a sense of loss, uncertainty and melancholy.

Activity

> Consider the tone of any Tennyson poem. Can you identity vocabulary that suggests an optimistic belief in the future, or is the tone of the poem one of melancholy? Is it possible to detect both moods in the poem?

His early poem *The Lady of Shalott* (1832 and 1842) shows a sympathetic attitude to women, which may have had its origins in his miserable childhood with a drunken and abusive father. The oppositions in the poem (female/male; passivity/activity; reflection/reality; isolated/social; private/public) emphasize the stultifying narrowness of the Lady's life, so that the poem appears to condone her breaking the rules. Who sets the rules? The Lady *knows not what the curse may be.* She is held in thrall by *a whisper.* The circles within circles of her restriction, a room in a tower on an island in a lake, and the reflective, removed, secondary nature of her occupation, seem symbolic of middle-class Victorian womanhood. The poem exudes longing: for sex, for activity, for a different kind of existence. It has been read as an expression of female sexual and emotional repression, and of women's exclusion from the public sphere of power and employment.

It has also been seen as expressing a more generalized regret at the loss of an ordered, rural, traditional way of life in the face of a commercial, work-orientated, nineteenth-century urban environment. The poem's setting is medieval, a setting it shares with many Victorian poems and paintings. The melancholy sense that religious faith was declining made many Victorians turn their eyes back to pre-Reformation times, when the Church was a unified Catholic institution and Christian ideals seemed more certain. The gothic revival started in the late eighteenth century and flourished in the nineteenth century in art and architecture. The Oxford movement in the late 1830s and 1840s encouraged a return to early traditions in religious architecture, which influenced many of the new Victorian churches, while public architecture – museums, banks, town halls and the Houses of Parliament – copied the style of medieval cathedrals. A full-scale retreat to the past was as impossible as the Lady's flight to Camelot is destructive. But what were her options? Lancelot is touched with emotion at her death, not with understanding. In the 1832 version, *the well fed wits at Camelot* are even less perceptive. Does the root cause of her oppression lie in her gendered isolation or in her repetitive, unending weaving? Weaving lay at the heart of early nineteenth-century industrial unrest. The poem subtly addresses both the 'Women Question' and the 'work ethic'.

The 'work ethic' is openly addressed in *The Lotos Eaters,* which asks: *Should life all labour be?* (87). A tone of weariness and longing for release from effort dominates the poem. *All things have rest: Why should we toil alone?* (60). The island has a mesmerizing effect on the exhausted mariners, and all is forgotten: *All things are taken from us, and become / Portions and parcels of the dreadful Past* (91–2). Are we meant to approve the oblivion into which the lotos-eaters are sinking, where *slumber is more sweet than toil* (171)? It hardly seems likely, yet the island is described in lushly attractive verse. Like mechanical labour in Carlyle's view, it renders men passive and mindless, and the poem can be read both as a blessed escape from repetitive toil and as a picture of the oblivious passivity to which repetitive toil reduces men until they are uncaring about their wives, children or any kind of engaged life. Excessive and mechanical work is estranging, exhausting and empties men and women of feeling. The seductive and morally disturbing tone of the poem shows Tennyson tapping contradictory nineteenth-century feelings about the value of work and its demands.

Many of his poems grapple with contradiction, and with the felt pressure of doing one's duty. *Morte d'Arthur* (1833) tries to come to terms with violent change. Images of desolation and waste in the darkening landscape of *barren land, juts of pointed rock* and *icy caves* contrast with images of plenitude, *great water, shining levels of the lake* and *full moon*. The fulfilment of God's plan requires the dissolution of the Round Table and Arthur departs, he hopes, for Avilion: *Where falls not hail, or rain, or any snow*. But a note of doubt creeps into Arthur's farewell, *if indeed I go*, and for Sir Bedivere, *the days darken*. Similarly, *Ulysses* (1833) for all its heroic call *To strive, to seek, to find, and not to yield* locates itself at the *still hearth* with an *idle king*, whose age is emphasized in images of waning light and setting day. The repetition of the provisional *may be* sounds a further, melancholy note of uncertainty about Ulysses's destiny.

Activity

> The ideology of duty, of doing the 'right' thing, was imposed upon Victorians by their education and culture. We see it in Robert Browning's *Childe Roland to the Dark Tower Came*, another poem that uses a medieval setting to promote the ideal of the unquestioning acceptance of duty. Consider the call of duty in a Victorian poem of your choice. Can you see any contradictions in the pressure to do one's duty? How might this relate to Victorian ideologies about the roles of men and women in society?

Ulysses and *Morte d'Arthur* were written while Tennyson was grieving over the sudden death in 1833 of his closest friend, Arthur Hallam, and both poems obliquely register Tennyson's personal loss. His most famous poem, *In Memoriam* (1850), records his grief directly. The series of short lyrics that make up his long elegy to Hallam meditate on the Victorians' deepest concerns about religious doubt, about death, about creation and evolution. *In Memoriam* was immensely popular from the moment of its publication and although, like most long Victorian poems, it is less widely read now, it has always been held in high critical esteem.

The poem records Tennyson's years of despair, three in the timescale of the poem, but far longer in the actual writing. His mental state moves from prostrate grief and religious doubt to renewed faith. While voicing the doubts about religious truth under scientific attack shared by many Victorians, the poem ends with a renewal of faith. Section 55, below, seemed to speak to the nation.

> I falter where I firmly trod,
> And falling with my weight of cares
> Upon the great world's altar-stairs
> That slope through darkness up to God,
>
> I stretch lame hands of faith, and grope,
> And gather dust and chaff, and call
> To what I feel is Lord of all,
> And faintly trust the larger hope.

Tennyson accepted the fact that Lyell's geological accounts contradicted the biblical account of creation, and also Chambers' evolutionary ideas which had appeared by 1844 in *Vestiges of the Natural History of Creation*. This meant that his poem remained intellectually relevant during the debates stimulated by the publication of Darwin's theories in 1859.

In section 35, Tennyson describes the slow process of erosion in the formation of the earth.

> The moanings of the homeless sea,
> The sound of streams that swift or slow
> Draw down Aeonian hills, and sow
> The dust of continents to be.

In section 56 he attacks the idea that life was individually created, each type treasured as unique by God. Instead, he paints a bleak picture of the ruthlessness of *Nature, red in tooth and claw*, who speaks through the fossils which the Victorians loved to collect and study.

> 'So careful of the type?' but no,
> From scarp'd cliff and quarried stone
> She cries, 'A thousand types are gone:
> I care for nothing, all shall go.'

Other Victorian poetry

Religious doubt and the struggle to come to terms with changing perceptions of God are central to much Victorian poetry. Robert Browning (1812–1889) used the device of imaginary personae to voice criticisms of the worldliness of the church and to explore proofs of the existence of God. Browning's Arab physician, Karshish, whose clinical training is disturbed by meeting Lazarus, is an expression of the Victorian longing for proof about God's miracles. Fra Lippo Lippi's fleshly passions and gift for art question the church's separation of soul and body and offer instead a belief in God's manifestation as physical beauty, natural or human.

The poems of Emily Brontë (1818–1848), Emily Dickinson (1830–1886) and Christina Rossetti (1830–1894) were written by women who were firm in their faith, but their writing also questions the nature of God, in varying degrees of anguish. For Brontë, a daughter of the parsonage, the natural world provided moments of intense beauty and violent destruction from which she longed to escape into 'Eternity' (*Death*) the 'night' world of 'solemn light' (*Stars*) and 'undying life' where 'Every Existence would exist in thee' (*No Coward Soul is Mine*). Christina Rossetti was a high-church Anglican. Her sister Maria became a nun and she herself, until her health failed, was a lay Sister at a home for 'fallen' women in North London. Her poems reveal confident faith, but an underlying yearning for rest and sleep.

Emily Dickinson, the American poet, was raised in a strict, Calvinist faith. She lived all her life in one of the houses her family built in New England, withdrawing gradually into total seclusion from all but her brother's next-door household. She refused to attend church, and her poetry questions and accuses God without ever denying his existence. Puritanical forbearance and moral restraint contend with a wry sense that God's 'justice' is inexplicable.

> Apparently with no surprise
> To any happy Flower
> The Frost beheads it at its play –
> In accidental power –
> The blonde Assassin passes on –
> The Sun proceeds unmoved
> To measure off another Day
> For an Approving God.

Activity

Compare Victorian poems of religious faith. What range of responses can you find? Do any of the poems suggest moments of doubt?

Elizabeth Barrett Browning is exceptional in the frankness of her feminist views. She was unafraid to express sexual passion openly (although she hid the sonnets written to her husband under the pretence that they were *Sonnets from the Portuguese*). Much of her best poetry is politically engaged and alert to contemporary issues with a committed, liberal agenda. Most women poets in Victorian times showed the limitations of their lives in their content and imagery, which depends on the domestic sphere and as much of the natural world as could be seen from a window or experienced on a country walk. For Emily Brontë, natural imagery tends to be tempestuous. Many of Emily Dickinson's lyrics are precise observations of nature and often these turn out to be revelations of a divine presence. The divine enters her natural or domestic space quietly, unexpectedly, like a courteous visitor or guest. It can be heralded by an alteration in the light (*A Light exists in Spring; There's a certain Slant of light; Presentiment – is that long Shadow*). Eternity is also glimpsed in images of entering and leaving houses (*Tho' I get home; We grow accustomed to the Dark*). The act of passing from or waiting in rooms becomes an image of the soul between life and death (*I heard a Fly buzz – when I died; The last Night that She lived*). A carriage ride takes the departing soul through familiar, personal countryside (*Because I could not stop for Death; 'Twas just this time last year I died*).

With Christina Rossetti too, nature is usually depicted in a gentle mood. The ripe imagery of *Goblin Market* makes it an exceptional poem in her work, but its undertones are not unique. *Cousin Kate, An Apple Gathering* and *Sister Maude* all show comradeship with the 'fallen' woman. *Goblin Market*, however, with its insistent call to *Come buy* from the *cat-faced* and *rat-paced, sly* and *leering* goblin men has proved particularly open to sexual readings. The activity of exchange and barter, Lizzie's resistance and Laura's addiction to the dangerously seductive fruit, all hint at adult meanings in what was long regarded as a child's poem.

That so much of their imagery centred on domestic activity and natural observation helped to diminish female poetry in critics' eyes until late in the twentieth century, when the work of feminist critics began. Christina Rossetti's poetry was dismissed until quite recently as simple, orthodox, lacking in intellectual depth and failing to address complex moral issues. Lionel Stevenson wrote in 1972 that her poetry *comes closer to the pure lyric mode than that of any other Victorian, male or female, for the obvious reason that it contains a minimum of intellectual substance*. Discussion of the sexuality of *Goblin Market* began to change attitudes towards her work. In the first half of the twentieth century Emily Dickinson was condemned for narrowness of imagery and technical insufficiency. Now her aberrant punctuation, multiple re-writings, brief lyrics and hesitant, ejaculatory, broken syntax are classed as innovatory female writing, fashioning its own forms, voice and style in opposition to male writing.

Activity

Do you notice differences between poems written by male and female authors in the nineteenth century? Do you think modern readers should take account of the gender of the author in their reading of Victorian literature?

7 Into the Twentieth Century

The term 'imperialism', or the phrase 'the new imperialism', began to be used towards the end of the nineteenth century to mean the policy of extending and securing the British Empire wherever trade interests required the protection of the flag. By this time Britain's economy had become global. British trade spread across the world, carried predominantly in British vessels. In the 1880s Britain had over a third of the world's shipping tonnage and over three times the tonnage of her nearest rival, the USA. The bulk of her trade was with the British Empire, which spanned the globe at the end of the century.

The British colonies

At first Britain acquired colonies haphazardly; sometimes, as with the West Indies, it was done to consolidate mercantile interests developed by traders and settlers; sometimes colonies were the spoils of exploration or of war. Canada fell to England at the end of the Seven Years' War with France, and victory in the Napoleonic wars brought further West Indian islands and Ceylon (today's Sri Lanka) under British rule. The Cape of Good Hope was secured early in the nineteenth century because it was desirable as a stopping place for ships on the long voyage to India. Prime Minister Benjamin Disraeli bought a major shareholding in the Suez Canal soon after it opened in order to safeguard passage through the new short route to India, and, somewhat reluctantly, Britain continued to occupy Egypt.

Australia was claimed by Captain Cook in 1770 and almost immediately became a destination for transported convicts. New Zealand was a whaling outpost until it was thought it might be useful for settling emigrants. Even then it was not until the French made moves to colonize the islands that the British government agreed to annex the country in 1840.

India was the treasured colony, 'the brightest jewel in the imperial crown'. Disraeli created the title Empress of India for Queen Victoria in 1876, and the ornately exotic Durbar Wing added for her to Osborne House is evidence of India's appeal to the British imagination. The East India Trading Company was formed as early as 1600 and, starting with ports and coastal forts, gradually extended its administration to large areas of inland India.

After the Indian Mutiny of 1857–8, the crown took over direct rule from the company. It was during the Indian mutiny that the massacre at Cawnpore occurred. Around 200 hostages, all women and children, were killed on the orders of the retreating Hindu leader, Nana Sahib, as the British army advanced on the town. The brutality of the massacre passed into legend, and a legend is what many of the grosser details may be, for historians have been unable to settle contending accounts of the incident. The Victorians, however, believed that women had been raped and mutilated before they were murdered, and Cawnpore became a notorious example of the barbarity that the British felt could break out at any time among the 'natives'.

The loss of the American colonies was not generally felt to be serious in the eighteenth century, but in the nineteenth century perceptions changed. Marxist historians argue that British imperialism had an economic impetus – the drive to find new markets abroad as the home market began to reach the limits of expansion. Victorians were aware of the profits to be made in colonial trade and also of the pioneering opportunities that the colonies offered to emigrants. Victorian ideology, however, stressed the 'white man's burden' – a sincerely held belief that Britain had a duty to bring civilization and Christianity to undeveloped countries. Wilberforce, with reference to India, spoke in 1813 of the

> endeavour to raise these wretched beings out of their present miserable condition, and above all, to communicate to them those blessed truths, which would not only improve their understandings and elevate their minds, but would, in ten thousand ways, promote their temporal well-being, and point out to them a sure path to everlasting happiness.

During the nineteenth century the 'white settler' colonies (Canada, Australia, New Zealand and South Africa) moved peacefully towards self-governing independence. For colonies whose indigenous populations were considered less 'civilized', independence came more slowly and pressure for 'freedom' built up locally while Whitehall debated when and to what degree it should be granted.

India was Britain's most prized possession. In 1858 Britain agreed to support the Indian princes, and two-fifths of the country consisted of independent states run by Princes and Maharajahs. Ultimate power lay with the British, and the British Raj were a social and political elite, but there was a feeling in Whitehall that India, like the 'white settler' colonies, should at some time become independent. India's significant contribution to the First World War, both in men and money, determined Britain to move, in the words of the Secretary of State to the House of Commons in August 1917, *to the gradual development of self-governing institutions with a view to the progressive realization of responsible government in India as an integral part of the British Empire.* In the early years of the twentieth century, liberation movements, the Indian National Congress (founded in 1885 by an English administrator), Gandhi's passive resistance movement, the Bengali nationalist movement and the first Indian communists were all agitating for independence. One of the difficulties was mistrust between the Hindu and Muslim communities. This difficulty was never solved, with the result that when independence finally came in 1947 the country was divided into separate states, a Moslem Pakistan and a Hindu India.

The First World War

Nowadays we call the 1914–1918 war between Europe's imperial powers the First World War, but until the Second World War destroyed European hopes that never again would fighting on such a scale take place, the 1914–1918 conflict was called the Great War. It was great in the numbers of casualties and great in suffering. It is estimated that some ten million men died, and of those over one million were from Britain and the Commonwealth. It was war on a scale never previously experienced. To this day, the centres of towns and villages throughout Britain have memorials to the local dead, and the names of those from the First World War outnumber those from the Second.

In August 1914, however, there was no expectation that the conflict would be long or difficult. It was confidently believed that fighting would be over by Christmas. The first troops sent from Britain, a small Expeditionary Force under Sir John French, halted the German advance at Mons, and in spite of heavy losses, the early battles of Marne and Ypres were technically victories. But by Christmas both sides had ceased to advance and were rapidly digging defensive trenches, preparing, in a new departure in warfare, to remain embattled through the winter. In 1915 the Allies and the Central Powers faced each other across the western front of 'No-Man's Land', and trenches stretched from Switzerland to the Channel. Through appalling winter conditions and brutal spring offensives, the war continued for another four years on the western front with few territorial gains for either side while, on the eastern front, fighting extended to Russia, Poland, Lithuania, Serbia and Macedonia. There were middle-eastern campaigns in Mesopotamia and Palestine, and at sea German and British fleets engaged in the Atlantic and Pacific. Fighting spread across the northern hemisphere, but it is the trench warfare in the fields of Flanders and Picardy that is most often represented in literature and art.

For the fighting men, the misery of rain-sodden, mud-filled trenches, and bombardment and sniping across a corpse-strewn No Man's Land was made worse by the fear of chlorine gas attacks which the Germans commenced in 1915. In December of that year Sir John French was dismissed and General Haig took command, determined to throw as many troops as were necessary into large-scale offensives. In 1916, compulsory conscription of men into the armed forces had to be introduced to keep up the numbers this strategy required. In July Haig launched his great offensive, the battle of the Somme, which in twenty weeks of fighting and at a cost of 600,000 lives (two-thirds of them British) advanced the western front by eight miles.

During 1917, Russia retreated before Germany and sued for peace after the Russian Revolution. As Russia left the war a new ally joined. In response to

Germany's renewed submarine attacks, the USA declared war in April 1917. The arrival of fresh American troops was a turning point in the war, but not before Haig won a grudging permission from Lloyd George to launch another large-scale offensive at Ypres in July 1917. Passchendaele, as the battle was named, has become a symbol for incompetent military planning leading to large-scale slaughter. Another 300,000 British troops died in an advance which achieved next to nothing in territorial gains.

In public rituals, and in churches and on cenotaphs throughout the country, the dead of later wars are commemorated alongside those of the 1914–1918 conflict, but it was the Great War that deeply changed the country's perception of battle. For the first time since the Civil War, poets and artists were again soldiers recording their experiences at the battlefront. They left a legacy of horror in their writings and paintings which contrasts with nineteenth-century portrayals of war. One of the Victorians' favourite war poems was Tennyson's *The Charge of the Light Brigade*. It celebrates a military disaster – yet 'celebrate' is what it does. With its galloping rhythm and impelling, repetitive rhymes and phrases, it creates a triumphant tone, helped by the forceful diction (*rode, volleyed, thundered, flashed, charging, plunged, stormed*) and imperative verbs (*charge; forward; honour*). The poem reinforces Victorian ideology at its most idealistic: unquestioning performance of duty, bravery in the face of overwhelming odds, dying for the honour of the country. Compare this with the tone of any of the poems which describe life and death in the trenches of the Great War, especially those written in the war's later years, and the change in attitude is clear.

Activity

Not all Victorian presentations of war were as glorifying as *The Charge of the Light Brigade*. Consider the illustrations on page 119. Elizabeth Thompson was only twenty-eight when her painting of the Grenadier Guards, *Calling the roll after an engagement, Crimea,* became the sensation of the Royal Academy Exhibition of 1874. The line of wounded soldiers dressed in sombre colours against a dull snowy sky and foreground, speaks of the suffering of war but also of Victorian ideals of duty, courage, fortitude and resolution. Compare this with Paul Nash's painting, *The Menin Road.* There are differences in style between the realism of Thompson and the modernism of Nash, which in its slashes of colour and unrealistic, geometric patterning deliberately draws attention to itself as a painting. What differences in mood can you find, and what similarities? You might like to consider the role played by landscape in each painting and the pictorial space given to the soldiers. Which of the paintings best conveys to you the sufferings of war?

Although the Great War is now renowned for the suffering and death it caused, the initial reaction in 1914 to the news that Britain was at war was jubilant. Historians have puzzled to account for the enthusiasm with which young men hastened to enlist – 750,000 volunteers in the first eight weeks. Battles in Victorian times, they point out, occurred in distant countries, were

*'Calling the roll after an engagement, Crimea (The Roll Call)' by
Elizabeth Thompson*

*'The Menin Road' by Paul Nash, a modernist representation of the horrors
of war*

fought by professional soldiers and supported by an ideology that presented war as a glorious opportunity for heroism. The realities of fighting were not a living memory to many Edwardians.

Moreover, class barriers were loosening in late Victorian England as the standard of living for the expanding middle class rose. An income of £400 a year provided a family with a nice house, servants, holidays abroad and ample leisure for the womenfolk and sons of the family. Virginia Woolf, in *A Room of One's Own* (1929), claimed that £500 a year gave a writer personal independence. The economic difficulties of the 1870s and 1880s, which had brought hardship to rural areas and swelled the numbers of emigrants, had disappeared by 1900. The years 1900–1914 were golden in memory, and with reason when one considers the strength of Britain's economy. Historians have suggested that the Victorian work ethic and belief in 'progress', and the imperialist ideology that taught young men they had a duty to strive to help less fortunate nations of the world, all contributed to the sense that life had become easy, comfortable and decadent.

Rupert Brooke (1887–1915) heard the news of the outbreak of war while on holiday in Norfolk. In *An Unusual Young Man*, he expressed his own feelings in his description of the reactions of an imaginary young man.

> With a sudden tightening of his heart he realised that there might be a raid on the English coast. He didn't imagine any possibility of it succeeding, *but only of enemies and warfare on English soil . . .*
>
> *His astonishment grew as the full flood of 'England' swept over him on from thought to thought. He felt the triumphant helplessness of a lover. Grey, uneven little fields, and small, ancient hedges rushed before him, wild flowers, elms and beeches, gentleness, sedate houses of red brick, proudly unassuming, a countryside of rambling hills and friendly copses. He seemed to be raised high, looking down on a landscape compounded of the western view from the Cotswolds, and the Weald, and the high land in Wiltshire, and the Midlands seen from the hills above Prince's Risborough. And all this to the accompaniment of tunes heard long ago, an intolerable number of them being hymns . . . To his great disgust, the most commonplace sentiments found utterance in him. At the same time he was extraordinarily happy.*

Several things strike one about this passage. Brooke chooses the word 'English' rather than 'British', although it was Britain that was called to war, and he embodies 'Englishness' in a rural vision. He is disquieted to find himself moved by religious, ideological sentiments, which his modern liberalism disdains and yet at the same time he registers his happiness in being so moved.

Brooke was not alone in opposing peaceful images of rural England with thoughts of threatening invasion and brutal war. Many poets shared his vision of essential 'Englishness', imaged in gently curving fields bounded by ancient woodlands, filled with wild flowers and farmed in traditional, pre-mechanized ways. Edward Thomas (1878–1917) in *As The Team's Head-Brass* uses similar rural features (fields ploughed by horses in the traditional manner, signified by the head-brasses worn by the team, and woods that shelter lovers) to suggest a humane way of life under threat of destruction. The blizzard that felled the elm on the night the ploughman lost his mate in France grows, through repetition, into a symbol of what has been lost and what, by association with the poet who sits in its crest, is still threatened with loss: arms, legs, lives, a better world. In a deceptively quiet manner, Thomas predicts his own death the following year in France. Instead of destruction, *Instead of treading me down,* the ploughing team turn the furrows, at one with the natural cycles of renewal which surround the two men as they converse companionably. The masterly structure of the poem gives a timeless air to the countryside, but Thomas never settled on a title. He considered calling the poem 'The Last Team', as though he sensed his image of rural peace was backward-looking.

Activity

> The 1914–1918 war poets often contrast the horrors of war and life in the trenches with peaceful, rural scenes. From the poems you have read, select several such scenes. What elements do the rural pictures share in common? What image of 'England' is presented?

Many poems written at the start of the war show excitement at being called to fight. *Now, God be thanked*, commences Brooke's sonnet *Peace*. In *Into Battle* Julian Grenfell writes of the *joy of battle.* Images brought to the foreground are of keenness and youth (recruits are *lads* or *children* or *sons* or *chaps*); the nobility of duty, *the grandeur of our fate* (Laurence Binyon: *The Fourth of August*); glory and proud death, *from failing hands we throw / The torch; be yours to hold it high* (John McCrae: *In Flanders Fields*). The older generation of poets whose poetry had celebrated the imperial wars, Thomas Hardy, Rudyard Kipling and Henry Newbolt, contributed poems less excitable in tone. In *Channel Firing* and *In Time of 'the Breaking of Nations'*, Hardy accepts war as sad, mad but inevitable. Kipling, after the death in battle of his only son, writes with understandable guilt and bitterness, and his *Mesopotamia* and *A Dead Statesman* condemn poor leadership as strongly as Siegfried Sassoon's *The General* and *Lamentations* – but they do so without the power that comes from Sassoon's direct experience of trench warfare. It is the sense of lived experience in the poetry of many of the Great War poets, of voices speaking directly to us from the battlefield, which is the new phenomenon.

Activity

> Contrast a poem written in the early months of the war with one written in the later years. What changes in tone do you find? You might like to read closely the work of one particular poet and see if his writing changes, in style, content or attitude, as the war continues.

In content and tone the best of the Great War poets are radically new. Even when written by a member of the officer class, the poems share a sense of companionship with ordinary soldiers, desolation at the loss of comrades and bitterness at the blindness of leaders and civilians to their situation. They often relate short incidents in which love and pity for individual loss preclude any recourse to vague idealism about honour or glory. Poems written towards the end of the war and after the Armistice register the intense weariness of the long campaign, for example Wilfred Owen's *Exposure* and *Disabled.* On war memorials and cenotaphs, lines from the war poets are engraved. The choice is usually from the early poems – favoured quotations are from Brooke's 1914 sonnets or from Laurence Binyon's *For the Fallen.* Brooke died of blood poisoning on his way to action in the Dardanelles. Binyon was 45 when war broke out. He joined up in 1916 as a Red Cross orderly, but he wrote *For the Fallen* at the very beginning of the war. It was published in *The Times* on 21 September 1914.

Activity

> Read Brooke's 1914 sonnets, especially I *Peace,* III *The Dead* and V *The Soldier,* and Binyon's *For the Fallen.* Can you identify the quotations that are used in memorial services and for inscriptions? Why do you think these particular lines have proved more popular than lines from poets whose work conveys the direct experience of life and death in the trenches?

Modernism

The term 'modernism' can be applied to a period, broadly 1880–1940 or more narrowly 1910–1930, or to the stylistic changes in literature which took place during this time. In fiction, there was a reaction against the realist novel – a feeling that its broad, social panoply of characters, minutely described appearances and plot-dominated structures failed to present reality. 'Real' life was a looser, less well-structured affair. Instead of 'closed' endings, which tied up all the threads of the plot, the modernist novel presented readers with 'open' endings, with less sense of characters being judged and rewarded, and more sense of life overflowing the bounds of the plot.

The novel captured *moments*, to use Virginia Woolf's word, or *epiphanies,* to use James Joyce's term for the significant moments of revelation that both writers felt lay at the heart of the novelist's art. In place of stories of resolution, in which plot episodes were linked in a causal sequence moving inexorably to a conclusion, novels became a succession of unexplained fragments of experience, moments of revelation. The author withdrew as a voice in his or her own writing, and ceased to interrupt the text with moralizing comments. A modernist text is apolitical. It does not exist *to preach doctrines, sing songs, or celebrate the glories of the British Empire,* wrote Virginia Woolf in 1924.

There was a move towards expressing characters' private feelings, a move away from objectivity towards subjectivity which grew out of a sense that the truth about other people, or even about oneself, was not simple and knowable but limited, partially graspable and incoherent. Authors developed new styles of writing – the 'interior monologue' and 'stream of consciousness' – in an attempt to convey experience as it filtered through the minds of their characters. The isolation of characters is striking. Difficulties and failures of communication are stressed, and society no longer offers clear goals or models of behaviour. Modernism can be seen as a literary response to the disillusionment brought about by the First World War, to the loss of religious and political certainties in the late Victorian period, and to a growing liberal disquiet about class differences in society.

Subjective experience, 'interior monologue', shifting points of view and the absence of overt, authorial guidance can all make for difficult reading. The reader has to make sense of the *moments*. Connective links are created by language, for the modernist novel is self-conscious about its artistry. Style is valued, almost above content. The writing of modernist novelists like Joyce and Woolf is polished, highly controlled, and at times obscure. Syntax is fragmented; conventional narrative signs are missing. Novelists used the stylistics of poetry – symbolism and allusions, repetition of imagery and motifs – to structure their texts. By deforming normal syntax and language codes, modernist writing drew attention to the fact that texts were artistic objects created from words, just as Nash's painting on page 119, by rendering the scene in unrealistic blocks and slashes of colour, immediately draws attention to the fact that it is a painting, whereas Thompson's painting on the same page tries primarily to draw the viewer's attention to a realistically presented scene. Modernist writers like Woolf, T. S. Eliot and E. M. Forster discussed technique more openly than previous authors. All published a considerable number of literary critical essays.

E. M. Forster

Forster wrote six novels and published five in his lifetime. The sixth, *Maurice*, is a homosexual love story. Forster knew it could not be published – not, anyway, until the arrival of the 'Happier Year' to which the novel is dedicated. His hero is a 'pervert'; *an absurd word* he calls it in a letter to Forest Reid, in which he writes of the *criminal blindness of Society* and how it *nearly destroys* his main character. Homosexuality was made illegal in Victorian times. Oscar Wilde was tried and imprisoned under this law. Attitudes began to change in the 1960s and, following the Wolfenden Report, the law was revoked in 1967. Forster continued to refuse to publish *Maurice*, although he agreed it could happen after his death and he wrote a 'Terminal' note to accompany the novel.

He always had supportive friends and found a liberal-minded community at Kings College, Cambridge, where he became a Fellow in 1945. His novels were written in an astonishingly condensed period between 1905 and 1914. Even *A Passage to India,* published in 1924, was started in 1912. He was writing, therefore, at time when social opprobrium against homosexuals was at its height. Only recently has criticism discussed this aspect of his writing and considered how the loneliness to which he openly admitted may surface in coded ways in his novels.

Modernist texts like James Joyce's *Dubliners* (1914) and *Ulysses* (1922), T. S. Eliot's *The Waste Land* (1922) and Virginia Woolf's *Mrs Dalloway* (1925) consist of episodes and fragments of experience. The structures of *Ulysses* and *Mrs Dalloway* are based on the events of a single, unremarkable day in the lives of the protagonists. The novels of E. M. Forster, written in the same period, do not belong in any simple way either to the older realistic tradition or to the modernist. They have elements of both genres, and show the transition between them. They have plots, discoveries, climaxes and endings that come to resolutions – marriage in *A Room with a View* (1908), inheritance in *Howards End* (1910) – and to acceptance of the effects of imperialism in *A Passage to India* (1924). The authorial voice is present and although less omniscient and moralizing than, for example, in a Dickens novel, it is intrusive, speaking directly to the reader. In *Aspects of the Novel*, Forster described this authorial intervention as a 'point of view': the relation of the narrator to the story.

> *The novelist . . . can either describe the characters from outside, as an impartial or partial onlooker; or he can assume omniscience and describe them from within; or he can place himself in the position of one of them and affect to be in the dark as to the motives of the rest; or there are certain intermediate attitudes.*

Activity

In any novel by Forster, select two or three authorial interventions. Do they fit Forster's definition of 'point of view' or extend it? Do you feel you are being directed in your judgement of characters by the authorial interventions? Is the 'point of view' a matter of character presentation, or does it also suggest a moral attitude towards the world created by the novel?

Another way in which Forster's novels are modernist is his poetic style, which uses images, symbolism, motifs and epiphanies. Themes are carried by repeating word clusters and imagery that helps to structure the text. In *A Room with a View,* references to rooms, sights, views, seeing and light accompany Lucy's slow discovery of the truth about her feelings, and the novel is structured on the opposition of lying and truth. In *Howards End,* houses, ownership, possession and the search for a spiritual home reveal a thematic opposition between the successful, financially acute, city-dwelling, empire-building Wilcoxes and the liberal, cultured, humane Schlegels. In *A Passage to India*, arches, caves and echoes carry messages about evil and ideals and the unresolved mystery at the heart of the story. Small motifs recur constantly: the violets in *A Room with a View*, the cars in *Howards End*, the wasp in *A Passage to India.* Careful reading of any heightened passage in Forster shows him crafting language, creating meanings by his poetic choice of vocabulary which carries meanings beyond the obvious. His epiphanies are examples of this. In *A Room with a View*, for example, moments of revelation occur when Lucy crosses the Piazza Signoria in

Chapter 4 and when George glimpses her among the violets in Chapter 6. On each occasion it is Forster's poetic use of language that heightens the scene and alerts the reader to the epiphany.

Activity

> How does the vocabulary of the opening chapter of *A Passage to India* relate to the themes in the novel? The geographical description mirrors the social structure of the society, beautifying the elevated area where the English live and concealing (from whom?) the Indian city, *scarcely distinguishable from the rubbish* deposited by the Ganges. The *overarching sky* introduces the idea of a shared, human existence which the novel will investigate. The *fists and fingers* of the caves introduce the threatening element that will form the climax of the plot. The word *extraordinary*, used in the first and last sentences, will repeat throughout the novel. Notice the negatives in the first paragraph, hinting at omissions, gaps and failures in understanding which will negate the best-intentioned efforts and end in a nullifying experience in the caves and the novel's closing words, 'No, not yet,' and 'No, not there'. Can you identify single words whose meanings are symbolic?

The sense of omissions, of gaps, of things left unresolved or not clearly stated, is strong in Forster's novels. Here is a group of words used about his writing by various critics: *complex, ambivalent, indeterminacy, enigmatic, omission, negation, ambiguities, evasive, reservation, muddle.* Quite a few are taken from the texts of the novels. Collectively they point to an important aspect of his work, an elusiveness or absence that can leave the reader baffled. The largest unanswered question is what happens in the caves in *A Passage to India,* but consider a smaller moment – the scene in Chapter 14 in *A Room with a View* where Lucy explains to Miss Bartlett that George's first kiss was *subconscious.*

> *'What I mean by subconscious is that Mr Emerson lost his head. I fell into all those violets, and he was silly and surprised. I don't think we ought to blame him very much. It makes such a difference when you see a person with beautiful things behind him unexpectedly. It really does; it makes an enormous difference and he lost his head; he doesn't admire me, or any of that nonsense, one straw. Freddy rather likes him, and has asked him up here on Sunday, so you can judge for yourself. He has improved: he doesn't always look as if he is going to burst into tears. He is a clerk in the General Manager's office at one of the big railways – not a porter! – and runs down to his father for week-ends. Papa was to do with journalism, but is rheumatic and has retired. There! Now for the garden.' She took hold of her guest by the arm. 'Suppose we don't talk about this silly Italian business any more. We want you to have a nice restful visit at Windy Corner, with no worriting.'*
>
> *Lucy thought this rather a good speech. The reader may have detected an unfortunate slip in it. Whether Miss Bartlett detected the*

> *slip one cannot say, for it is impossible to penetrate into the minds*
> *of elderly people.*

What 'slip' should we have noted? The comment brings us up short. Forster's disingenuous suggestion that a reader 'may' have detected a slip is more likely to worry the reader into a search for it. Everything about Forster's authorial intervention is disingenuous. He addresses the reader conversationally, in an open admission that an act of decoding is taking place upon a text he created and which the reader is deciphering. Yet he pretends not to be able to 'penetrate' the mind of his own creation.

Activity

> What is Lucy's 'slip'? In a novel based on lies and truth is it her self-deceiving claim that George doesn't admire her? Or could it be the pronoun 'him' in the phrase, *when you see a person with beautiful things behind him unexpectedly*? Instead of recalling the scene as herself being perceived against the rivulet of violets by 'him', has she slipped into revealing how she saw George? She had in Chapter 7 confessed to Miss Bartlett that she 'slipped into those violets' and was 'a little to blame' and that George appeared to her at that moment like a hero or a god. Another suggestion from recent 'queer' readings of the text has pointed out that if the slippage is in the personal pronoun and the eliding of 'him' and 'her', it could indicate an authorial slippage and the possibility that in much of Forster's writing it is love between man and man rather than man and woman that interests him.

Friendship between men is treated with good-humoured comedy by Forster and becomes, at its best, an ideal of moments of comradeship and unity, like the swim in the sacred Pool in *A Room with a View,* or Aziz and Fielding's *gracious interlude* in Chapter 27 of *A Passage to India*. These moments do not last. It is elderly women who carry the sustaining sense of wisdom and goodness. Types rather than individualized characters, Forster's benevolent older women have an influence in his novels far beyond their place in the plots. In *Howards End*, Mrs Wilcox's presence pervades the book and her search for a *spiritual heir* (Chapter 11) for Howards End, the search that the Wilcoxes fail to understand when they decide not to honour her dying wish, ends only at the close of the novel when Margaret, her chosen inheritor, takes possession of the house. The house seems to be a symbol for what Forster values in England, the *English farms* where *one might see life steadily and see it whole* (Chapter 29) in contrast to what he deplores, *the continual flux of London* (Chapter 20), and this comes together in the female figures who pass the care of the house from one to another.

Activity

> Helen claims that Mrs Wilcox *knew . . . everything* (Chapter 4) and Margaret echoes this later, *She knows everything* (Chapter 40). Miss Avery foresees that Margaret will live at Howards End. In *A Passage to India*, Adela claims *Mrs Moore – she did know* (Chapter 29). What kind of sympathetic understanding and mystic insight do Forster's elderly women possess? Do you think he makes it clear or leaves it vague and undefined?

A Passage to India has been read as Forster's condemnation of the destructive effects of imperialism. In his essay *Notes on the English Character* he blames the public school system for training Englishmen to conceal and suspect emotion, and then sending them

> *forth into a world that is not entirely composed of public-school men or even of Anglo-Saxons, but of men who are as various as the sands of the sea; into a world of whose richness and subtlety they have no conception. They go forth into it with well-developed bodies, fairly developed minds, and undeveloped hearts. And it is this undeveloped heart that is largely responsible for the difficulties of Englishmen abroad. An undeveloped heart – not a cold one. The difference is important.*

Imperialism in India kept alive the memory of the Indian Mutiny. Forster's novel alludes to the event when McBryde, *the most reflective and best educated* of the officials, tells Fielding to *Read any of the Mutiny records* (Chapter 18). Just before Forster completed *A Passage to India* another atrocious massacre occurred at Amritsar in 1919 when the British commander, General Dyer, ordered his troops to fire on a crowd at a public meeting, killing and wounding large numbers of unarmed, unprotected Indians. The fear of massacre is dissipated in *A Passage to India* by locating it in the comic presentation of the more hysteric and racist members of the British community, but the myth of the oriental desire to rape Victorian womanhood (a myth held up to brutal ridicule by Aziz's reaction to Adela's ugliness) lies behind the plot's climax.

'Orientalism' is a term created by Edward Said to describe the way in which the East was perceived by the West as beautiful, feminine, desirable, seductive, mysterious and alluring but also as devious and untrustworthy. The myth of native rape on white womanhood was, new-historical and cultural materialist critics have argued, a useful ideological belief, justifying harshly punitive measures of imperialist control. Both views of the sexuality of the East described by Said's Orientalism underlie Forster's novel. He denigrates the hostile view by making it the opinion of characters we condemn as racist and despise as ridiculous. The mysterious, seductive image of the East, the view Forster foregrounds, is conveyed in paragraphs of lyrical description and in the way the privileged characters respond to the landscape and to each other.

Activity

Do you find you want to know what happened in the caves in *A Passage to India*, or do you prefer to leave the event a mystery? Critics have suggested that any answer a reader provides reveals more about the reader's own ideas of East and West, and that the novel's indeterminacy is Forster's way of rejecting imperialist discourses of power in favour of a receptive willingness and openness to non-Western ideas.

Recently criticism has looked again at the indeterminacies and silences in the novels and at the way Forster disclaims the possibility of ever knowing the truth. Instead of interpreting this as a modernist style feature or as registering historical and political evasions, 'queer' criticism considers the possibility of coded and concealed homosexuality. The male comradeships, the sense of ideal, personal relationships, glimpsed but deferred, and the knowledge implied but unspecified, remind the reader of the conditions under which Forster wrote – of the novel in which he openly declares his desires and the impossibility of publishing it at the time. Some of the most challenging recent criticism allies Forster's open questioning of imperialist ideology and political power with a hidden questioning of the same power as it bore down on personal relationships.

Section II
Genres and Critical Approaches

8 Theatres and Playing Spaces

● ●

The Middle Ages

From the Middle Ages to the Renaissance, drama in England was predominantly religious. The Church was the 'patron' of drama, in the sense that 'holy' days or holidays were the main occasions when plays were performed. Churches were the spaces in which performances usually took place and the plays themselves were Christian in content, acting out biblical stories, the lives of the saints, and moralities. The audience was the local community, which often provided the actors as well. The plays were performed in the vernacular at a time when church services were in Latin, and they were popular with both the Church and the populace.

There is evidence that as early as the fourteenth century professional players visited churches and cathedrals to present plays. They were paid for their performances – in fact the payment record is often the only evidence we have of their existence. The players would have been members of royal and aristocratic households, employed to arrange revels for the household on special occasions like Christmas or a wedding. In Tudor times the universities, schools and lawyers at the Inns of Court revived classical Latin plays and encouraged pupils and students to perform and write their own plays in Latin. Like the household revels, these would have been private or privileged performances. Public theatre was associated with the Church and with religious festivals.

Within this strong tradition of plays performed in churches, there was one type of religious drama that always took place out of doors: the Corpus Christi or 'Mystery' play cycle, performed on Corpus Christi Day alongside religious ceremonies. The Mystery cycles were a series of individual episodes called 'pageants', telling the history of the world from its creation to the Last Judgement. The separate episodes were acted on mobile stages dragged from station (stopping-place) to station along a prescribed way through the town. The players halted their pageants at fixed sites, repeating each episode many times in the course of the day.

The routes of the processional pageants were part of the ritual of performance. On Corpus Christi Day in York the religious procession bearing the Host started at Holy Trinity Priory, visited York Minster, and ended at St Leonard's Hospital, visiting the town's three chief religious foundations. The pageants followed the same route as far as the Minster but then moved along a different route to take in the merchant and artisan areas. They ended in the market square, York's first paved open space, called the Pavement. Here the Mayor's wife and friends watched the plays (the Mayor and Council saw them earlier at the Common Hall). Performed and watched among neighbours, taking place during a church festival which was celebrated by twin processions, one religious and one pageant, in spaces that were integral to people's daily life and work, the Corpus Christi plays must have been a powerful community experience of Christian devotion and civic pride.

When Henry VIII broke from Rome in 1536, taking England into the Protestant faith, all things Catholic, including religious plays, became suspect. In 1548 celebration of the Feast of Corpus Christi was banned, removing the occasion for the Mystery cycles, and when Elizabeth I came to the throne local officials were ordered to forbid any play *wherein either matters of religion or of the governance of the estate of the commonweal shall be handled or treated.* By the 1580s York, Chester, Coventry and Wakefield had all ceased performing their Mystery cycles. But as opportunities for religious theatrical performances diminished, a new form of drama came into existence. It was public, commercial and professional.

Renaissance theatre

When they were no longer tied to church holidays and religious festivals, actors could perform on working days and charge for admission. For this to succeed they needed a protected space. Strolling players and sponsored companies performed in town halls, rooms at inns and in the halls of great houses, as well as continuing to perform in churches – often the biggest indoor space in a village or small town. Long before the Mystery cycles ceased, morality plays like *Magnificence* and *Everyman* were welcomed. Protestant leaders recognized the propaganda value of drama. Thomas Cromwell organized theatrical events in the 1530s for Henry VIII, and professional acting companies continued to enjoy the patronage of the crown and the nobility. Companies toured throughout the century; indeed, they were forced to do so whenever plague drove them from London. In the late sixteenth century they began to build or convert buildings into permanent playing spaces. The first playhouse in London of which a record survives, the Red Lion, was built in Stepney in 1567. It was an open-air amphitheatre put up as a business venture, and does not seem to have succeeded, but it was soon followed by others that did: the Theatre (1576), the Curtain (1577), the Rose (1587), the Swan (1595), the Globe (1599), and the Fortune (1600), all in London.

As well as the amphitheatres, five indoor theatres were fitted out as commercial ventures between 1575 and 1629. The 'private' playhouses were indoor theatres where the actors performed by candlelight. They charged higher prices than open-air theatres and attracted a relatively well-to-do audience. They continued in public the tradition of the private Court and great hall performances. It was the open-air playhouses like Shakespeare's Globe that were London's innovatory playing spaces. Nothing like them had been seen in England, and it is unclear where their design came from. One idea is that they were modelled on Elizabethan bull- and bear-baiting houses, but current scholarship considers this less likely than the theory that James Burbage, the theatrical impresario who built the Red Lion and the Theatre, was trying to construct a playhouse of classical Roman design. It was Burbage who named his playhouse (which was the Elizabethan word) the *Theatre*, introducing the Latin term which to this day denotes a building in which plays are performed.

The Globe was built as a wood and plaster polygon, shaped like a doughnut with an open central yard where the 'groundlings' stood, thatched galleries with bench seats and a huge stage thrusting out into the yard. It has become so familiar through its many (often inaccurate) pictorial representations that it stands as an icon for the Elizabethan theatre. Because it was the theatre where Shakespeare acted, in which he had a part share and for which he wrote his greatest plays, it has always attracted the greatest interest, culminating in a scholarly reconstruction in 1997 on the south bank of the Thames near the site where the original playhouse stood. Such attention to one playhouse tends to disguise the extent to which the Elizabethan open-air amphitheatres were short-lived, experimental spaces. They did not survive Parliament's closure of the theatres between 1642 and 1660. When drama returned to the public stage with the Restoration of the monarchy, it was the indoor, candlelit theatres that provided the model for the new theatres. Indoor theatre, artificially lit, with a fully seated audience, has continued to be the standard setting for drama to the present day.

Audiences for the open-air playhouses were large. The Globe and the Fortune each held about 3,000 people. They came from all social classes except the very highest. Plays were performed in daylight, on a stage bare of scenery except for a few properties and painted hangings across the openings in the *frons scenae* (the back wall of the stage). The actors (no actresses – the female parts were played by boys) were costumed in a variety of contemporary dress. A company's costumes were its most valuable assets, along with the 'playbooks' and 'parts', i.e. scripts of whole plays and the acting parts that showed the individual's lines and cues. Flute in *A Midsummer Night's Dream*, unaccustomed to acting, speaks all his 'part' at once, *cues and all*, as Quince complains.

The playing companies which settled in London in the last years of the sixteenth century consisted of about fifteen actors. The leading members were sharers in the company's property, the costumes and playscripts. Each company had its own playhouse, usually owned by an impresario, although at the Globe the leading actors took part shares. The playhouses were richly decorated on the inside, and the players' costumes were equally rich. It was the actors' costumes, and their custom of ending each performance with a dance or 'jig', that struck Thomas Platter, a Swiss tourist who visited London in 1599:

> *The actors are most expensively and elaborately dressed; for it is the English usage for eminent lords or knights at their decease to bequeath almost the best of their clothes to their serving-men, which it is unseemly for the latter to wear so that they offer them for sale for a small sum to the actors.*

In the absence of scenery and with few properties, costume was a vivid system for signifying identity. There were about fifteen actors in a company, and (apart from the leads) each played several roles. Costume helped to identify characters and reveal their social status – very important in a society as hierarchical as the Elizabethan one.

The companies performed daily in the afternoons, except on Sundays, offering a different play at each performance. They attracted large crowds, which gave opportunities for theft and prostitution, the possibility of fights and even riots, and the spreading of disease. They also drew apprentices and artisans away from their work. All these things troubled the civic authorities, who banned plays whenever they could, both in London and the towns that the travelling companies visited. Whenever recorded deaths from plague in London rose above thirty a week, the playhouses were automatically closed. To avoid the Lord Mayor's displeasure and escape his control, the playhouses were built on the outskirts of the city, in the suburbs to which his jurisdiction did not extend. They were positioned on or close to busy roads so that audiences could reach them on foot, or in the case of the playhouses on the south bank, by ferry. The players' real protection, however, was royal favour. Elizabeth I, James I and Charles I all enjoyed plays and those performed at Court were not specially written for the monarch but drawn from the repertory of the playing companies.

The evolution of the open-air amphitheatres coincided with an astonishing outburst of dramatic creativity. Shakespeare was one among many authors writing for the new playhouses. Each wrote for a particular company. Christopher Marlowe wrote for the Lord Admiral's Men at the Rose. Shakespeare wrote for the Lord Chamberlain's Men at the Theatre and at its later reconstruction as the Globe. Ben Jonson wrote public plays for the Globe, private plays for the company of boy actors at Blackfriars, and masques for the Court at Whitehall. Before a play could be staged it had to be licensed by the Master of the Revels, who censored any passages that he felt to be blasphemous (such as swearing, or using the name of God) or seditious (for example, any mention of killing or deposing kings was suspect). The licensed version of a play, with the Master of the Revels's signature, was a company's most valuable possession after their costumes. This became the company prompt book. From it, parts were written out for the actors. It went with the company on tour and was used to reassure civic authorities that no unlicensed material was being performed.

What effect did open-air playing spaces have on the plays performed in Elizabethan amphitheatres? Lacking the signals that scenery provides, authors had to use language to create settings. Where and at what time a scene takes place is revealed by characters' speeches as they enter. *'Tis now struck twelve. Get thee to bed, Francisco*, says Barnardo at the beginning of *Hamlet*, and we know from their words that we are seeing two soldiers on midnight watch. *What country, friends, is this?* asks Viola in *Twelfth Night*, and we learn from the Captain's reply that we are in Illyria. To read the conventions correctly required an active suspension of disbelief because playgoers attended in broad daylight. Shakespeare's plays abound in appeals to the audience to use their imagination. *Play with your fancies*, begs the Chorus in *Henry V*, *Work, work your thoughts*, and *eke out our performance with your mind*. Apologizing for the inadequate staging of the battle of Agincourt, the Chorus says *Yet sit and see / Minding true things by what their mockeries be*. In other words, the audience must create the true scene in their minds, ignoring the 'mockery' of *four or five most vile and ragged foils*, the few actors who represent the armies of France and England. The appeal to the mind, to the imagination, is through language, not vision. Plays were energized by the intensity, speed, complexity and immediacy of the spoken language.

Both public and private playhouses thrived during the early part of the seventeenth century (until drama was banned by the Puritans in 1642). Audiences began to separate along class lines, rich and poor, catered for separately by the two forms of playhouse. Increasingly the indoor playhouses, with their superior musical resources, became the up-market, desirable form of new drama, while the amphitheatres offered more old-fashioned blood-and-thunder plays. A more elaborate form of drama developed at Court: magnificently staged masques with splendid scenic effects, transformations, music and courtly dancing.

Alone of all the companies the King's Men, the one for which both Shakespeare and Jonson wrote (renamed when King James took over the patronage of the Lord Chamberlain's Men) performed both types of commercial drama, because they owned both types of playhouse, the Globe for public performances and the Blackfriars for those staged indoors. The Blackfriars did not come into their hands until 1608, and only Shakespeare's last play, *The Tempest* (1610), was written for this type of playhouse. We can see the influence of the masques at Court in his presentation of Juno and Ceres in that play.

The closure of the playhouses in 1642 was not completely effective. Occasionally and illegally, actors put on plays at various surviving theatres in London, sometimes running them for several days before the soldiers were sent in to shut them down and confiscate the costumes. But Parliament's embargo severely limited performances. One by one, the playhouses were pulled down. Actors went abroad and boy actors were no longer trained. Very few new plays were written, until in 1658 Sir William Davenant found a way round the ban on stage plays.

Davenant was an enterprising man. A playwright since the 1630s, he claimed to be Shakespeare's illegitimate son. He succeeded Ben Jonson both as Poet Laureate and as producer of masques at Court. He fought on the royalist side in the Civil War and went into exile in France with Charles's Queen in 1640. While sailing for Maryland in 1647, where the King had appointed him governor, he was captured by Cromwell's navy and imprisoned in the Tower. His release in 1654 was probably due to the efforts of John Milton. Always a man of the theatre, Davenant realized that by producing plays as musical events (rather like the masques he had organized for Charles I) he might succeed in circumventing the ban. In 1656 he wrote *The Siege of Rhodes*, a mixture of heroic drama and opera of a kind not seen before in Britain. He produced it with scenic effects at an indoor venue. As he charged admission and anyone who could pay was admitted, this was in truth the beginning of the re-emergence of public theatre.

Restoration theatre

Charles II loved the theatre. Shortly after his return to claim the throne in England he licensed two playing companies, who played in disused and converted tennis courts until new theatres could be built for them. The custom-built Restoration theatres were not like the open-air Tudor playhouses. They were small, indoor, covered spaces with horseshoe-shaped pits, surrounded by three tiers of balconies and boxes, facing a proscenium arch that divided the stage between an inner curtained-off section and a front section thrusting out into the pit. Their design recalled the private playhouses and Court theatres that Davenant knew so well, but they were also influenced by the advances in scenic staging and stage machinery which the exiles had seen abroad in France and Italy.

The curtain opened after the Prologue and remained open until after the Epilogue. It revealed an inner, scenic stage with flats painted in perspective (and sometimes built in diminishing scale to increase the illusion), leading the eye to the back of the stage, also painted in perspective. From above, there hung borders of trees or clouds or sky for an outdoor scene, or architectural decoration for an indoor scene. The stage floor had grooves along which shutters were slid to change the scenes. While one scene was playing in front, another could be set up behind. Restoration plays abound in 'discoveries', where a new scene is revealed by sliding open the shutters.

The main acting, especially in comedies, did not take place on the scenic stage but on the front stage which projected forward of the proscenium arch into the pit, as Elizabethan stages had done. On either side, and in front of the proscenium arch, a pair of doors gave entry for the actors. Restoration theatres were thus a kind of halfway house between the bare Elizabethan stage, where actors were close to their audiences, and the later eighteenth- and nineteenth-century illusionistic stages where actors were distanced inside the picture-frame of the proscenium arch.

The Elizabethan groundlings had inexpensive standing places in a yard. In Restoration theatres the pit was a fashionable, sociable space with bench seating, where gallants and their ladies could meet, mingle and converse throughout the play, perfectly able to see each other in the candle-lit interior. Both the King and his brother the Duke of York had reserved boxes (which were sold when they did not attend). Prices were four shillings for a box, two shillings and sixpence for the pit and first gallery, one shilling and sixpence for the middle gallery, and one shilling for the upper gallery, the cheapest place. Even in the upper gallery where servants went, these admission prices were relatively high. We do not know the size of the audiences. Scholars' estimates vary between 300 and 1,000, with most agreeing that it was probably not above 500 even when full. Shakespeare's Globe had held 3,000. The Restoration audience was courtly, especially under Charles II (neither William and Mary nor Anne were interested in plays) but not exclusively aristocratic. The professional middle class, both men and women, attended, many on a regular basis. According to his diary for 1668, Pepys went to the theatre 73 times between 1 January and 31 August. He often took his wife, and like many women of a similar station she was quite happy to go on her own with a servant or with female friends.

The small audience, the limited number of theatres (down to a single theatre for some years) and the high admission prices indicate that playgoing was no longer a mass, popular event. The public Restoration theatre belonged to a select and cohesive group, well-to-do, courtly, educated and middle-class.

The two major innovations of Restoration drama were the use of changeable scenery and the introduction of female actors. Neither were completely new, since women had performed in the magnificently staged masques at the Courts of James I and Charles I. Even the Queen took part on occasions. Those, however, were private events. In Restoration drama, for the first time audiences could see female actors and illusionistic scenery on a public stage.

The elaborate scenery, with its painted flats, shutters and borders and machinery had a major effect on the content and presentation of the plays. Tragedies had ornate and exotic settings, in keeping with the high artificial style of the language (often in rhymed verse). In comedies, the indoor scenes were set in realistically painted dressing rooms, parlours, coffee houses and gaming rooms. Outdoor scenes took place in painted vistas representing St James's Park, Hyde Park, the Spring Gardens, the piazza at Covent Garden or the New Exchange, and very occasionally at a country estate or in the streets of towns beyond London. No longer were comedies located imaginatively in Illyria or magical woods outside Athens. Restoration comedy reflects the familiar daily world of its audience, and besides operating as a sign of location, scenery helped to signify the play's meaning. In *The Country Wife* most scenes are set in the lodgings of either Horner or Pinchwife. The unattached, liberated, successful rake is set in opposition to the rule-bound, restrictive, physically violent, defeated, jealous, possessive husband. The similar settings emphasize what they share, with each other and with the audience. Basically they inhabit the same living space and the question is how, in this shared environment, they should behave in order to live well with each other. The actors and actresses, speaking from the forestage in prologue and epilogue, claim the right to comment on current morals and manners, bonding the play to the audience even more closely.

The introduction of actresses may have had an even greater effect on drama. In spite of the professional opportunities it offered to women, acting was not a 'respectable' job for them. Females were paid less than males and were denied the lucrative opportunity of becoming a shareholder in the company – since Tudor times, the most profitable side of acting. They were regarded as easy sexual game. Most actresses had a string of lovers and their affairs were common gossip. On 14 January 1668, Pepys records the comment of one of his wife's friends about the actress Moll Davis, whom she had seen performing the previous evening: *the most impertinent slut . . . and the more now the King doth show her countenance and is reckoned his mistress.* Elizabeth Barry, the most powerful actress of her day, was described in print as *that mercenary, Prostituted Dame.* Anne Bracegirdle, her younger rival, was renowned for her chastity (she favoured chaste, coquette roles) but the fact that this was a matter of note in itself reveals the prurient public interest in actress's affairs. The language in which she was addressed by one anonymous writer is offensively suggestive: *a haughty, conceited Woman, that has got more Money by dissembling her Lewdness, than others by professing it.* Nell Gwyn was famed more for her social rise from mistress to a leading actor through a series of affairs to mistress of the King, than for her undoubted comic skills in acting.

Sexuality was displayed on stage. Restoration tragedies featured rape or near-rape scenes, where actresses were 'discovered' with their garments torn in a revealing manner (see illustration on page 68). Disguising women as men, in the 'breeches' role, was another way to display parts of the female body, legs and hips, normally concealed beneath long dresses. Disguising a girl as a boy was not a plot novelty, but in a Shakespearian play the part was taken by a youth. Restoration drama deliberately plays on and displays the sexual attractiveness of women. Consider how much the success of any Restoration comedy arises from the knowing sexual banter of the heroine and hero, the seductions and near-seductions, and the comical flirtations of older women who fail to accept that they are no longer alluring.

The relationship of Restoration audiences to each other and to the players was a close one, and this added a frisson to performances. Actors and actresses became associated with certain role-types, and authors wrote with this in mind, sometimes slipping in real-life references. Prologues and epilogues in particular blurred the line between role and real life. Nell Gwyn was cast, unusually because she was a comic actress, as a tragic heroine in Dryden's *Tyrannick Love* (1669). Having died at the end of the play, she hopped off her bier saying *Hold, are you mad? You damn'd confounded Dog / I am to rise and speak the Epilogue*. In the epilogue she openly mocks the difference between her stage role and her known personality.

> *To tell you true, I walk because I dye*
> *Out of my Calling, in a Tragedy.*
> *O Poet, damn'd dull Poet who could prove*
> *So Senseless! To make Nelly dye for Love.*

Eighteenth-century theatre

In 1728 John Rich, manager of the Lincoln's Inn Field theatre, agreed to produce John Gay's *The Beggar's Opera*. Against all expectation it was a huge success. A fashionable joke at the time went *it made Rich gay and Gay rich*. In fact both men did well out of the play, and Rich used his profits to build Covent Garden Theatre, where he continued to produce musical drama, pantomimes and operas. When David Garrick – the most famous actor of the mid-eighteenth century – became manager of the rival Drury Lane Theatre in 1747, he deliberately chose to stage mainstream drama in contrast to the fare offered by Rich. In keeping with 'reformed' eighteenth-century taste, Garrick altered and re-wrote many of the older plays. *There seems indeed an absolute Necessity for reforming many Plays of our most eminent Writers*, he wrote, *For no kind of Wit ought to be received as an Excuse for Immorality*.

Prime Minister Walpole was annoyed by the political satire in *The Beggar's Opera*, and brought in a Licensing Act in 1737, re-activating the censorship powers of the Lord Chamberlain. Anything considered obscene or politically dangerous could not be performed on stage. Not until the mid-twentieth century would playwrights regain the freedom of expression enjoyed in the Restoration period – the Act stood until 1968. Although primarily aimed at controlling political satire, the Act helped to turn the 'taste of the Town' against anything that offended middle-class morality. Increasingly, theatre depended on scenic effects rather than wit and language to attract its audience. Garrick banished spectators from the fore-stage and commissioned a leading artist of the sublime, Philip de Loutherbourg, to take control of scenic design, including lighting. Loutherbourg's salary was twice that of the leading actors, a clear indication of the growing importance of scenic illusion. During the late eighteenth century the stage area retreated behind the proscenium arch (see the illustrations on the next page) and realistic, illusionary settings became fashionable.

Theatre Royal, Haymarket in 1821. There is a forestage, proscenium doors and boxes above them

Theatre Royal, Haymarket in 1880. Forestage and proscenium doors have been removed, and the proscenium arch frames stage 'pictures'

Nineteenth-century theatre

Like many other advances in the nineteenth century, theatrical innovation was driven by engineering and scientific discoveries. Nineteenth-century stages moved out of the flickering shadows as gas and electricity replaced the candles and oil lamps of the eighteenth century. New flexibility in stage lighting and machinery combined with the nineteenth-century love of realism to produce settings of extraordinary elaborateness. The acting area was now behind the proscenium, like a painting inside a frame. Stages increased in size to accommodate in-depth illusions of grandiose scenes. Long grooves were opened in the floors and tall towers built overhead to allow scenery to be raised up or flown in. Sea and river scenes were acted in large, shallow containers and the effect of stage lighting on expanses of water was admired. Expensive sets could be built because the earlier system of repertory companies performing a new play every few days changed to a system of actor-managers organizing and starring in long-running productions. When Irving took on the management of the Lyceum, he is reputed to have employed over eighty carpenters, fifty property men and thirty gasmen.

The nineteenth-century theatre of scenery and music, of spectacle and sensationalism, drew large audiences from all social classes. New forms of drama became popular: music hall, circuses and melodrama, the latter

A set for Charles Kean's production of The Merchant of Venice, *1858, showing the exterior of Shylock's house (painting by W. Telbin)*

Charles Kean's 1858 production of The Merchant of Venice: *actors could stand on the bridges and float in gondolas on the canals*

utilizing to the full the theatre's spine-chilling and nerve-tingling scenic effects. Shakespeare's plays were performed with lavish scenery. *A Midsummer Night's Dream* acquired seascape, background music and forest scenes filled with gnarled, leafy trees and banks of real flowers, tapping into the Victorian fascination with fairyland. Silent episodes were added which depended upon mime, setting and lighting to make their point. Major productions of the history plays ran to casts of over a hundred in the crowd scenes, and sets showing embattled castles and towering city walls hung with rich tapestries and banners. The showy costuming and 'story-book' scenery were historically inaccurate, although they encouraged an interest in historical accuracy. The deeper reality that these settings were reflecting and reinforcing was the Victorians' image of themselves as an imperial, world power.

Modern theatre

Early twentieth-century plays influenced by Henrik Ibsen and Anton Chekhov became less sensationalist and more naturalistic, but realistic sets remained in fashion. The proscenium arch was like the non-existent, fourth wall of a meticulously re-created interior. Seated in a dark auditorium, audiences seemed to be in the privileged position of having a secret view into dramas played out in private spaces. Avant-garde theatre, however,

Act II Scene 1 from Herbert Beerbohm Tree's production of Shakespeare's
Henry VIII, *1912*

turned away from realism and illusionism to experiment with stripping the
stage almost bare, relying on a few symbolic structures and mood-enhancing
lighting to create the setting. We can see this in the work of Gordon Craig,
who argued that theatre was an art, an abstraction disengaged from reality.
His innovatory designs used a synthesis of lighting and forms which hinted
at architecture (see the illustration on the next page). In Germany in the
1920s and 1930s, Bertolt Brecht was working with anti-illusionist designers
who produced expressionist, minimalist sets. A few curtains, sometimes
with words scrawled across them, a bare stage, text or images projected onto
a screen – these were the basic elements of his theatre. From his experiences
of working in an aggressively anti-illusionistic mode, he developed a theory
of alienation, the idea that audiences should never be permitted to forget that
they are watching, not life, but an act in a theatre.

Today, theatre performance is eclectic. Sophisticated lighting and
engineering, aided by computerization, can produce almost any illusion. At
the same time, film and television challenge theatrical illusion by their
greater power of reproducing the appearance of reality. The changes in
production styles over the past century have not had the effect of excluding
or cancelling each other out, and currently anything goes in theatre design.
We are still able to watch plays in the realistic and naturalistic settings that
were popular at the start of the century. Settings can be symbolic and moody,
elaborate and artificial, sparse and bare, decorative and stylish. Costuming
can be historically accurate, wildly fantastic, simple 'uncostumed' jeans and

E. Gordon Craig's set design for Hamlet, *1908*

T-shirts, or a mixture of periods and styles. These choices tend to depend on the space in which the play is performed, the audience at which it is directed, and the company for which it is designed.

There are questions you should consider about any modern production. Was the text written for stage, for radio, for film or for television? Was it performed by one of our major national companies with all the resources modern theatre can provide, or by a small touring group in a school or community hall, with the minimum of scenery and no artificial lighting? Or was it out of doors at the re-created Globe on the south bank of the Thames, where the audience is in full view and provides part of the entertainment? What kind of audience did it play to – the small numbers who attend live theatre in London, Stratford and the regional cities, or the huge international audience who watch film?

Economics have dictated that contemporary stage plays tend to use tiny casts while films can involve casts of thousands. The super-realism of film and television has encouraged meta-theatrical devices on stage, which deliberately draw attention to stage drama's unreality and 'staginess': for example, the direct address to the audience by Tom at the opening of Tennessee Williams's *The Glass Menagerie*, or the joint presence on stage of characters from 1809 and the present day in scene 7 of Tom Stoppard's *Arcadia*. The text of any play is affected by the theatrical conditions for which it was originally written and by the way it is produced in later realizations when theatrical conditions may have changed radically. Jonathan Miller has called this the 'afterlife' of a play, paying tribute to theatre's power to create new interpretations of classic plays through new modes of presentation.

9 Approaches to Drama: Shakespeare

• •

In the critical study of literature, we always need to remember that there is more than one way of interpreting a text. Texts are not stable entities. Directors of Shakespeare's plays will cut and alter lines to suit their productions. Actors will play the parts in radically different ways. Members of the audience have their own personal responses. And differing critical approaches produce alternative readings of texts.

This Unit describes ways in which you could start to look at a text from different viewpoints. There are many different critical theories. Some of the more significant ones are outlined here and given a very brief explanation, to show you how approaching a text from a theoretical or formal standpoint can open out meanings that might not otherwise have occurred to you. If you become interested in these approaches and wish to pursue critical theories more fully, you will find they are sophisticated and extensive. On even a simple level, however, applying the following ideas to any single text may suggest many alternative readings, including ones with which you may not agree.

Plot

The terms **story** and **plot** are both used to describe the way an author arranges a chronological series of events in a text, be it a narrative poem, novel, short story, play or even a factual account. 'Story' refers to the events as they unfold, logically and with a causal relationship, while 'plot' is used to describe the way in which the events are narrated, and this may include disrupting the time sequence, giving prominence to some episodes at the expense of others, and presenting the events from a limited or biased point of view. (Confusingly, some critics reverse the terms – but this is how they will be used in this book.) One story can provide many possible plots, depending on how the events are presented. The story of Shakespeare's *Antony and Cleopatra*, for instance, could provide the basis of plays on 'The Tragedy of Octavia' or 'The Triumph of Octavius', if an author chose to select different events and make Octavia or Octavius the hero.

Plots are not normally told in a straightforward manner, not even the simplest of children's tales. Think how repetition in *The Three Little Pigs* lengthens the episodes where the pigs' houses are blown down, while years pass in an instant after the Sleeping Beauty falls asleep. Some episodes will be lingered over, some will be ignored or rushed through, and some will be concealed from the reader in order to create a mystery. Many episodes will be left out entirely, because an author selects from all possible events the ones he or she will use in the text.

The chronological sequence of events may be radically altered, with the plot starting in the middle, or even at the end, and moving backwards and forwards across the timespan of the text. Novels often play around with the time sequence, while Shakespeare's plays tend to narrate their plots chronologically, one event in time following another.

Multiple stories may be told. The term **sub-plot** describes additional stories the author includes but wishes to keep as secondary to the main story. By structuring the way in which events unfold, the author focuses and controls our attention. Structure is a powerful device in the overall effect of a text.

Structuralism and formalism

Structuralism is a complex theory grounded in the belief that human societies function within systems, structures or codes (for example, language systems) and that in any system the parts derive meaning from their relationship to and difference from other parts in the structure. In this section we will consider only one aspect of the theory, the aspect that relates to literary genres. It has links with **formalism**, a literary approach that developed in Russia in the early part of the twentieth century. This approach assumes that there is a limited number of literary structures and plots, which experienced readers learn to recognize. Understanding the rules that govern structures provides us with expectations which the text fulfils or fails to fulfil, since one of the qualities of literature is its power to refuse to conform to our expectations, to 'deform' the literary structure. We expect a fairy story beginning 'Once upon a time' to end with 'and they lived happily ever after', and we are pleased with the familiar conclusion, but equally we can be surprised and delighted by an unexpected twist in the tale. We recognize from the start of a Shakespearian play that we are in the world of comedy or tragedy, and our expectations of how the play will end (in marriage or in death) influence the way we respond to the various parts.

Shakespearian comedy is romantic, in contrast to the satirical comedy of a writer like Jonson. In satirical comedy, people make fools of themselves and love is unimportant, while romantic comedy is centrally about love and ends in marriage. In Shakespeare, young people fall in love at first sight, with a passion that brooks no interference from parents or state. The lovers' path is not initially smooth. Shakespearian comedy commences in loss, disruption and despair, but ends in reconciliation and harmony, usually represented by marriage. The harmony is wider than the private world of lovers, for Shakespeare sets them in a social world where all are gathered into unity by the successful resolution of difficulties. In his early comedies the harmony of society is complete. In later comedies some characters cannot be included in the reconciliation, like Malvolio in *Twelfth Night* and Antonio in *The Tempest*.

In a comedy, the initial, unhappy situation of the heroine or hero (Orsino, Viola, Katherine, Hermia, Rosalind) does not upset us because we recognize that the structure of the play will bring about a happy resolution. How do Benedict and Beatrice fit this theory? They appear content with their situation at the start of the play. The disruption to their settled state is caused by interfering, well-meaning friends and it is none of their own making. The expected resolution, however, suggests that their apparent contentment and expressed dislike of each other may have been a self-denying refusal to admit the true state of their dissatisfaction with bachelor life. Ask yourself: if we believed they disliked each other as much as they claim to, would we go along with the comedy plot as light-heartedly as we do? Is not our enjoyment of their bewilderment and growing affection based on our privileged position, of understanding them better than they do themselves? Our recognition that the structure of the play requires them to be brought together, rather than any psychological insight into their characters, gives us this privileged understanding.

Aristotle defined tragedy as the fall of a great man who, through a tragic flaw in his noble nature, was the ultimate cause of his own downfall and death. All tragedies end with the death of the hero. Revenge tragedies, in which the innocent hero is set the task of committing murder in revenge for an act perpetrated by others, end with the death of most of the cast. In many ways Aristotle's theory fits Shakespearian tragedy. Othello is a noble Moor betrayed by the tragic flaw of jealousy. Hamlet is a morally delicate, intelligent, promising prince betrayed by indecision, by *thinking too precisely on th'event*. Antony is a world leader betrayed by passion. But it seems an insufficient explanation of the power with which Shakespeare involves nature in his hero's fall. With the death of Hamlet or Macbeth or Lear, we feel a cosmic presence, and that the world of the play is shaken by the loss.

That the outcome will be fatal is apparent early in the plays. In the opening scenes, the ghost of Hamlet's father, the witches in *Macbeth* and the relay of messengers to Antony from Rome all point the tragic way the hero will go, while Lear's folly in dividing the kingdom and his brutality in casting out Cordelia immediately suggest an impending catastrophe. Comments by trustworthy lookers-on, such as Horatio, Banquo, Philo and Kent, confirm the audience's understanding of the hero's initial decision, and experience of the structure of tragedy tells us this will be fatal. Unusually, Othello makes no early act towards his tragic end, but Iago is on stage from the start, letting us know the evil he intends.

Some plays have structures that do not fit so readily into the genres of comedy and tragedy. *The Winter's Tale* starts in tragic mode, and keeps this until Perdita is discovered by the shepherds, at which point the play swings into comic mode. You might like to consider what structural indications there are in the first half of the play that it is heading towards a tragic conclusion, and how we recognize, in the second half, that we have moved into the world of comedy. In fact, the structure opposes the two genres, as winter is opposed to spring, and the movement towards rebirth, regeneration and renewal which drives the play depends upon the structural opposition of life and death so apparent in the action and in the language. It is always interesting to see where directors place the interval that marks a change in mood and style. It must come near the end of Act III and the beginning of Act IV, but directors have chosen to break the play before the scene in which Antigonus abandons the baby, at the entrance of the bear, and after the discovery by the shepherds, before Rumour arrives. Where do you think the structural hinge is best located, and what is there in the language to indicate the transition from one genre to another?

Measure for Measure is another play that does not fit easily into the genre of comedy or tragedy. Its structure is a journey of discovery, which spirals downwards to the depths before ascending again. Accompanying the Duke, we traverse society from palace to prison. Individuals discover that they are capable of committing shameful acts. The spiral begins to reverse in Act IV when the Duke says *Look th'unfolding star calls up the shepherd*, but does the play end with our expectations fulfilled? This may depend upon how the play closes in performance. A director can choose to close with a mime in which Isabella either accepts or rejects the idea of marriage, but if we are left with an uneasy sense that all is not resolved, then we are responding to a structure which set up certain expectations and chose not to satisfy them completely.

Character

The most powerful pull of character is towards realism. In both drama and the novel, most interpretations discuss character as though the words on the page relate to living human beings. The author's skill in creating character is judged in great part by the degree to which we are given the illusion that we are meeting real people and learning to know them in greater depth than is possible in reality.

In drama, the possibilities for character interpretation are extended by the numerous ways in which actors can realize a part. In *Antony and Cleopatra*, for example, Cleopatra can be played as younger than Antony or similarly aged. She can be treacherous, vain, fickle and foolish. She can be alluring, seductive, gracious and noble. She can be presented as attractively skittish or as an irritating, provocative tease. Evidence for any interpretation needs to be based in the text, but in a play much of the evidence is provided by the opinions of other characters, and a complex character like Cleopatra evokes differing responses. What does Enobarbus really think of her? Does Octavius change his opinion in the course of the play?

Nineteenth- and early twentieth-century criticism was predominantly character based, treating Shakespearian stage characters as though they were real people, analysing them psychologically and giving them previous

Mark Rylance as Cleopatra in an all-male production of Antony and Cleopatra *at Shakespeare's Globe Theatre in 1999*

histories and subsequent fates. Character analysis remains a fascinating and fruitful way of studying a text so long as you remember that these are literary artefacts and not real people, and that their characteristics may conform to traditional **types**. From medieval morality plays, English drama inherited the concept of characters representing a moral quality, like Mercy or Faith or Everyman. Falstaff, in *Henry IV Parts 1* and *2*, develops from the medieval Vice or Riot figure – the jovial, robust enjoyer of life who leeches on others and leads them into sin. The Duke in *Measure for Measure* has a character so mysterious that it is difficult to reconcile his actions into a satisfying unity. Critics have suggested that he stands for the quality of justice, as Perdita in *The Winter's Tale* can be interpreted as the symbolic embodiment of spring.

Language

All texts are realized in language. And language, through rhythm and rhyme, through vocabulary and syntax, through imagery and symbolism, has power to create meaning. On the bare Elizabethan stage it was language which created the illusion of the settings for the plays. *Antony and Cleopatra* moves constantly between Rome and Egypt, and only through language do we know where the scene is set. In the words associated with each domain, an opposition is presented, so that we perceive Rome as rational, legalistic and orderly, but also cold and ruthless, while Egypt is mysterious, irrational and disorderly but also warm, seductive and beautiful.

Character is established by language, both by giving characters an **ideolect**, or individual style of speaking, and by creating an aura around them. Falstaff's inventiveness, Iago's cynicism and Hamlet's soliloquies could not be mistaken for the speech of any other character. Othello's imagery, drawing on the sea and exotic lands, helps to establish him as an *extravagant and wheeling stranger*.

Metaphorical language casts an atmosphere across a whole text. The two opposing worlds of *The Winter's Tale* are imaged in language that repeatedly refers to winter and spring, while the restoration of Hermione gains a sense of wonder from language associating it with magic and spells. In *Hamlet*, images of death and disease reiterate the idea that *something is rotten in the state of Denmark*, and the theme of act, action and acting, both in the sense of doing a deed and playing a role, runs right through the play. In *King Lear* words cluster around two ideas of nature – the animal nature and the moral nature of human beings – while language associated with clothing, disguise and nakedness reflects Lear's growing appreciation of human need. Language clusters express themes, and imagery can provide another way of organizing the text.

Feminist criticism

Feminist critics have taught us to look at texts from the woman's point of view. Most early texts were written by men. It was not until the nineteenth and twentieth centuries that women writers began to emerge in significant numbers. Feminist critics have done much to re-discover women writers from earlier centuries and made us aware that women have always been writing even if, at times, their writing dropped out of the literary canon.

Another area that feminist critics have explored has been the question of language. Feminists argue that in patriarchal societies women are subordinated by language oppositions (female/male, active/passive, rational/emotional, adventurous/timid) which place them in a secondary, negative category. They have asked whether women naturally write in a different style from that of men and whether they feel constrained expressing their perceptions and interests in male-dominated language and literary forms. The novel, which partly developed from letter and diary forms of writing, has been claimed as a literary form particularly suited to women.

Feminism has isolated three areas in which sexual differences may be perceived. There are biological differences, and all the constraints on women of the lack of safe birth control until the mid-twentieth century. There are political differences, with the exclusion of women from political power until the twentieth century. Lastly there are cultural differences, and the possibility that girls are brought up with different aspirations from boys.

Feminist criticism looks carefully at how female characters are portrayed in literature. What is their social position in the world created by the text? What kinds of lives can they lead compared to those on offer to men? What power do they have, what goals do they strive for, and what does this do to their relationships with the male characters? What image of womanhood do they project, and is it one that women would accept for themselves today?

In *Henry V*, Princess Katherine is a pawn in a diplomatic game, demanded in marriage by Henry to make his conquest of France more secure. She is utterly biddable. *Dat is as it shall please de roi mon pere* is her answer to Henry's proposal. Modern productions often soften the chauvinism of Act V by playing it for laughs, with Henry moving from bashful nervousness to signs of real affection, but they rarely show an equal interest in how Katherine feels. *The Merchant of Venice*, *Twelfth Night* and *King Lear* all have female characters of considerable power, authority and spirit. Portia and Olivia run their own households, and Cordelia commands an army. But all suffer a loss of independence as the plays end.

In *The Taming of the Shrew* we have a heroine who is out of control. The wild, unruly Katherine is forced into marriage by her father and tamed into submission by a husband who holds all the power. If her final speech is sincere, it reinforces the cultural model of the submissive wife. If, however, we approach the play from Katherine's point of view, can we be sure that she submits willingly? Her final speech may be ironic as she learns how to tame a wild, unruly husband. It is also interesting to think about the reasons for her shrewishness and whether she is happier under her father's domination or her husband's. Even more enigmatic is the heroine in *Measure for Measure*. Shakespeare gives her no lines to speak in answer to the Duke's proposal of marriage. If the play is given a resolution in which harmony is restored, Isabella will accept. If you look at the play from a feminist point of view, however, what choice do you think she will make?

Marxist criticism

To be a Marxist critic does not imply holding left-wing views or a political commitment to the ideas of Marx and Engels, but it does involve looking at texts in a way that is based on their economic theories. Marx argued that humans are first and foremost economic beings and that the **base** of any society is the manner in which it organizes its modes of production – its economy. All the other social institutions, like government, law, religion and education, are the **superstructure** of society and reflect and sustain the economic power base. Culture belongs in the superstructure because Marx felt it was actively implicated in supporting the **dominant ideology**. By 'dominant ideology' he meant the set of beliefs that the majority of society subscribe to, uncritically and often unconsciously, and a network of practices and institutions that work to make the social order acceptable. The dominant ideology serves to keep the ruling group in power and encourages those who do not possess power to remain willingly disempowered. Marxist critics try to show how literature organizes the individual consciousness of the reader into an acceptance of the dominant ideology.

At its simplest, Marxist criticism has drawn attention to the ways in which texts can reflect the imbalance of power between economic classes in a society. But Marxist criticism goes further, beyond the idea that literature is a reflection of reality, to argue that texts themselves are implicit in creating the illusions that constitute the prevailing ideology.

To look at Marxist criticism in practice, let us consider *Henry V*, a play normally performed in a way that idealizes Henry as a warrior king. His rousing speech before Agincourt offers universal brotherhood to all who will fight with him, *be he ne'er so vile*. The night before the battle, the ordinary soldiers are apprehensive and frightened. They believe, as the King's subjects, that they have no option but to follow him (*to disobey were against all proportion of subjection*, IV.1.132–3) in a war whose justness they cannot measure. Henry's response calms and enthuses Williams, but does it answer his case that *few die well who die in a battle*?

Henry himself is sufficiently disturbed by Williams's accusations to move immediately into an anguished soliloquy in which he contrasts the burdens of kingship with the carefree life of the *wretched slave*. Emotionally, the play re-directs our sympathy away from Bates and Williams and back to Henry, but are we being swayed by language? The soliloquy subtly displaces kingship onto the empty trappings of ceremony, addressed as a separate, personified 'thou' by Henry, who claims to be *but a man*. Should we accept Henry's assertion that a wretch sleeps soundly and *Never sees horrid night*? We have just witnessed the sleeplessness of the frightened soldiers.

And does Henry live up to his promises of brotherhood? When Williams keeps his word and challenges the glove worn by Fluellen, unaware that it was a gift from Henry, he has to plead for his life when Henry reveals the truth. His plea is eloquent and just, Henry's response apparently generous and gracious, and Fluellen's twelve-penny joke ends the scene in good humour. But for all the familiar language, the distance between king and subject is strongly re-established. The power of life and death lies with the King, and for a moment Williams is allowed to believe that Henry might use it, although these are the men he called *brothers, friends and countrymen* (IV.1.34) before the battle. Reading 'against the grain' of the text, in a famous Marxist phrase, we can discover a different Henry, self-pitying, self-seeking, pragmatic, conniving, ruthless, and a clever orator when he needs to persuade men to follow him. His determined will to win and rule is evidenced in the execution of Cambridge, Scroope and Grey, the hanging of Bardolph and the killing of the French prisoners. In order to make Henry uniformly heroic, Laurence Olivier cut the second of these incidents from his film and reversed the sequence of events in the third so that the order to kill the prisoners followed the murder of the baggage boys, giving Henry an excuse that Shakespeare's text does not allow him.

Although it is possible to justify a harsh political interpretation of Henry, this is not the effect of watching a performance. Marxist criticism argues that this is precisely the point. The text does not conceal his less attractive qualities but, through literary strategies, it impels us to accept them as part of an idealized portrayal. The text reinforces a willing acceptance by the characters in the play and the audience of the dominant ideology of Tudor times, which was a belief in the absolute authority of the monarchy.

New historicism

One of the newer approaches of the 1980s and 1990s, new historicism shares with Marxism a belief that power is ideological, but it is interested in the way this is formed by language. Dominance in society is partly a matter of possessing absolute power, but it is also a matter of being perceived as having moral or intellectual leadership. New historicism believes that in liberal, peaceful societies government is sustained by texts more than by guns, and control is exerted in the family, school and media through language. New historicism relates texts to their historical context, and investigates how texts serve to subvert, contain and assimilate those areas that challenge or question the structures of society.

Culture influences the way people view their society, and the production of any piece of culture involves more than a creating artist. Its outcome is influenced by the occasion of its creation, the audience for which it was designed and the genre form the artist selected. In studying the literature of the past, new historicists argue that we are inevitably brought into contact with these influences, whether we recognize them or not. If we consider the political and social struggles, and the anxieties of the period in which texts were created, we can see that literature registers the values and concerns of its society. The approach of new historicism has been particularly influential in recent Shakespeare studies.

How would this theory affect a reading of *Henry IV Part 2*? New historicism begins not with the text, but with the concerns of its historical period. The context of Shakespeare's history plays includes the anxieties of the Tudor regime about the transfer of political power. The Tudor Henry VII won the throne in battle from Richard III, and the Tudors were anxious to secure and legitimize their dynasty. With the country destabilized by the religious upheavals of the Reformation and under threat of a foreign invasion, they were fearful of rebellion. Shakespeare's history cycles, argue new historicists, do more than reflect a Tudor obsession with legitimacy and rebellion. They are implicit in the ruling power's use of texts to bolster their image.

Henry IV Part 2 is the hinge of the Lancastrian history cycle. Power passes from a guilt-ridden Henry IV to Henry V, his son who acquires the throne *with better quiet / Better opinion, better confirmation; / For all the soil of my achievement goes / With me into the earth* (IV.3.315–8). The play opens with the efficient, capable Prince John firmly crushing rebellion. Why does Henry

IV, so worried by Prince Hal's fecklessness, never think of giving the throne to John, his younger son? Because the play supports and endorses legitimate rule. With his dying words, Henry IV stresses the legitimate transfer of power: *What in me was purchased / Falls upon thee in a more fairer sort. / So thou the garland wear'st successively* (IV.3.327–9).

Prince Hal must reform if hereditary rule is to be seen as ideal. An alternative, charismatic leadership which could stir rebellion is exemplified by the heroic daring of Hotspur, who is doomed to fail in *Henry IV Part 1* because rebellion cannot be seen to be successful. In *Henry IV Part 2*, justice is represented by the Lord Chief Justice. It is above rank and privilege (he arrests Prince Hal) but not above the King. Falstaff is renounced, along with his attractive, ludic, subversive ways, so that Henry V can appear the image of justice and fair, legitimate rule.

In an influential essay, 'Invisible Bullets' (1988), the new historicist Stephen Greenblatt argued that Shakespeare's history cycle voiced subversive ideas not to undermine Tudor propaganda but to support to it by assimilating and containing oppositional views. Of *Henry IV Part 2*, he writes,

> *actions that should have the effect of radically undermining authority turn out to be the props of that authority. In this play even more cruelly than in* 1 *Henry IV, moral values – justice, order, civility – are secured through the apparent generation of the subversive contraries. Out of the squalid betrayals that preserve the stage emerges the 'formal majesty' into which Hal at the close, through a final definitive betrayal – the rejection of Falstaff – merges himself.*

10 Approaches to Prose: *Wuthering Heights*

The novel is a late developer among literary genres since it requires literate readers; poetry and drama could be enjoyed by an illiterate population. The emergence of the novel in the late eighteenth century accompanied the spread of education, and its popularity in the nineteenth century owes much to the development of cheap printing. Plots were long – novels were usually 'three-deckers' (three volumes) or serialized in monthly magazines – and were concerned with realistic depictions of the humble particulars of 'ordinary' people's lives.

The dominant style of nineteenth-century fiction was **realism** (sometimes called **classic bourgeois realism** or **concrete realism**). Realist writing attempts to replicate in words the external appearance of the physical world. We learn about characters and settings through concretely observed details. In realist fiction, time is causal – the past informs the present. Although the links are sometimes concealed until late in the plot, events are seen to inter-relate in a chain of cause and effect. Narrative time and the linked causality of events persuade the reader to agree with the moral rightness of a **closed** ending – closed in the sense that the text imposes a single point of view on the reader, in contrast to **open** endings, which offer the reader the possibility of different interpretations.

Who tells the story, and from what point of view? This question is of prime importance in the novel, where the story can be told by an **omniscient narrator** who stands outside the narrative, God-like in his or her knowledge of all that is going on in the minds of the created characters. We have faith in the omniscient author, and we trust the words on the page. But the narrator may be a character within the story. In an autobiographical novel like *Jane Eyre*, we see everything from the single **first-person** viewpoint of the main character, so we have to take possible bias into account. How well do the autobiographical heroes and heroines know themselves? How much of the truth are they willing to disclose?

A novel can also be a composite of many voices, each telling the story from his or her own limited viewpoint, and not necessarily reliably. How well do characters within a novel know each other? In the case of an **unreliable narrator**, we have to be on our guard against a limited viewpoint which may all too easily mislead us. Detective fiction relies upon this narrative device, because the murderer rarely tells the truth.

Within the late eighteenth- and nineteenth-century novel genre there were sub-genres: **detective** stories, like Arthur Conan Doyle's *Sherlock Holmes* stories; **ghost** stories; **science fiction** like Jules Verne's *Twenty-Thousand Leagues under the Sea*; **historical novels** like Walter Scott's *Ivanhoe*; and **gothic novels**, like Horace Walpole's *The Castle of Otranto*. You can probably think of contemporary examples of all these sub-genres except the last. Gothic novels were romantic stories set in remote, haunted castles where the isolated heroine was at the mercy of a dangerously attractive hero-villain, usually a nobleman with a secret past. Their style was florid and extravagant, easy to parody as Jane Austen showed in *Northanger Abbey*. Gothic novels like those of the late eighteenth century have not survived as a genre, although elements of the gothic style have carried over into modern horror stories and films.

Modernism describes works which, at the beginning of the twentieth century, rejected the realism of nineteenth-century fiction and art and sought for ways of expressing the 'reality' of the world as it was experienced in the minds of human beings. The influence of Sigmund Freud and the development of psychoanalysis affected writers and artists' ways of looking at the world. The modernist novel is less concerned with describing the external, concrete world than in showing how this is perceived in the consciousness of the main characters. This led to new styles of writing, such as **interior monologue** and **stream of consciousness**, which attempted to replicate the mental processes by which we assimilate our sense impressions.

Interest in mental processes also changed the ways in which artistic objects were themselves viewed. Instead of writing and painting being regarded as mirroring 'reality', as creating a parallel world that bore a faithful resemblance to the 'real' one, they were seen as artefacts, things made of words and paint. Modernist writing is self-conscious, and it draws attention to its own literariness. It 'deforms' style, to remind the reader of the artificiality and artistry of its creation. This does not mean that a modernist novel is any less 'real' than a realist novel. In its avoidance of closed endings, its loosening of plot, its interest in revealing moments or **epiphanies** in characters' lives, a modernist novel can get closer to the way people experience life as an unstructured flow rather than an organized, pre-determined pattern, with a clear beginning and a morally defining end.

The turning away from realism as a literary style to focus on the creative artistry of texts increased in the later part of the twentieth century. Writers began to play with the novel form, upsetting earlier assumptions that readers should be directed on the way to approach a text and shown how far they could trust the meanings they read in the words on the page. Novels teased readers with increasingly sophisticated deformations of viewpoint, character and plot. Fantastic and fairy-tale elements entered, and a new sub-genre called **magic realism** appeared.

The geographical spread of writing in English is acknowledged in terms like 'American literature' or 'New Zealand literature', but the term **postcolonial**

novel is usually applied to writing from ex-colonial countries of the third world that had to struggle for their independence. Signs of a country's cultural and political history are a feature of this genre.

Wuthering Heights

As an illustration of a way of studying a novel, this Unit will use the approaches outlined below to look at different ways of interpreting Emily Brontë's *Wuthering Heights*. None of the approaches stands alone. One approach will merge into another, and concentrating upon a single approach may falsify your overall impression of a novel. Nor are all approaches equally applicable to any particular text. For example, **new historicism** has been influential in the re-interpretation of Elizabethan literature, but less helpful in the literature of other periods. Studying formal qualities in isolation, however, may help you to understand how a novel achieves its effects.

The opening pages of a novel introduce us to its tone and genre, and these formal features set up resonances and expectations in an experienced reader. What genre and tone are presented at the start of *Wuthering Heights*? A Victorian reader might have mistaken the opening for that of a gothic novel. There is a remote setting, the hint of an attractive, threatening, secretive hero-villain (*erect and handsome* yet *morose* and *exaggeratedly reserved*), a haunted house and extravagances of style (*the atmospheric tumult to which its station is exposed; inspecting the penetralium*). Yet the external physical description of setting and character indicate a novel in the realist style. The ambiguity of tone and genre is part of a general unsettling of expectation at the start. *Wuthering Heights* is not a novel that invites clarity of response from the reader – rather, the opposite.

Plot

The plot of *Wuthering Heights* alters the chronology of events. Although we cannot be aware of it on our first reading, the novel begins near the end of the story. It is not until Chapter 30 that the reader can fully understand the complex situation into which the narrator Lockwood walks on his first visit. In the main, the story is told in retrospect by Ellen Dean. The older generation of the Earnshaws and Lintons, Edgar and the first Catherine (whom I will refer to hereafter as Cathy) have died before the novel begins, and we learn their histories from Nelly as she relates the story to Lockwood. The little we do not see through her eyes comes to us from the viewpoint of Lockwood, with a few episodes related by Isabella and Zillah.

Our initial impression of Wuthering Heights and Thrushcross Grange derives from the period when the Grange was uninhabited, apart from Nelly, and the Heights inhabited by an elderly Joseph, a morose Heathcliff, an uncared-for Hareton, and a depressed, withdrawn Catherine. The picture is at odds with happier times in the two houses, but we will not learn about those times until later. Moreover, we see through Lockwood's eyes, and he is quickly signalled to be an **unreliable narrator**. If we miss the first clues to his self-deceiving, sexually timid personality in the account of his panic flight from the young lady with whom he flirted at the sea-coast, his series of blunders over relationships at the Heights must alert us to his unreliability as a witness. Lockwood obviously gets things wrong. We have no other way into the text except through his eyes, and, interestingly, we never doubt the accuracy of his realist descriptions, but we would be naïve to trust his interpretation of what he sees.

Through Lockwood's eyes, we have a vivid picture of the wildness of the storm that forced him to spend the night at the Heights, and of the blanked-out moors the following day. But natural, realist description operates throughout the novel in a metaphoric way. The loss of the lime-daubed markers which define the safe path across the moors is another indication to the alert reader that Lockwood will not find the right way into the story, and that we should not trust him as a guide. His inhospitable reception, his bewilderment over Cathy's alternative names, his horrified repulsion of the ghost and Heathcliff's strange behaviour all create an atmosphere of anguish and violence at the Heights, of things effaced, crossed out, left unexplained. We are forced to suspend our certainty that the world of the novel is knowable or judgeable.

Another effect of the plot's alterations to the chronology of events is to delay the account of Heathcliff opening Cathy's coffin. As early as Chapter 17 we learn of Heathcliff's behaviour on his return to Wuthering Heights on the evening of Cathy's funeral, but it is not until Chapter 29 that we understand why he is driven frantic when Isabella and Hindley try to prevent him from entering the house. In the first account, provoked though he is to violence, his reactions fit Cathy's description of a *fierce, pitiless, wolfish man*. The second account of the same event, told to Nelly from his point of view, reveals the limitations of Isabella's understanding and invites us to reassess the incident, even to sympathize with Heathcliff. As so often in the novel, our judgement is unsettled by the way in which the plot presents the events of the story.

Structure

Is *Wuthering Heights* a love story? The question might be better rephrased: is *Wuthering Heights* only a love story? But when we consider the structure of the novel, problems arise even with the first question. Whose love story is it? Cathy and Heathcliff? Catherine and Hareton? The novel invites comparison between the love of the elder pair and the younger. If we read the novel as the story of the first couple, Cathy's death becomes the structural climax of a plot which contrasts wild, eternal passion with gentler, domesticated love. Wuthering Heights is rightly left to the ghosts of the more intense love, while Catherine and Hareton retreat to the safer, subsidiary Thrushcross Grange. If we read the novel as the story of the second couple, Catherine and Hareton reconcile in a fulfilling union the fractures and failings of the destructive passion of their elders. In either interpretation, we note that it is love that structures the plot.

In the 1920s, C. P. Sanger researched the nineteenth-century laws on property and inheritance before the Married Women's Rights and Properties Act was passed in 1870, and he drew attention to Heathcliff's devious methods of acquiring legal ownership of both houses. He demonstrated that Emily Brontë was meticulous in plotting the timescale and legal niceties of the novel, which suggested that the structure was based not on love but on revenge. Heathcliff, overhearing Cathy's remark that it would degrade her to marry him, believes he has lost her. He runs away and does not return until he has acquired the education and means of a gentleman. By then it is too late, and his revenge takes the form of ruining Hindley and dispossessing and degrading the Earnshaw and Linton heirs. Socially, in Victorian terms, Heathcliff succeeds – only to discover at the climax of his achievement that he has lost interest in material rewards and punitive revenge. With his recognition of where his true desire lies, his spirit is united at last with Cathy.

Both of the structures outlined above are plot-driven, and novels are not necessarily structured by their plot. They can be structured by feeling, by language and by symbolism. From the first storm that blots outs the landscape, the descriptions of nature hint at cosmic forces more potent than human beings. Lord David Cecil (1935) argued that *Wuthering Heights* was structured on the opposition of 'storm' and 'calm', imaged in the two houses. He related character to cosmic principles; some children are of the storm (Cathy, Heathcliff) and some are of the calm (Edgar, Isabella). When characters attempt to unite against their symbolic natures they come to disaster. Catherine and Hareton, a mixture of the best elements of storm and calm, reconcile the cosmic tensions in their ultimate union.

Further symbolic readings have been suggested (eternal versus ephemeral; exposure versus inclosure). Van Ghent (1953) traced the recurring use of apertures and openings to illustrate her thesis that the structural opposition was between raw natural energy (which was inhuman, alien, 'other') and civilized but restrictive manners. The human world is 'inside'; the alien world is 'outside'; and characters try unsuccessfully to cross from one to the other through barriers of windows, doors, and coffin lids. These ideas throw light on certain powerful episodes (Cathy's ghost at the window; Cathy's insistence on opening the window in her illness; Heathcliff's forced entry on the evening of Cathy's funeral; the strange calm that descends on him after opening the coffin, and his death beside the open window). It suggests that these are the climactic moments in a symbolic structure.

Because the structure of *Wuthering Heights* has proved to be susceptible to differing interpretations, it appears to fit the theory of **deconstruction**, which questions the structuralist idea that texts offer readers repeating, recognizable plots leading to expected, closed conclusions. Deconstructionists argue that texts contain multiple possible meanings and are open to plural readings.

The discrepancies between what Lockwood sees and what he thinks he sees could be signs that the text articulates more than appears on the surface. Structuralist efforts to arrive at a single interpretation involve highlighting some features of the text and ignoring others. Instead of seeking an explicable conclusion or a single meaning, perhaps we should accept that the text is contradictory and open, and cannot be reduced to a rational explanation.

Character

We view the characters mainly through Nelly's narration. Some critics argue that her common-sense, limited viewpoint is essential to give credibility to the story. For other critics, Nelly's narration sets up ambiguities. Her limitations prevent her from understanding Cathy or from sympathizing with her. In her hallucinations, Cathy sees Nelly as a *witch* who betrays her and although she is raving, she is also perceptive. Nelly can be accused of bias – the children she raises from birth, Catherine and Hareton, are her favourites. Nelly is less than fair to Cathy in her illness; she admits to disobeying Edgar's instructions and misjudging the seriousness of Cathy's state. The reader is required to see beyond Nelly's narrative, and the effort of doing so creates sympathy for Cathy.

Character appraisal can be approached either psychologically – treating them as real people – or formally, treating them as literary types. The most mysterious character, deliberately so in his origins, is Heathcliff. If we approach him psychologically, his missing early years are important. A 'gypsy' boy who speaks 'gibberish', found *starving, and houseless, and as good as dumb, in the streets of Liverpool*, is likely to have been the half-caste, illegitimate child of a foreign sailor and local mother, abandoned when very young. (There have also been suggestions that Earnshaw is himself the father.) Such a start in life would account for his uncomplaining acceptance of suffering and his opportunistic, ruthless determination to seize what he covets, which we see in his early struggle to possess Hindley's pony. In the light of what we now know of the importance of a child's earliest years, it is interesting to compare the upbringing of all the main characters and consider the effect this has on their later development.

If, however, one approaches the character of Heathcliff as a linguistic artefact, a piece of fiction, one needs to focus on how his character is created by the words on the page. As a literary type, he is a demonic figure. Brontë was the daughter of a parson and, as we can see in her poetry, she experienced the religious doubt felt by many Victorians, but her Christian faith was firm. The religious references in the novel, the presence and importance of church-going and church rituals in the community, Joseph's Calvinist sermonizing and the characters' individual definitions of heaven and hell, all encourage us to see Heathcliff as an image of the powers of darkness. He enters Wuthering Heights as an inhuman 'it', not a human 'he': *as if it came from the devil*, not *a gift of God*. Throughout the novel he is referred to in language that associates him with hell and the devil. The judgement of characters within the novel condemns him to hell. Nelly urges him near the end to send for a minister and repent. He refuses to do this, and Joseph is convinced the *divil's harried off his soul*. But we already know that Nelly and Joseph lack insight. Heathcliff has his own definition of heaven, and close to death he tells Nelly that he has *nearly attained* it. The *gaze of exultation* in his dead eyes makes us wonder if he succeeded. The way in which the novel holds the reader's judgement at bay suggests that his 'otherness' is unfathomable, unknowable and beyond Christian morality. He seems to lack an ethical dimension. Lockwood believes his spirit is at rest, but are we to believe Lockwood? The reader must judge whether Edgar, Heathcliff and Cathy have *unquiet slumbers*.

Language

Emily Brontë's choice of diction is one of the most important formal features of the novel and any detailed study requires attention to her style. Her use of dialect gives it an unusually vigorous tone. Servants speak in dialect – Joseph uses it all the time, and Nelly favours dialectal phrases. Hareton is her *bonny little nursling*; her narrative is *dree*. The shepherd lad sees the ghosts *under t'nab*. Other characters use country images. Heathcliff compares his nerves to *catgut*, and his son to a *puling chicken . . . reared on snails and sour milk*. Cathy sees Nelly *gathering elf-bolts to hurt our heifers*. Hareton swears he will have nothing to do with Catherine's *mucky pride*. Again and again, this homely, farmyard diction, and use of dialect for vocabulary and accent, invigorate the language of the novel.

Brontë's style is full of similes and metaphors drawn from nature. Nelly compares Heathcliff and Edgar respectively to a *bleak, hilly coal country* and a *beautiful fertile valley*, and describes the wedded Cathy's reception by the Lintons as *honeysuckles embracing the thorn*. Cathy expresses her love for Heathcliff and Edgar in imagery based on foliage and rocks. Catherine, discovering that Linton's love letters are missing, utters *anguished cries and flutterings*, like a bird *flying back to a plundered nest*. The day of her father's illness is *watery* and *cold* and the natural details on the walk she takes with Nelly (moist, withered leaves; grey streamers of cloud; stunted oaks; one lonely bluebell; blanched grass; fungus) build the sense of her melancholy mood. When she explains to Nelly her idea of heaven and Linton's, she gives two contrasting pictures of the moors on a summer's day, perceptively illustrating the differences in their personalities. At many points in the novel, the natural world is a reflection of the characters' feelings – the fine June day of Hareton's birth; the storm on the night of Heathcliff's flight; the cold winter blasts at Cathy's illness; the momentary brightening at her daughter's birth; and the fall of snow at her funeral.

The natural descriptions which mirror human emotions help to convey characters' feelings and moods, but they also establish the landscape in its own right. Few scenes are set on the moors, yet their presence broods over the novel because the diction of *Wuthering Heights* uses so many images drawn from them. Landscape in turn becomes imagistic. The most natural details can be read symbolically; for instance, Cathy is buried *on a green slope in a corner of the kirkyard, where the wall is so low that heath and bilberry plants have climbed over it from the moor*, as though her spirit wishes to escape from the traditional burial ground out into nature.

Feminism

Feminist criticism has produced radically new readings of many Victorian novels, revealing how debilitating and destructive a severely restrictive, patriarchal society can be for women. In *Wuthering Heights* the revenge plot turns on the fact that married women were forbidden to hold property. Cathy has no share in the property of Wuthering Heights. Hindley inherits all, and reduces Heathcliff to servitude. Cathy is trapped by her gender and chooses a socially advantageous marriage because, as she tells Nelly, marrying Edgar will get her the money *to aid Heathcliff to rise*. In the society of Brontë's time, she can find no other way.

Catherine is brought up as a typically Victorian, protected girl. It is unlikely any son of Edgar's would have been restricted to the park around the Grange. But she has spirit and breaks the bounds of her father's restraints. Like her mother, she yearns after *the golden rocks* of Peniston Crags. Her solo expedition, however, only succeeds with male leadership – Hareton shows her the way. She has a degree of power in the love relationship, in that she is the better educated, but in the end she accepts without demur her domesticated role in a patriarchal society. It is Cathy who challenges the Victorian ideology of the dominant male. She addresses Heathcliff in her hallucination of death: *You are slow!*, and claims leadership: *Be content, you always followed me*. She rejects society's right to regulate her choices, but she fails to solve the conflict between her desires and society's restrictions on women. Her temper tantrums, her illness and her death can be seen as a female response to irreconcilable male pressures.

Marxist criticism

Marxist critics argue that the novel's tensions are social and relate to the historical conditions of the times. Kettle (1951) considered the novel *an expression in the imaginative terms of art of the stresses and tensions and conflicts, personal and spiritual, of nineteenth-century capitalist society*. He argued that Heathcliff uses the same ruthless capitalist methods that have been used against him by Edgar and Hindley – marriage and property ownership – to lift himself from exploited worker into the property-owning class. Kettle felt that Heathcliff never loses our sympathy entirely, even at his most inhumane, because we recognize *a rough moral justice* in his revenge. But in the struggle between oppressor and oppressed, Heathcliff loses sight of the human values that are at the heart of his love for Cathy. They have been soul-mates in childhood and are brought closer by their rebellion against Hindley. When Hareton in his turn supports Catherine in her rebellion, Heathcliff recognizes in the younger pair the yearning towards something better than power and property which he has shared with Cathy. Revenge dies in him.

Terry Eagleton (1975) felt that the pivotal event in the novel was Cathy's choice between Edgar and Heathcliff, between retaining her social position among the gentry, the land-owning class, and joining the disempowered class of farm labourers to which Heathcliff has been reduced by Hindley. By denying Heathcliff an education, Hindley uses culture to dominate him. Eagleton associated Wuthering Heights with the declining class of yeoman farmers, men who still worked their own small estates but were a disappearing class during the nineteenth century. He associated the Grange with the rising class of landowners who were divorced from the labour that sustained them. Heathcliff represents the victory of capitalist property-dealing over the traditional yeoman economy of the Earnshaws. His rise to power symbolizes the triumph of the oppressed over capitalism but it is also, Eagleton argued, the blunt instrument by which the Earnshaw world is transformed into fully fledged capitalism.

11 Approaches to Poetry

• •

Lyric poetry

I sing of a maiden
That is makeles
King of all kings
To her son she chose.

He came all so still
There his mother was
Like dew in April
That falleth on the grass.

He came all so still
To his mother's bower,
Like dew in April
That falleth on the flower.

He came all so still
There his mother lay,
Like dew in April
That falleth on the spray.

Mother and maiden
Was never none but she;
Well might such a lady
Godes mother be.

makeles: matchless

I sing, starts this lyric, because that is exactly what would have happened in the Middle Ages when these words were written – a lyric was written to be sung. We still use the term 'lyrics' today for the words of a song.

The subject of lyrical poetry is personal emotion – love or an impassioned response to a thought, momentary happening or natural scene. Because lyrics were originally set to music, their form usually consists of a series of repeating, rhyming stanzas, sometimes with a chorus. Phrases and words also tend to be repeated. In time, lyrics separated from their musical settings and stood alone as poems, and this freed them to become less regular in form. Brevity, repetition, rhyme, simple diction and personal feeling are the hallmarks of lyric poetry. Although it is brief and apparently simple, a lyric can convey complexity through its imagery, as, for example, in Blake's

Songs of Innocence and Experience. The bulk of twentieth-century poetry is lyrical – the brief expression of personal feeling and thought.

Sigh No More

Sigh no more, ladies, sigh no more.
Men were deceivers ever,
One foot in sea, and one on shore,
To one thing constant never.
Then sigh not so, but let them go,
And be you blithe and bonny,
Converting all your sound of woe
Into hey nonny, nonny.

Sing no more ditties, sing no more
Of dumps so dull and heavy.
The fraud of men was ever so
Since summer first was leafy.
Then sigh not so, but let them go,
And be you blithe and bonny,
Converting all your sounds of woe
Into hey nonny, nonny.

William Shakespeare

Activity

> What stylistic features show that *Sigh No More* is a lyric and what evidence is there that it was written as a song?

Song

When I am dead, my dearest,
Sing no sad songs for me;
Plant thou no roses at my head,
Nor shady cypress tree:
Be the green grass above me
With showers and dewdrops wet;
And if thou wilt, remember,
And if thou wilt, forget.

I shall not see the shadows,
I shall not fear the rain;
I shall not hear the nightingale
Sing on as if in pain:
And dreaming through the twilight
That doth not rise nor set,
Haply I may remember,
And haply may forget.

Christina Rossetti

Activity

> What stylistic features show that Rossetti's *Song* is a lyric?
>
> How, from the feeling expressed, could you deduce that Rossetti was a devout Christian?

To Make a Prairie

To make a prairie it takes a clover and one bee,
One clover, and a bee,
And revery.
The revery alone will do,
If bees are few.

Emily Dickinson

Activity

> What stylistic features show that *To Make a Prairie* is a lyrical poem, and what evidence is there that it was not written originally as a song?
>
> The parallel balancing of 'one' and 'a' lock the *clover* and the *bee* into a unity, broken by the surprise of the word *revery*. As so often with Dickinson, the simplest diction is interrupted by one sophisticated word which turns out, as in this instance, to be important. If *revery alone will do,* if the limitless expanse of pioneering fruitfulness conveyed in the word *prairie* can be reduced to a single clover and one bee, and then further emptied of any physical presence, what does this suggest the poem is describing? Do you think the lyric can be read metaphorically?

Ballads

Like the lyric, the ballad is a sung, pre-literate poetic form, although it is thought to date back only to the sixteenth century. Ballads are narrative poems, simple in style and diction, and, like the lyric, they use repetition of stanzas and phraseology. The four-line stanza of alternate iambic tetrameter (four-beat) and iambic trimeter (three-beat) lines, rhyming on the second and fourth lines, is so standard as to be known as 'the ballad stanza'. The stories are usually romantic, heroic, tragic or comic, told in selective episodes which move quickly to the climax. There is no comment, no character analysis, and no explanation of events. Narrative is all-important, and it is told in dialogue and action. The reader is sometimes left to puzzle out the full story from a few episodes. Although primarily a folk form, the ballad became a popular poetic genre in the nineteenth century, used for example in Wordsworth and Coleridge's *Lyrical Ballads* and Oscar Wilde's *The Ballad of Reading Gaol.*

Ballad

O! shairly ye hae seen my love
Doun whaur the waters wind;
He walks like ane wha fears nae man
And yet his e'en are kind.

O! shairly ye hae seen my love
At the turning o' the tide;
For then he gethers in the nets
Doun be the waterside.

O! lassie I hae seen your love
At the turning o' the tide;
And he was wi' the fisher-folk
Doun be the waterside.

The fisher-folk were at their trade
No far frae walnut grove;
They gethered in their dreepin nets
And fund your ain true love.

William Soutar

Activity

What stylistic features show this poem is a ballad?

This is not a traditional folk ballad. Soutar was a Scottish poet of the late nineteenth and early twentieth century, and his spelling conveys the Scottish accent. What, however, in the diction and content of this poem gives the sense of a poem springing from folk culture?

At what point in the story does the poem commence?

Repetition is a major stylistic device in the poem. Using a grid to help you, mark the repetitions as they occur in the four stanzas. Notice how they form a pattern. Which repetitions break the pattern and why do you think this is done? Do any important words occur in all four stanzas?

Elegies

The tone of lyrical poetry is normally celebratory. The inspiration, whether it is love, a small, inspiring moment in life or a pleasing glimpse of a natural scene, is usually accompanied by emotions of affection and joy. Grief is the subject of a particular type of lyric, the elegy, which is a lyric poem mourning someone's death. The formal characteristics are lyrical but the tone is naturally more sombre.

Elegy for Himself

Written in the Tower before his execution, 1586

My prime of youth is but a frost of cares;
My feast of joy is but a dish of pain;
My crop of corn is but a field of tares;
And all my good is but vain hope of gain;
The day is past, and yet I saw no sun;
And now I live, and now my life is done.

My tale was heard, and yet it was not told;
My fruit is fall'n, and yet my leaves are green;
My youth is spent, and yet I am not old;
I saw the world, and yet I was not seen;
My thread is cut, and yet it is not spun;
And now I live, and now my life is done.

I sought my death, and found it in my womb;
I looked for life, and saw it was a shade;
I trod the earth, and knew it was my tomb;
And now I die, and now I was but made;
My glass is full, and now my glass is run;
And now I live, and now my life is done.

Charles Tichborne

Activity	What stylistic features show that this elegy is lyrical in form?

Sonnets

The sonnet is another specialized type of lyric, consisting of a tightly patterned form of fourteen lines of rhymed iambic pentameters. The Petrarchan sonnet was introduced from Italy into England in Tudor times. The rhyming pattern uses only two rhymes in the first eight lines, or **octave**, following a strict *abba, abba* pattern. The remaining six lines, the **sestet,** use a varying combination of three further pairs of rhymes. Shakespeare invented a looser rhyming scheme for the type of sonnet that bears his name, the Shakespearian sonnet. It uses seven pairs of rhyming words instead of the Petrarchan five, in a pattern of three quatrains and a closing couplet: *abab, cdcd, efef, gg*. The subject of sonnets was, like the lyric, primarily love, but the sonnet expressed a more thoughtful attitude. Although short, sonnets can be serious poems, offering brief philosophical statements. The progression of the poet's thoughts can be traced through the argument of a sonnet, which sometimes makes surprising twists in logic and even complete reversals of thought and feeling.

When my love swears that she is made of truth
I do believe her though I know she lies,
That she might think me some untutored youth
Unlearned in the world's false subtleties.
Thus vainly thinking that she thinks me young,
Although she knows my days are past the best,
Simply I credit her false-speaking tongue;
On both sides thus is simple truth suppressed.
But wherefore says she not she is unjust,
And wherefore say not I that I am old?
O, love's best habit is in seeming trust,
And age in love loves not to have years told.
Therefore I lie with her, and she with me,
And in our faults by lies we flattered be.

William Shakespeare, Sonnet 138

When I consider how my light is spent,
Ere half my days, in this dark world and wide,
And that one Talent which is death to hide
Lodg'd with me useless, though my Soul more bent
To serve therewith my Maker, and present
My true account, lest he returning chide,
Doth God exact day-labour, light deni'd,
I fondly ask; But patience to prevent
That murmur, soon replies, God doth not need
Either mans work or his own gifts, who best
Bear his milde yoke, they serve him best, his State
Is Kingly. Thousands at his bidding speed
And post o'r Land and Ocean without rest:
They also serve who only stand and waite.

John Milton

When I have fears that I may cease to be
Before my pen has gleaned my teeming brain,
Before high-pilèd books, in charactery,
Hold like rich garners the full ripened grain;
When I behold, upon the night's starred face,
Huge cloudy symbols of a high romance,
And think that I may never live to trace
Their shadows with the magic hand of chance;
And when I feel, fair creature of an hour,
That I shall never look upon thee more,
Never have relish in the fairy power
Of unreflecting love; then on the shore
Of the wide world I stand alone and think
Till love and fame to nothingness do sink.

John Keats

Activity

Odes

The ode is a longer, more serious form of the lyric, written in praise of a person or abstract subject. Like the lyric, the form is often a series of repeating stanzas, but the tone is more elevated and the diction more sophisticated. The ode form derives from two Roman poets: Pindar, whose odes were written in praise of the winners of the Olympic games, and Horace, whose stanzas are more regular than those of Pindar and whose tone is more personal and philosophic. The subject matter of an ode is usually given in the title (*Ode to . . .*) and the subject is often addressed in the opening stanza. The first three stanzas of Marvell's *Ode to Cromwell*, below, commence in adulation. But the poem includes a sympathetic account of the behaviour of Charles I on his execution: *He nothing common did nor mean / Upon that memorable Scene*, and ends with an appeal to Cromwell: *Still keep thy Sword erect* and a warning: *The same Arts that did gain / A Pow'r must it maintain.*

An Horatian Ode Upon Cromwell's Return from Ireland

The forward Youth that would appear
Must now forsake his Muses dear,
Nor in the Shadows sing
His numbers languishing.
'Tis time to leave the Books in dust,
And oyl th'unused Armours rust,
Removing from the Wall
The Corslet of the Hall.
So restless Cromwel could not cease

> In th'inglorious Arts of Peace,
> But through adventurous War
> Urged his active Star.

Andrew Marvell

Activity

The stanzas of Marvell's ode are regular but run together without breaks. Can you identity the stanza form and the rhythm and rhyme pattern?

What in the diction of the poem is in an elevated style of praise? Select two or three words or phrases which are more sophisticated than you would expect to find in a simple love lyric.

The ode contrasts the activities which Cromwell *must now forsake* (singing and reading, the arts of peace) with those he must take up. Find words that describe Cromwell and his activities. You will need to consider both adjectives and verbs. Notice how they invigorate the portrait of Cromwell and oppose the arts of peace with those of war.

Epic poems

The classical epics, Homer's *Iliad* and *Odyssey* and Virgil's *Aeneid*, were long narrative poems, possibly oral, whose style was elevated and whose subjects were grand and momentous – the destruction of Troy, the wanderings of Ulysses and the founding of the Roman Empire. The only English epic in true classical style is Milton's *Paradise Lost*, although Spenser's *The Fairie Queene* and Wordsworth's *The Prelude* owe much to the epic form. Following the example of Virgil, Milton commenced his narrative in the middle of the story, with an invocation to the Muse. The passage below is taken from the opening to Book III, lines 1–49, in which Milton, having completed in Books I and II his account of the fallen angels in Hell (the *Stygian* Pool) appeals again to the Muse.

1   Hail Holy light, offspring of Heav'n first-born,
     Or of th' Eternal Coeternal beam
     May I express thee unblam'd? since God is Light,
     And never but in unapproached Light
     Dwelt from Eternitie, dwelt then in thee,
     Bright effluence of bright essence increate.
     Or hear'st thou rather pure Ethereal stream,
     Whose Fountain who shall tell? before the Sun,
     Before the Heav'ns thou wert, and at the voice
10   Of God, as with a Mantle, didst invest
     The rising world of waters dark and deep,
     Won from the void and formless infinite.
     Thee I revisit now with bolder wing,
     Escap't the *Stygian* Pool, though long detained
     In that obscure sojourn, while in my flight

Through utter and through middle darkness borne
With other notes than to th' *Orphean* Lyre
I sung of *Chaos* and *Eternal Night*,
Taught by the heav'nly Muse to venture down

20   The dark descent, and up to reascend,
Though hard and rare: thee I revisit safe
And feel thy sovran vital Lamp; but thou
Revisitst not these eyes, that roul in vain
To find thy piercing ray, and find no dawn;
So thick a drop serene hath quencht thir Orbs,
Or dim suffusion veild. Yet not the more
Cease I to wander where the Muses haunt
Clear Spring, or shadie Grove, or Sunnie Hill,
Smit with the love of sacred song; but chief

30   Thee *Sion* and the flowrie Brooks beneath
That wash thy hallowd feet, and warbling flow,
Nightly I visit; nor sometimes forget
Those other two equald with me in Fate,
Blind *Thamyris* and blind *Maeonides,*
And *Tiresias* and *Phineus* Prophets old.
Then feed on thoughts, that voluntarie move
Harmonious numbers; as the wakeful Bird
Sings darkling, and in shadiest Covert hid
Tunes her nocturnal Note. Thus with the Year

40   Seasons return, but not to me returns
Day, or the sweet approach of Ev'n or Morn,
Or sight of vernal bloom, or Summers Rose,
Or flocks, or herds, or human face divine;
But cloud in stead, and ever-during dark
Surrounds me, from the cheerful ways of men
Cut off, and for the Book of knowledge fair
Presented with a Universal blanc
Of Natures works to mee expung'd and ras'd,
And wisdom at one entrance quite shut out.

John Milton

The blank verse rhythm, the sophisticated diction, full of classical references, and the complex syntax of the lengthy sentences are signs of the epic style, as is the lofty subject matter and the appeal to the Muse.

Activity

The epic style is difficult for a modern reader. The first task is to unpack the meaning: try reading the passage aloud, ignoring for the moment the words you do not understand. What sense do you make of it? Milton addresses the *Light*, associating it with the first day of Creation when God separated night from day, and also with the sun, the *sovran vital Lamp* which lights the earth, and finally with his own blindness and loss of sight.

Once you feel you have mastered the general sense of the passage, choose one or two long sentences and try to unpack their syntax. You might like to consider lines 40–49, noting that *cut off* and *presented* are past participles, acting as adjectives.

Similarly with vocabulary. Choose a few lines, for example, the second sentence or lines 21–26, and look up the words you do not understand. Why does Milton use the word *increate?* What does the phrase *dim suffusion veild* mean?

The heroic couplet

The eighteenth-century taste was for decorum and politeness, for clarity and order, and there is a sense of discipline and propriety in the regularity of these poets' verse and diction. They used classical genres with regular, highly patterned forms. The heroic couplet, which Chaucer had used for *The Canterbury Tales*, was a favoured eighteenth-century form. It consists of a pair of rhyming iambic pentameters. When Pope came to write his mock-epic, *The Rape of the Lock*, he chose the heroic couplet, as he does in the poem below.

The regularity of the form increases a reader's expectations and creates possibilities of 'deforming' the structure, of overturning and frustrating expectations. The slight jar we experience when this happens serves to draw attention to language, to the unusual placing of a word or to the use of an image which we did not expect. Pope is a master of this device and many of his jokes arise from his deft reversal of language expectation.

Epistle to Miss Blount, on her Leaving Town, After the Coronation

1   As some fond virgin, whom her mother's care
     Drags from the town to wholesome country air,
     Just when she learns to roll a melting eye,
     And hear a spark, yet think no danger nigh;
     From the dear man unwilling she must sever,
     Yet takes one kiss before she parts for ever:
     Thus from the world fair *Zephalinda* flew,
     Saw others happy, and with sighs withdrew;
     Not that their pleasures caus'd her discontent,
10   She sigh'd not that They stay'd, but that She went.
       She went, to plain-work and to purling brooks,
     Old-fashion'd halls, dull aunts, and croaking rooks,
     She went from Op'ra, park, assembly, play,
     To morning walks, and pray'rs three hours a day;
     To pass her time 'twixt reading and Bohea,
     To muse, and spill her solitary Tea,
     Or o'er cold coffee trifle with the spoon,
     Count the slow clock, and dine exact at noon;
     Divert her eyes with pictures in the fire,
20   Hum half a tune, tell stories to the squire;
     Up to her godly garret after sev'n,

There starve and pray, for that's the way to heav'n.
  Some Squire, perhaps, you take delight to rack;
Whose game is Whisk, whose treat a toast in sack,
Who visits with a gun, presents you birds,
Then gives a smacking buss, and cries – No words!
Or with his hound comes hollowing from the stable,
Makes love with nods, and knees beneath the table;
Whose laughs are hearty, tho' his jests are coarse,
30   And loves you best of all things – but his horse.
  In some fair evening, on your elbow laid,
You dream of triumphs in the rural shade;
In pensive thought recall the fancy'd scene,
See Coronations rise on ev'ry green;
Before you pass th'imaginary sights
Of Lords, and Earls, and Dukes, and garter'd Knights;
While the spread Fan o'ershades your closing eyes;
Then give one flirt, and all the vision flies.
Thus vanish sceptres, coronets, and balls,
40   And leave you in lone woods, or empty walls.
  So when your slave, at some dear, idle time,
(Not plagu'd with headachs, or the want of rime)
Stands in the streets, abstracted from the crew,
And while he seems to study, thinks of you:
Just when his fancy points your sprightly eyes,
Or sees the blush of soft *Parthenia* rise,
Gay pats my shoulder, and you vanish quite;
Streets, chairs, and coxcombs rush upon my sight;
Vext to be still in town, I knit my brow,
50   Look sow'r, and hum a tune, – as you may now.

Alexander Pope

Activity

This is a poem of opposition and balances, mirrored in the balanced pattern of the heroic couplet. Town and country are one example of pairing. Can you list the ways in which they are opposed? You might like to look for examples of elegance and coarseness, excitement and dullness, sophistication and roughness, variety and routine, eloquence (the poem is itself an example of the wit of the poet) and inarticulacy.

Pope is in town while Miss Blount is in the country, leading opposed lives. What do they share in common? You might like to consider their mood, their dreams, and the implications of the final line. (*Gay*, who interrupts Pope, was his friend.)

Pope's ironic wit subtly undercuts the meaning of certain words and phrases with a juxtaposition of expected and unexpected language which the heroic couplet encourages. Consider the opening couplet. Who believes the country air is *wholesome*? Can you discover other couplets where the joke arises from either an unexpected word or an ironic implication? You might like to consider lines 3–4, 21–22 or 29–30.

Narrative verse

Narrative verse is poetry that tells a story. Epics are narratives and so are ballads. The nineteenth century was particularly fond of narrative verse. Not only was the ballad revived as a poetic genre, but many long narrative poems were written, like Tennyson's *The Idylls of the King* and Robert Browning's *The Ring and the Book.*

Cousin Kate

I was a cottage-maiden
Hardened by sun and air,
Contented with my cottage-mates,
Not mindful I was fair.
Why did a great lord find me out
And praise my flaxen hair?
Why did a great lord find me out
To fill my heart with care?

He lured me to his palace-home –
Woe's me for joy thereof –
To lead a shameless shameful life,
His plaything and his love.
He wore me like a golden knot,
He changed me like a glove:
So now I moan an unclean thing
Who might have been a dove.

O Lady Kate, my Cousin Kate,
You grow more fair than I:
He saw you at your father's gate,
Chose you and cast me by.
He watched your steps along the lane,
Your sport among the rye:
He lifted you from mean estate
To sit with him on high.

Because you were so good and pure
He bound you with his ring:
The neighbours call you good and pure,
Call me an outcast thing.
Even so I sit and howl in dust
You sit in gold and sing:
Now which of us has tenderer heart?
You had the stronger wing.

O Cousin Kate, my love was true,
Your love was writ in sand:
If he had fooled not me but you,
If you stood where I stand,

He had not won me with his love
Nor bought me with his land:
I would have spit into his face
And not have taken his hand.

Yet I've a gift you have not got
And seem not like to get:
For all your clothes and wedding-ring
I've little doubt you fret.
My fair-haired son, my shame, my pride,
Cling closer, closer yet:
Your sire would give broad lands for one
To wear his coronet.

Christina Rossetti

The story is the familiar Victorian tale of a 'ruined' woman, familiar even in the slight touches of medievalism which the Victorians favoured and in Rossetti's sympathy for her 'fallen' heroine. What is unusual is the heroine's sense of triumph, even if she is bitter towards her cousin. Thomas Hardy (who subtitled his novel *Tess of the D'Urbervilles: a Pure Woman Faithfully Presented*) adopts a more ironically understanding attitude to the 'ruined' woman.

The Ruined Maid

'O 'Melia, my dear, this does everything crown!
Who could have supposed I should meet you in Town?
And whence such fair garments, such prosperi-ty?' –
'O didn't you know I'd been ruined?' said she.

– 'You left us in tatters, without shoes or socks,
Tired of digging potatoes, and spudding up docks;
And now you've gay bracelets and bright feathers three!' –
'Yes: that's how we dress when we're ruined,' said she.

– 'At home in the barton you said "thee" and "thou",
And "thik oon", and "theas oon", and "t'other"; but now
Your talking quite fits 'ee for high compa-ny!' –
'Some polish is gained with one's ruin,' said she.

– 'Your hands were like paws then, your face blue and bleak
But now I'm bewitched by your delicate cheek,
And your little gloves fit as on any la-dy!' –
'We never do work when we're ruined,' said she.

– 'You used to call home-life a hag-ridden dream,
And you'd sigh, and you'd sock; but at present you seem
To know not of megrims or melancho-ly!' –
'True, One's pretty lively when ruined,' said she.

– 'I wish I had feathers, a fine sweeping gown,
And a delicate face, and could strut about Town!'
– 'My dear – a raw country girl, such as you be,
Cannot quite expect that. You ain't ruined,' said she.

Thomas Hardy

Activity

> What genre do you feel *The Ruined Maid* belongs to?

The repetitive stanza form suggests a sung piece. Form and brevity are lyrical but the ironic tone is unusual in a lyric, as is the content, which is a little story, but seems too brief to qualify as a narrative poem. Perhaps it is closest to a ballad. Most nineteenth- and twentieth-century poetry is lyrical, and it would be perfectly appropriate to call this a lyric. Poems do not always fit neatly into a particular genre. Like this one, they may include stylistic elements from several genres.

Dramatic monologues

A monologue is a speech, whether on stage or in poetry, spoken by a single person. In a sense, any lyrical expression of a poet's feelings is a monologue, but in a dramatic monologue a character either speaks to a silent listener, or voices his thoughts aloud. The dramatic monologue is a nineteenth-century poetic form. As interest in mental processes developed, along with recognition that thought could be self-deceiving as well as hidden, poets like Browning and Tennyson perfected this genre in which a character 'speaks' his thoughts and reveals what is concealed not only from the people he or she lives among but also, more intriguingly, from the speaker himself or herself. The Duke in Browning's *My Last Duchess* may intend to reveal to the Count's envoy, to whom he is speaking, that he has caused the death of his last Duchess, but he is unaware that he is also revealing his self-absorbed, egocentric, murderous arrogance to readers who will be repelled by it. Thought, reflection, self-revelation and the conversational tone of the speaking voice are all stylistic features of the dramatic monologue.

Soliloquy of the Spanish Cloister

GR-R-R – there go, my heart's abhorrence!
Water your damned flower-pots, do!
If hate killed men, Brother Lawrence,
God's blood, would not mine kill you!
What? Your myrtle-bush wants trimming?
Oh, that rose has prior claims –
Needs its leaden vase filled brimming?
Hell dry you up with its flames!

Robert Browning

Activity

> The lines above are the first stanza of a much longer poem. What in the syntax belongs to spoken rather than written language?
>
> Although these are only the opening lines, you will already have a sense of the character of the monk who is speaking. What kind of man do you think he is? What, in his use of language, creates the sense of his personality?

Free verse

Free verse was written in the early twentieth century by poets who broke away from the constraints of regular rhyme and rhythm patterns, concentrating instead upon imagery and cadence. Lines are printed as poetry, not prose, but their rhythm and length are irregular. Free verse was a major verse form during the modernist period and greatly influenced later twentieth-century poetry, leading to a general loosening of metrical patterns.

Oread

Whirl up, sea –
Whirl your pointed pines.
Splash your great pines
On our rocks.
Hurl your green over us –
Cover us with your pools of fir.

H.D.

Activity

> What stylistic features show that this is free verse?
>
> How do imagery and syntax help to give the poem a form?

Index